# Social Entrepreneurship in the Middle East

# Social Entrepreneurship in the Middle East

## Volume 1

Edited by

Dima Jamali and Alessandro Lanteri
*American University of Beirut, Lebanon*

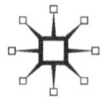

First published 2015 by
PALGRAVE MACMILLAN

Palgrave Macmillan in the UK is an imprint of Macmillan Publishers Limited,
registered in England, company number 785998, of Houndmills, Basingstoke,
Hampshire RG21 6XS.

Palgrave Macmillan in the US is a division of St Martin's Press LLC,
175 Fifth Avenue, New York, NY 10010.

Palgrave Macmillan is the global academic imprint of the above companies
and has companies and representatives throughout the world.

Palgrave® and Macmillan® are registered trademarks in the United States,
the United Kingdom, Europe and other countries.

ISBN 978–1–137–39534–4

This book is printed on paper suitable for recycling and made from fully
managed and sustained forest sources. Logging, pulping and manufacturing
processes are expected to conform to the environmental regulations of the
country of origin.

A catalogue record for this book is available from the British Library.

Library of Congress Cataloging-in-Publication Data
Social entrepreneurship in the Middle East / [edited by] Dima Jamali,
   Alessandro Lanteri.
      volumes   cm
   Includes bibliographical references.
   ISBN 978–1–137–39534–4 (hardback)
   1.  Social entrepreneurship—Middle East.    I. Jamali, Dima.
   II. Lanteri, Alessandro.
   HD60.5.M53S63 2015
   338'.040956—dc23                                      2015003466

*This book is dedicated to Gregory Dees, whose untimely and unexpected passing left us very saddened. Gregory, who was credited as the father of social entrepreneurship, had graciously agreed to write the Foreword to this book, and we were really shocked, beyond words can convey, by the news of his passing away on 20 December 2013.*

*We also dedicate this book to our fellow citizens of the Middle East and invite them to continue in steering their efforts in taking social entrepreneurship forward in a region where it is desperately needed.*

# Contents

# Figures and Tables

## Figures

## Tables

# Foreword

It was Mohammad Yunus, back in the 1970s, who first invested in the proposition that the poor are *bankable* entrepreneurs. He took a small risk on 42 hard-working village women, lending each $27 at no interest. The women got their businesses running and the loans were paid back, giving nascent shape to the powerful notion that entrepreneurship could be just as passionately deployed towards positive social impact as it is towards profitable business innovation.

Across the border, Bunker Roy, a young graduate student around the time Yunus was establishing Grameen Bank, felt the same fervour about access to education in marginalized villages in India, and so he founded The Barefoot College to educate illiterate and semi-literate rural Indians. More than 37,000 dedicated men and women – doctors, dentists, architects, designers, engineers, chemists, mechanics, masons, and teachers – are now engaged in training villagers throughout the country.

No one thought then to call Yunus' and Roy's endeavours social entrepreneurship – a term the late Gregory Dees defined best in the late 1990s. Today, these pioneers are but two of a growing army of social entrepreneurs developing inventive answers to social problems, oftentimes moving full force into the many gaps long neglected – if not created – by governments and development agencies.

But 40 years into experimentation with social businesses, the field has only recently begun to gain serious traction in emerging countries. The reasons are many, but there is little doubt that technology is key among them. An estimated two billion people have access to the Internet, and around six billion are connected via mobile devices. Technology is helping democratize development, and social entrepreneurs are positioning themselves as game changers in an area long dominated by public actors. Essentially private sector activists, these entrepreneurs are galvanizing impactful, scalable solutions to complex social and economic challenges.

For us, in the Middle East and North Africa (MENA), the trends hold tremendous promise. Widespread unemployment, chronic poverty, environmental corrosions, food insecurity, water scarcity, and disenfranchised populations have long haunted Arab economies and confounded even the most well-intentioned public servants. It is this tableau of entrenched realities that has given impetus to social innovation in the region. And remarkably, we are witnessing a method that is grassroots and community driven. It might be early days yet, but, already, the effect on old, depleted development paradigms is perceptible. Our social entrepreneurs have begun to chip at the walls of one of the most stubborn Arab monopolies: the business of development.

However, this space in the Arab World (much like the case remains outside) is in serious need of critical thought and investment. Instruments that can reliably measure impact evaluation mechanisms that sort out the real from the bogus and strategic private sector support would give a significant boost to social entrepreneurship's ambitions to become a main driver of change.

Clearly, without a system of collaboration between social entrepreneurs and the private and public sectors, the sustainability and scalability of the work become all the more difficult to achieve. Although we are seeing examples of private sector partnerships with social businesses, there is as yet no concerted effort to invest in and capitalize on the commitment, energy, and talent of Arab social entrepreneurs. The role of the Arab private sector, as an enabler in this arena – as an independent source of investment, expertise, and knowledge – is, in fact, vital. It can tip the scales for social entrepreneurship, which makes this volume extremely timely.

Dima Jamali and Alessandro Lanteri have assembled a very impressive group of field experts, academicians, and practitioners, addressing an exciting regional trend and mapping the social entrepreneurship landscape in the Arab World. These groundbreaking contributions are an essential reference for anyone interested in social and economic development of the Arab region.

Fadi Ghandour
Founder of Aramex, Executive Chairman of Wamda Capital

# Acknowledgements

This book is an extension of an effort we started two years ago to take stock of and compile an overview of the happenings in the Middle East and North Africa (MENA) region in relation to the latest responsible business trends pertaining to corporate social responsibility (CSR) and social entrepreneurship (SE). The first book on CSR in the Middle East was published with Palgrave in 2012, and this book constitutes an extension of this effort, zooming on other manifestations of responsible business among smaller organizations and entrepreneurial ventures scattered across the region.

As we embarked on this effort, we were overwhelmed and pleasantly surprised by the positive vibe and enthusiasm the book had generated within a span of a short few months. We are lucky that the majority of the contributors have acted on this enthusiasm and made meaningful and substantive contributions to our edited volume. We were fortunate to have had the opportunity to work with a select group of authors who are immersed in social entrepreneurship in the region. As we embraced this enthusiasm, we ended up with two volumes for our edited book, rather than one!

We hope the two volumes will give our readers a rounded and comprehensive understanding of the current practice and landscape of social entrepreneurship across the region. We feel confident that in combination, the two volumes reconcile breadth with depth and provide a solid overview of the social entrepreneurship ecosystem in this region. In this regard, we wish to extend our most sincere thanks to the authors of the chapters, who have been generous with their time and effort, providing key insights in relation to an important topic and showing willingness to rewrite and craft their chapters to perfection. We feel fortunate to have worked with each of you and hope that our collective effort contributes to advancing existing knowledge in this important area of research and invite or entice more writings on this topic.

We also take the opportunity to extend our most sincere gratitude to the various research assistants whose help was instrumental in compiling this edited volume. Primary among them is Farah Matar, whose commitment, dynamism, and perfectionism are simply unmatched. We also wish to extend our sincere thanks to Nadine Mohanna, who, although joined the team at later stages, made an instrumental effort in filling final gaps and helping us bring the project to successful completion. Finally, we wish to acknowledge the great support from the Palgrave publisher team for the professional assistance and follow-up throughout the various phases of this project.

# About the Editors

**Dima Jamali** is a professor at the Olayan School of Business (OSB), American University of Beirut (AUB), Lebanon, and is currently serving as the Kamal Shair Endowed Chair in Responsible Leadership. She holds a PhD in Social Policy and Administration from the University of Kent at Canterbury, UK. Her research/teaching revolves primarily around corporate social responsibility (CSR). She is the author/editor of three books (*CSR in the Middle East*; *Social Entrepreneurship in the Middle East*; and *Development Oriented CSR*) and more than 50 international publications focusing on different aspects of CSR in the Middle East, all appearing in highly reputable journals. Her research record has won her a number of scientific awards and honours, including the Abdul Hameed Shoman Award for Best Young Arab Researcher for the year 2010 and a member of the Eisenhower Fellows, a global network of leading professionals committed to collaborate for a more prosperous, just, and peaceful world.

**Alessandro Lanteri** is an assistant professor at OSB, AUB, Lebanon. He holds an MA in Economics from Bocconi University, Milan, Italy, and a PhD in Philosophy and Economics from Erasmus University Rotterdam, The Netherlands. His research focuses on ethics and economics. He has been a speaker on these subjects across Europe and the United States. His research has been published by international academic journals (including: *Journal of Business Ethics, Journal of Social Entrepreneurship, Philosophical Studies, Philosophical Quarterly*) and publishing companies (Cambridge University Press). He is also a certified public accountant and has served as consultant to the United Nations Joint Program Against HIV/AIDS and to several social enterprises both in Lebanon and in Italy.

# Contributors

**Fatimah S. Baeshen** is a GCC socio-economic expert with an Islamic finance specialization. She has over 12 years' experience operating in, analysing, and advising on GCC regional developments – across social, political, and economic spheres to private, government, NGO, and non-profit entities, such as AON, Emirates Foundation for Youth Development, the Islamic Development Bank, the World Bank, regional municipalities, local family-owned businesses, and international investors. She is passionate about applied research and developing strategic models that both resonate culturally and are organically implementable. She operates in several spheres, including, but not limited to, enterprise and innovation development, Islamic finance, and market entry advisory/investor relations. She is especially passionate about applying her expertise towards initiatives related to women's empowerment. She holds a BA in Sociology from the University of Massachusetts and an MA from the University of Chicago's Center for Middle Eastern Studies.

**Iman Bibars** is Vice President and Global Diaspora Leader of Ashoka: Innovators for the Public and Regional Director of Ashoka Arab World. She is a social entrepreneur, activist, and a specialist in women's development. She is also the co-founder and current chairperson of Egypt's very first microfinance organization, Association for the Development and Enhancement of Women (ADEW), a citizen sector organization (CSO) that provides credit and legal aid for impoverished female heads of household. With an international career spanning from UNICEF to Catholic Relief Services (CRS) and the World Bank, she is a globally respected social development expert. She is also the author of several books on gender issues including *Victims and Heroines: Women, Welfare and the Egyptian State* and *The Women of Tahrir*, which details the most recent experiences of women during the Egyptian uprising. She has published one of the first books written in Arabic on US President Barack Obama – *Dreams of a Good Fellow*.

**Samantha Constant** is an international consultant focusing on social inclusion and economic development in the Middle East and North Africa (MENA) region. Her portfolio includes The World Bank, International City/Council Management Association, Save the Children International, FIKRA Research & Consultancy, among others. Prior to her current position, she was special advisor to James D. Wolfensohn and was a director of the Middle East Youth Initiative at the Wolfensohn Center for Development, Brookings. She has led community-based trainings with youth in Morocco and Sri Lanka on the use of media for development. Her case study entitled *Broadband in Morocco: Political Will Meets Socio-Economic Reality* highlighted Morocco's achievements in the information and communications technology (ICT) sector and opportunities for bottom-up innovations. She holds a Master's in International Affairs: Middle East and North Africa Comparative and Regional Studies from the School of International Service, American University, Washington DC.

**Ali El Idrissi** is a senior member of J.P. Morgan Social Finance (JPM SF), a unit launched in 2007 to service the growing impact investing market. Over the last few years, he and his team have pioneered new ways to attract private capital to achieve social progress. He has co-authored many landmark reports on impact investing, notably the annual JPM Impact Investor survey. Besides his JPM role, he assists a few impact ventures with their strategy and growth plans. Previously, he worked in Investment Banking at JPM, in London, New York, and Dubai, where he helped establish the bank's coverage of sovereign wealth funds. He holds an MA in Economics from Columbia University, an MA in International Affairs from Sciences Po Paris, and a BA in Philosophy from La Sorbonne. He currently teaches Impact Investing for an MA class at Sciences Po Paris.

**Diana Greenwald** is a PhD candidate in Political Science at the University of Michigan, where she focuses on the politics of revenue mobilization in transitional settings, including newly independent and post-conflict states. She is a 2014–2015 Jennings Randolph Peace Scholar at the US Institute of Peace. She is the founder and graduate student coordinator of the Workshop on Modern Middle East Studies at the University of Michigan. She was a 2010–2011 Weiser

Center for Emerging Democracies Student Fellow. Prior to joining Michigan, she was a research assistant for the Middle East Youth Initiative at the Brookings Institution, where she co-authored the 2010 report, "Social Entrepreneurship in the Middle East: Toward Sustainable Development for the Next Generation". She graduated from Georgetown University (BA 2006, magna cum laude), where she majored in government and minored in Arabic and studio art.

**Rebecca Hill**, with a background in communications, has an international career that stretches 25 years, starting in financial PR, progressing into corporate communications for global financial institutions, and then as the executive director for a non-profit trade association for communications professionals in the Middle East. More recently, she has taken on consultancy projects, moderated conferences, and facilitated company strategy sessions, in addition to advising start-ups and social entrepreneurs. She first became interested in sustainability while managing the Middle East Public Relations Association and undertook an MSc in Sustainability and Responsibility at Ashridge College to further her understanding. It was during this period that her interest in social enterprise grew, and she is now a strong advocate for this form of business enterprise.

**Irene Kapusta** serves as an innovation executive at Orange Labs UK, London. She is a startup mentor at Seedcamp and coaches young social entrepreneurs as a guide at the Resolution Project. She is a member of the Executive Committee of Think Palestine, an event dedicated to Palestinian entrepreneurship. Previously, she carried out a diaspora study for arcenciel, a leading social enterprise in Lebanon; she co-organized the 2014 NYU Abu Dhabi International Hackathon for Social Good in the Arab World. She started her career in strategy consulting. As a module leader at Monitor Group, she advised clients on innovation and growth in EMEA. She worked with multinational companies, start-ups, public entities, universities, and nonprofits. She holds a triple Master's in Management from ESCP Europe and a Master's in International Affairs focused on social entrepreneurship from Columbia University.

**David Munir Nabti** works to support high impact innovation and entrepreneurship and youth/alternative media. He is co-founder and CEO (Chief Entrepreneur and Organizer) of AltCity (www.altcity. me), a new media/tech/social impact collaboration space and start-up accelerator/support space in Beirut, and he previously founded/ran a separate co-working space in Beirut from 2008 to 2011. He is also Co-Founder, Chairman, and General Director of Boot Camp SAL, a new joint venture supported by Lebanon's central bank (Banque du Liban) working to build the pipeline of early-stage, investable, scalable ventures in the technology, knowledge, and creative sectors in Lebanon. He studied political economy at UC Berkeley, worked at the UN-FAO in Syria, Stanford University (Communication Department, Journalism Program), UC Berkeley (Education Department, Service-Learning Research & Development Center), and Google, as a freelance journalist, and interned at Cisco Systems HQ and KQED (the largest public media outlet in the US). He worked at his first tech start-up at 18 before going to university. He also conducted research on social entrepreneurship and the relation between regime interests, the education system, and economic development in Egypt.

**Medea Nocentini** is Vice President, Corporate Development, at OSN, the leading Pay TV platform in the MENA region, where she is responsible for corporate strategy and planning, market intelligence, and research. While at OSN, she founded C3 – Consult and Coach for a Cause, a UAE-based social enterprise fostering the social enterprise movement in the MENA region by mobilizing corporate professionals to support emerging social entrepreneurs on a volunteer basis. Before joining OSN, she worked in Business Development at McGraw-Hill and prior to that she spent several years at Booz & Co developing strategies for media, consumer, and social sector's clients across Europe, the United States, and Middle East. She holds an MBA from Columbia Business School, New York; a BA in Mechanical Engineering from Politecnico di Torino, Italy; and an Engineering Diploma from Ecole Centrale Paris, France.

**Clare Woodcraft-Scott** is CEO of Emirates Foundation, UAE's national foundation that creates social enterprises for youth development. She has 20 years' experience in sustainable socio-economic development in MENA as a development practitioner, a journalist, and a corporate executive. Prior to Emirates Foundation, she was Deputy Director of Shell Foundation that angel invests in social enterprises related to the energy sector. Earlier, she worked as the Regional Director of Communications for Royal Dutch Shell in MENA, managing Shell's social investment portfolio and issues related to sustainability. Before that, she was Head of Public Affairs CEMEA for Visa International working closely with governments and financial sectors on the role of electronic payments in socio-economic development. She has written extensively on socio-economic development and sustainability and has a BA in Arabic and French from Salford University and MSc in Development from LSE.

**Jamil Wyne** is the Manager of the Wamda Research Lab, the research arm of Wamda (wamda.com). He has worked for over six years on various aspects of economic and social development in the MENA, with a particular focus on entrepreneurship ecosystem development and social enterprise. Before Wamda, he worked as the Special Projects Manager at INJAZ Al Arab, where he ran projects on online entrepreneurship education for Arab youth and policy research on MENA education reform with the Arab League and World Bank. He is also a Fulbright Fellow, former research and outreach officer at Ashoka Arab World, and a researcher at the American Chamber of Commerce in Egypt and the Brookings Institution. He is a graduate of Bowdoin College.

**Soushiant Zanganehpour** is the former Strategy and Operations Manager of the Skoll Centre for Social Entrepreneurship at the University of Oxford. He currently advises multinationals, foundations, and impact startups seeking financial growth and social impact opportunities on strategic and operational matters. His professional experience spans the fields of management and strategy consulting, policy research, and entrepreneurship in London, Paris, Vancouver, and Dubai. He is an adjunct lecturer at Sciences Po Paris, teaching a masters-level course on social entrepreneurship and impact investing. He co-founded Vancouver's World Economic Forum Global Shapers Community and sits on the board of Opportunity Collaboration and RADIUS Ventures, a social innovation and venture accelerator based within Simon Fraser University's Business School. He holds an

MPP from the University of London's School of Oriental and African Studies, a BA in Political Science and International Relations from the University of British Columbia, and a Diploma in International Affairs from Sciences Po Paris. The UK Foreign Office selected him as one of four Canadian Chevening Scholars in 2010.

# Abbreviations

| | |
|---|---|
| ADB | African Development Bank |
| AIDS | Acquired Immune Deficiency Syndrome |
| AUB | American University of Beirut |
| AUC | American University of Cairo |
| BCG | Boston Consulting Group |
| BRD | Beyond Reform and Development |
| BSC | Big Society Capital |
| CEO | Chief Executive Officer |
| CGAP | Consultative Group to Assist the Poor |
| CIC | Community Interest Companies |
| CSR | Corporate Social Responsibility |
| C3 | Consult and Coach for a Cause |
| DF | Development Funds |
| DFI | Development Finance Institution |
| EIB | European Investment Bank |
| EU | European Union |
| FAO | Food and Agriculture Organization |
| GCC | Gulf Cooperation Council |
| GDP | Gross Domestic Product |
| GEM | Global Entrepreneurship Monitor |
| GIIN | Global Impact Investment Network |
| GNI | Gross National Income |
| HFHE | Habitat for Humanity Egypt |
| HIV | Human Immunodeficiency Virus |
| ICRF | Investment and Contract Readiness Fund |
| ICT | Information and Communications Technology |
| IDC | International Development Community |
| IFC | International Finance Corporation |
| IFI | International Financial Institutions |
| ILO | International Labour Organization |
| IPO | Initial Public Offering |
| JAW | Junior Achievement Worldwide |
| LFE | Lebanon For Entrepreneurs |

| | |
|---|---|
| MCISE | Moroccan Center for Innovation and Social Entrepreneurship |
| MENA | Middle East and North Africa |
| MFI | Microfinance Institutions |
| MIV | Microfinance Investment Vehicle |
| NESsT | Non-profit Enterprise and Self-sustainability Team |
| NGO | Non-Governmental Organization |
| NPO | Non-Profit Organization |
| OCP | Office Chérifien des Phosphates |
| OECD | Organisation for Economic Co-operation and Development |
| RISE Egypt | Realizing Innovation through Social Entrepreneurship in Egypt |
| ROI | Return on Investment |
| SE | Social Entrepreneurship |
| SETG | Social Enterprise Task Group |
| SITF | Social Investment Taskforce |
| SME | Small and Medium Enterprises |
| STC | Saudi Telecom Company |
| SWF | Sovereign Wealth Funds |
| TCSE | Tunisian Center for Social Entrepreneurship |
| UN | United Nations |
| UNDP | United Nations Development Programme |
| UNHCR | United Nations High Commissioner for Refugees |
| USAID | United States Agency for International Development |
| VC | Venture Capital |
| WDI | World Development Indicators |
| WEF | World Economic Forum |
| WES | Women's Enterprise for Sustainability |
| WOCMES | World Congress for Middle East Studies |
| WTO | World Trade Organization |

# Introduction

*Dima Jamali and Alessandro Lanteri*

Social entrepreneurship is a new trend that has taken the world of business by storm. Across the globe, social entrepreneurship (SE) continues to advance and seems to be increasingly recognized as a welcome addition to the traditional business lexicon, given its immense potential for shared value creation. According to Gregory Dees, who is credited as the father of social entrepreneurship and to whom we dedicate this book, given his untimely passing earlier this year, "A social entrepreneurial organization places a *social mission* as the *priority* over creating profit or wealth, tackling *social issues* with a business-like approach" (Dees, 2001). SE thus brings much needed entrepreneurial energy into the social space, harnessing the power and ingenuity of business to generate positive social innovations and social change across the world.

Despite soaring interest in recent years, knowledge of SE is still nascent across the Middle East. Our excursion in this book is intended to document the evolving understanding and practice of SE in this part of the world. Through the voices of scholars, practitioners, and social entrepreneurs who are anchored and working across the region, we document how SE manifests itself in practice and both the constraints and opportunities facing social entrepreneurs across this region. The contributors to this book make clear that while there is significant progress towards mainstreaming SE and harnessing its potential in addressing some of the thorny social issues afflicting the region, there are also enormous salient challenges and constraints, accentuating the fact that the potential for SE to contribute to the region's economic and social development remains, to date, largely untapped.

The Arab Spring served to highlight deep-seated socio-economic challenges facing countries of the Middle East and North Africa (MENA) region. With a population of over 345 million, half of whom are under the age of 25, unemployment continues to haunt generation after generation of Arab youth (World Bank, 2014; Roudi, 2011). With an estimated 20 million unemployed across this region (the unemployment regional average was estimated at 44 per cent in 2011), the World Economic Forum estimates that the region needs to create 75 million jobs by 2020 just to uphold the present employment levels (World Economic Forum, 2011). Specifically, the youth bulge in the region represents a noteworthy demographic challenge, but it can equally serve as an opportunity for development and change. Accordingly, the creation of sustainable jobs through private sector growth and investment is recognized as a prime avenue to harness the entrepreneurial energy of the youth, who lie at the heart of any future value creation across MENA.

Aside from unemployment, the region continues to grapple with a myriad of social and economic problems, including scattered pockets of poverty across MENA, elitist access to quality health care and education, and gender inequality among others. Poverty, for example, is a growing problem across the region, with poverty afflicting between 30 and 40 per cent of non-oil-producing countries (Ghandour, 2013). According to recent statistics, 23 per cent of the 345 million MENA residents live on less than $2 per day. Public health coverage extends to just about 30–40 per cent of the population in non-oil-producing countries (Jawad, 2014). Female labour force participation is estimated at about 26 per cent, one of the lowest in the world (and half of the global average of 51 per cent). There are salient economic inequalities across the region, with the nominal GDP for most non-oil-producing countries well below $10,000 per capita compared to over $20,000 for Gulf countries (Sirkeci et al., 2012). The estimated income per capita of Qatar, for example, considered to be the highest in the region, is over 30 times that of Yemen, which is among the poorest countries in the world (World Development Indicators, 2014).

These staggering social and environmental ills unfortunately also create tremendous opportunities for positive change through SE, which is much needed to complement the efforts of governments, civil society organizations, and the budding corporate social responsibility (CSR) initiatives across the region (Jamali and Sidani, 2012). According to Chapter 6 of Volume 2, the region is currently home to approximately 78 recognized social entrepreneurs, mostly males between 35 and 44 years and holding a post-secondary education degree. Also, as nicely highlighted through the various contributions to this book, the majority of social entrepreneurial activities in the MENA region are devoted to education and talent development, health care, and women empowerment. The contributions to this book also make clear that social entrepreneurial activities are thriving in the stable countries of the region, such as the Gulf area, rather than the turbulent and conflicted environments, such as Libya and Syria. Many of the Gulf countries are capitalizing on this new trend and partnering with international institutions to support the efforts of young entrepreneurial talent.

In this context, SE presents significant potential and hope for charting new ground and redefining new beginnings in a region where social value creation is most needed. Many believe that aside from highlighting the deep-seated inequalities in the region, the Arab Spring has also sparked a flow of entrepreneurial energy and increased sense of empowerment among the youth, translating into an array of social entrepreneurial ventures tackling cultural activities, health, agriculture, water and sanitation, and women empowerment among others. Also, as described in Chapter 8 of Volume 2, we have seen a substantive increase in the number of support institutions, as in dedicated centres, social incubators, and accelerators, working in this space. This coincides with a time that the technology market in the MENA countries is at a turning point which can serve as a booster for technology-oriented social entrepreneurial investments (Anderson, 2014). SE has also strong affinity with the culture of philanthropy and giving anchored across the region (Jamali and Sidani, 2012). Hence, there are various building blocks that could contribute positively to fostering a supportive ecosystem for SE in the years to come.

Yes, the contributors to this book have aptly highlighted some significant challenges that continue to hinder the progress of SE in the MENA region. Primary among these is the limited access to finance, with Arab investors still favouring traditional equity investing with short-term financial return; foreign aid investment also continues to be curtailed because of the risk and uncertainty across the region. As highlighted by various contributors, SE is also impeded by tight legal restrictions, time-consuming and expensive registration procedures, and the absence of a formal designation for social enterprise companies across most countries in the region, generating practical logistical challenges and constraints. Brain drain is also a challenge across the region, making it especially difficult for young entrepreneurial ventures to attract and retain human capital with the right talent and experience. Other aspects that are interfering with the ability of social enterprises to thrive include poor infrastructure, slow speed of Internet, lack of freedom of speech, lack of market research, and the scant supply of relevant knowledge pertaining to SE and sustainability, all compounded by protracted conflicts in various parts of the region. Facilitation by governments through enabling regulation, tax incentives, and nurturing supporting institutions is also key going forward.

## About the contributions to this book

It is clear from the above that this is an opportune time for researching SE across the MENA region. To sharpen our understanding of SE in this region, we present two volumes that draw on the insights and experiences of practitioners and scholars who are working across the region. Each author provides an important insight into SE from his/her unique vantage point. As highlighted below, the two volumes are complementary: one providing a generalist focus and the other one providing case-based supporting insights and evidence.

*Volume 1* provides much of the framing of the broad contours of SE in the region, in terms of commonly used definitions, leading SE ventures on offer, and regional and international organizations supporting these nascent efforts. Moreover, Volume 1 helps in delineating the drivers of SE and assessing the promise and potential of SE in addressing social issues through new and innovative business models, thus contributing to the region's broader and longer term transition to prosperity. Volume 1 also highlights some of the key priorities to nurture an entrepreneurial ecosystem, dwelling specifically on various mechanisms for scaling the social enterprise model, generating increased momentum in the field of impact investment, and engaging diasporas more closely in the emerging regional SE ecosystem.

*Volume 2* takes on a more practical case-based approach, providing detailed examples of the practice of SE in different countries in MENA, including Egypt, Lebanon, Saudi Arabia, and Morocco. By providing various examples of the practice of SE from across a spectrum of countries in the region, the authors of Volume 2 help synthesize a practical assessment of the opportunities and constraints on the ground, as well as a range of more practical recommendations for taking the sector forward, including increasing entrepreneurial skills, providing access to venture capital, providing technical advice and access to a network of partners and support institutions, including incubators and funders, all while harnessing vision, values, volunteerism, and engagement in pursuit of the greater social good.

The two volumes are complementary and together provide a more rounded understanding of SE across various parts of the MENA region, its distinctive manifestations, challenges, and opportunities, and priorities for the region going forward, building on insights from a variety of MENA countries. While some countries are featured in detail (e.g. Lebanon, Egypt, Saudi Arabia, Morocco), the volumes also draw insights from Palestine, Libya, Tunisia, Qatar, Yemen, Jordan, Syria, Iraq, United Arab Emirates, and Kuwait. Together, the two volumes go a long way in unfleshing the vibrant discourse around SE in a context that has received scant attention and capturing the immense potential of social enterprise as a viable model for innovation, transformation, and change in MENA at a time when the region is grappling with a myriad of social and economic challenges.

In the section that follows, we provide the main highlights and a succinct roadmap to each of the chapters included in the first volume.

## Chapter 1: A decade of social entrepreneurship in the region

As aptly pointed out in the first chapter, the field of SE has experienced an exponential growth, but the proliferation of terminology with varying nuances and definitions has impeded the effective progress of SE in the Middle East. Therefore, in Chapter 1, Iman Bibars begins by examining various definitions of SE, elucidating its distinguishing characteristics and differentiating it from similar terms and descriptions that are commonly – and wrongly – associated with SE. The chapter then makes a strong case why SE is crucial for the future development of the entire Arab region and provides various examples of leading social entrepreneurial ventures led by Ashoka Fellows across the region and how this in turn is creating an enabling development-oriented environment. Iman posits that the social business model has evolved as an essential avenue or platform for addressing the social and political turbulences afflicting the region, particularly with the advent of Arab Spring. The society-wide impact that these social entrepreneurs create needs more recognition and channelling of investment, as we develop collective awareness in this region that financial returns on investments are accrued by long-term social and economic development just as much as short-term monetary gains.

## Chapter 2: The context for social entrepreneurship in the Middle East

In Chapter 2, Diana Greenwald and Samantha Constant provide a broad brush assessment of the institutional and macroeconomic environment for SE in the MENA. Their chapter nicely describes the region's socio-economic landscape, noting both important variation in characteristics across countries, such as income level, population, and nature of export, and some shared development challenges, including large youth populations and high unemployment. In addition to the pre-existing challenges, the authors highlight the economic and social spillovers of recent uprisings and political frustrations. Drawing on interviews with key stakeholders consisting mainly of individuals in the entrepreneurship support sector and in some of the leading international and regional organizations supporting SE, the authors note that more can be done to practically connect the discourse and activities surrounding SE to national and regional priorities. The chapter evaluates the respective roles of governments, investors and support organizations, and educational institutions in shaping the SE ecosystem in MENA. The cases of Tunisia, Libya, and Palestine are explored in detail. The chapter concludes by outlining broad principles for those seeking to support the growth of SE in the region as a separate entity from the traditional private or non-profit sector. Particularly, the authors suggest that while the policy environment and funding mechanisms remain constrained, the "socialization" of SE in public governance can result in a better mainstreaming of SE, as part of a menu of priorities for MENA to enable stakeholders to embrace it and utilize it.

## Chapter 3: The rise of social entrepreneurship in the Middle East: A pathway for inclusive growth or an alluring mirage?

As highlighted by Soushiant Zanganehpour in Chapter 3, the Arab World is now at an important socio-political and economic inflection point. On one hand, it faces compounding social and environmental challenges. On the other hand, many across the region have developed a renewed sense of pride and optimism about its future. Soushiant explores, in this chapter, the rising interest in the concept and practice of SE across the Arab World. The author explains how SE has recently resonated across the Arab World as an innovative trend for dealing with today's complex social needs, blurring the traditional boundaries among public, private, and non-profit sectors. Furthermore, the chapter highlights the extent to which SE can help facilitate change in the near term while considering the extent to which it may contribute to the region's broader and longer term transition to prosperity. However, the author concludes that, in order for SE to provide an effective arsenal of sustainable solutions, social entrepreneurs and other stakeholders should collaborate to build an ecosystem of support, which entails the involvement of key institutions and economic actors, such as government, educational institutions, and the private sector, which can all actively engage in creating a conducive innovation environment. We also need to work concomitantly on alleviating a range of obstacles facing social enterprises including low awareness, lack of funding, the limitations of existing legal frameworks, and the absence of technical support.

## Chapter 4: Social enterprise in the MENA region: False hope or new dawn?

As members of MENA's emerging social enterprise community, Rebecca Hill and Medea Nocentini, the authors of Chapter 4, foresee a bright future for the social enterprise sector, given the increasing significance of key drivers such as the prevalence of pressing social issues requiring sustainable solutions, the favourable demographic structure, and the development of technology infrastructure. Another sign for social enterprise prosperity is the growing convergence of different stakeholder efforts including regional and international support, governmental efforts and investments, and CSR initiatives. Given the limitations of existing "social good" initiatives, the authors posit SE as a key platform that can contribute to MENA's social, environmental, and economic growth. Rather than demonstrating a new dawn, the authors posit that SE is not a false hope – there are enough companies and entrepreneurs contributing to solve social issues via business models that both grow the enterprise and address underlying challenges. In other words, the authors suggest that the social enterprise model is certainly viable for the MENA region. While this business model is valid in its own right, it is its resilience to market volatility that makes it a compelling option for this region. Despite the overall optimistic outlook and rhetoric, the authors acknowledge that being an entrepreneur in MENA is not easy and propose a series of recommendations to build a collaborative framework and a fostering ecosystem. Hill and Nocentini identify some of the key priorities to be addressed in this respect, including providing a legal structure conducive to SE, conducting additional research about consumer preferences and other market data, and raising general awareness regarding SE. Finally, the authors conclude that SE may well be the missing link for generating the much-needed social impact in this region and devising disruptive solutions and systemic solutions to endemic social and economic issues.

## Chapter 5: Social enterprises: A panacea for engaging youth and inspiring hope?

Entrenched in the Arab world, neither youth unemployment nor disengagement is unique to this region. Capitalizing on this key insight, Chapter 5 by Clare Woodcraft-Scott and Fatimah S. Baeshen emphasizes the promising role of the social enterprise in providing a solution for development-related challenges across MENA. The authors aptly point out that Arab human capital tops many corporate agendas and yet the region has the highest percentage of disengaged employees in the world, with youth unemployment reaching around 30 per cent. Businesses complain about the mismatch between youth skills and industry needs, and job creation is often cited as the biggest regional challenge. These factors are juxtaposed with the rapid growth of social enterprises that have evolved from being an obscure jargon to a trend that even formal businesses now embrace. According to Woodcraft-Scott and Baeshen, the flaws of capitalism have perhaps fuelled this appetite for more responsible business models and inspired new hope in Arab youth. Accordingly, they explore, in their chapter, the complex links between traditional socio-economic constructs, the disaffection and alienation of the youth, and the prospect of social enterprises creating a new regional paradigm. Based on different examples of local entrepreneurs, the contributors explain how social enterprises are reducing the dependence on governments and focusing on regional development. The authors then reveal a number of reforms needed in the region to build an enabling environment for social enterprises to prosper and respond to different challenges. Such reforms include designing legislations that allow the construction of social purpose businesses, establishing laws that are convenient for social enterprises, implementing formal mentorship structures for start-up social enterprises, and raising awareness about the concept of SE and its benefits.

## Chapter 6: Scaling social enterprises and scaling impact in the Middle East

Chapter 6 ponders ways to maximize the public benefit of entrepreneurial activity and increasingly engage the strengths of the private sector in boosting social impact in the Middle East through stimulating the growth of scalable social enterprises. The general framework proposed by David Mounir Nabti is that, although riskier than for-profit small businesses, scalable start-up social enterprises have much more potential benefits to both the entrepreneur and the community. Accordingly, the chapter examines internal and external challenges to social enterprise scaling in the Middle East. External challenges include entity registration, access to finance, infrastructure, and business processes and transactions, while internal challenges are mainly associated with the social entrepreneur's personal traits, such as risk aversion and innovation limitations. The highlights of this chapter, however, are the different recommendations for enhancing the scalability of social impact and social enterprises through using tools and adaptations of tools that have been developed for use in for-profit entrepreneurship and that address the specific challenges facing social enterprises in the region. Some of the key recommendations for increasing scalable social enterprises in the Middle East identified by Nabti include increasing the availability of financing, introducing legal reforms to make registration procedures simpler, and improving educational curricula to nurture SE at a young age. In addition to the former interventions, Nabti emphasizes that one critical consideration for social entrepreneurs is whether to choose an organization-focused scaling or a non-organization-focused scaling based on the challenges faced and available resources.

## Chapter 7: Bridging impact and investment in MENA

As pointed out by Jamil Wyne in Chapter 7, though a young field globally, impact investment is gaining momentum, through the buy-in from the private sector, grassroot organizations, and even governments as a viable way of deploying capital to deliver profitable solutions for social and environmental challenges. At the heart of this movement is a belief that companies can be profitable to investors while having a scalable impact on their countries and communities. However, the MENA region, despite having a growing entrepreneurship ecosystem and large demand for development solutions, has yet to fully embrace and effectively utilize impact investment. In this chapter, Jamil Wyne explains why investors in MENA are just beginning to explore the impact investment space. According to the author, this gap is due to several factors including low public interest, an underdeveloped venture capital sector, the limited amount of investment traditionally directed to social enterprises, and the lack of success stories related to funds invested in social enterprises that meet expected financial and social returns. Finally, the author identifies a range of solutions for practitioners looking to generate momentum in the field of impact investment. In particular, supporting impact investment would require mobilizing the diaspora, increasing research and knowledge sharing, adopting a gradual approach, focusing on capacity building, and encouraging and incorporating impact investment as part of a larger economic development agenda.

## Chapter 8: From necessity to opportunity: The case for impact investing in the Arab World

In Chapter 8, Ali El Idrissi points out that while the bulk of impact investments are directed to emerging markets, some regions such as the MENA are still under-represented and attract less capital than other regions. Starting with a definition of impact investment as the practice of investing for positive social and/or environmental impact while also targeting a financial return, the chapter explores the rise of impact investment globally and the reasons behind the under-representation of MENA. Ali El Idrissi notes that the current level of impact investment in MENA is not surprising, as investment opportunities are still limited and the main conduits through which it developed in other regions, such as sustainable investing, microfinance, and venture capital, are underdeveloped in MENA. However, the author also notes that the current cultural shift and momentum behind social business in the region can create vast opportunities to accelerate economic growth and social progress, if a robust and holistic ecosystem is built over the next decade. In this respect, while the demand for impact investment is increasing, there should be a focus on expanding and deepening the range of services provided to ventures as well as the scope of those ventures. Accordingly, the author suggests that capacity-building organizations should be equipped to provide high-quality business support including financial management, intellectual property, and access to investors. Other initiatives include addressing regulatory challenges, supporting early-stage ventures to grow, increasing the supply of capital to entrepreneurs, and leveraging recent experience from similar cases abroad.

## Chapter 9: Arab diasporas: A catalyst for the growth of social ventures in the Middle East?

Arab diasporas (from Egypt, Lebanon, Palestine, Syria, Jordan, Iraq, and Yemen) have shown throughout history their resilience, capacity, and interest in supporting their country of origin or descent. As emphasized by Irene Kapusta in Chapter 9, the level of remittances and humanitarian support that diasporas regularly channel to the Middle East provides hope to also engage diasporas in the emerging regional SE ecosystem. Recent Arab diaspora initiatives for start-up growth offer interesting involvement models. For example, Lebanon For Entrepreneurs (LFE) was launched in 2013 by three US-based Lebanese diaspora entities (LIFE, LebNet, and SEAL) and was set up "to accelerate the development of the Lebanese IT start-up ecosystem through the active involvement of diaspora organizations". Yet, Irene notes that the literature on Arab diasporas is scarce. Above all, the lack of diasporic trust in Middle Eastern entities (not least, governments and non-profits) and the fragmentation of Arab diasporas require original diaspora engagement models. Accordingly, Irene Kapusta demonstrates, in this chapter, how diaspora contributions to regional SE should go far beyond philanthropy. According to the author, diasporas can be involved in setting up engagement schemes, and mobilization should be incremental. SE, in turn, would benefit from dedicated communication channels (diasporas networks, social media, and physical places for meetings) and from communities of supporters, to effectively mobilize diaspora communities. The author suggests several models to engage diaspora communities in SE in the Middle East. The first model is rallying diasporas on their own terms by involving them in setting up and defining the project, building a feedback process, and creating electronic involvement options for diasporas' virtual participation. The second model is creating an SE platform to educate diasporas on the role and mission of social enterprises and build trust in Middle Eastern social enterprises. The third and final model focuses on forming an initial circle of supporters for Middle Eastern social ventures in order to, later on, reach out to other diaspora members. Such engagement should not be limited to financial support but should be spread to meet the needs of the different parties of the SE ecosystem.

## References

Anderson, B. (March 2014). As Arab Startups Get More Serious, So Too Does VC Investment. *Wall Street Journal*, available at http://blogs.wsj.com/middleeast/2014/03/04/as-arab-startups-get-more-serious-so-too-does-vc-investment/.
Dees, Gregory J. (Original Draft: 31 October 1998 Reformatted and Revised: 30 May 2001). The Meaning of "Social Entrepreneurship", available at http://www.caseatduke.org/documents/dees_sedef.pdf.

Ghandour, F. (2013). Corporate Entrepreneurial Responsibility (CER), available at http://www.wamda.com/2013/01/corporate-entrepreneurship-responsibility-by-fadi-ghandour.

Jamali, D. and Sidani, Y. (Eds.) (2012). *CSR in the Middle East: Fresh Perspectives.* Palgrave Macmillan.

Jawad, R. (2014). Social Protection in the Arab Region: Emerging Trends and Recommendations for Future Social Policy. United Nations Development Programme, Regional Bureau for Arab States, Arab Human Development Report, Research Paper Series, available at http://www.arab-hdr.org/publications/other/ahdrps/Final_Rana%20Jawad_Social%20Policies%20(ENG).pdf.

Moayed, T. T. (2011). *Middle East and North Africa – Regional Brief.* Washington, DC: World Bank, available at http://go.worldbank.org/1JVC0DGRS0.

Roudi, F. (2011). Youth Population & Employment in the Middle East & North Africa: Opportunity or Challenge. UN/POP/EGM-AYD/2011/06.

Sirkeci, I., Cohen, J. and Ratha, D. (2012). *Migration and Remittances during the Global Financial Crisis and Beyond.* Washington, DC: World Bank.

The World Bank (2014). Data: Middle East & North Africa, available at http://data.worldbank.org/region/MNA.

World Economic Forum (WEF) (2011). *Accelerating Entrepreneurship in the Arab World.* World Economic Forum (WEF) with Booz & Company.

World Development Indicators (WDI) (2014). The World Bank, available at http://data.worldbank.org/products/wdi.

# 1
## A Decade of Social Entrepreneurship in the Region

*Iman Bibars*

This chapter gives an overview of social entrepreneurship, both as a concept and as a practice in the Arab World. It has two main focuses: to interrogate and define the term "social entrepreneurship" and differentiate it from other, related, concepts; and to demonstrate why social entrepreneurship is an essential tool for solving social challenges, which has particular relevance for the Arab World in the light of the "Arab Spring" (or Arab Awakening).

I have been working with Ashoka: Innovators for the Public for 11 years, having established Ashoka Arab World, our regional office in Cairo, in 2003. My long experience with this organization, the platform for social innovation, has led me to the understanding that in order to be able to examine any of the issues listed above, we first need to agree on definitions.

Social entrepreneurship and what has come to be known as the Arab Spring are very loaded concepts that have been defined and understood differently by activists, social and business entrepreneurs, and academics alike. The different, and sometimes contradictory, definitions encountered have adversely affected the progress of social entrepreneurs working in the Arab World. It is important to have a clear understanding of the terminology used by different sectors – the social sector, the private sector, educational institutions, government bodies, and other stakeholders – if they are to collaborate in order to support social entrepreneurs and facilitate progress.

This chapter begins with an introduction of different definitions as understood by the leading social entrepreneurship institutions, explaining the history of the term "social entrepreneurship" through the story of Bill Drayton, the founder of Ashoka who originally coined the term, and reclaiming the true spirit of entrepreneurship that has been somewhat distorted by the business sector. Following that, the chapter explains why it is important and represents sound business and economic sense to invest in social entrepreneurs (male and female) whose work leads to significant long-term economic and social returns. Finally, the chapter argues that we need to change the social investment framework and create an enabling environment for social entrepreneurship in the Arab World in order to achieve these long-term returns that will benefit all sectors of society, business included.

## Definitions and terminology

There are three leading global organizations that seek to promote and encourage social entrepreneurship: Ashoka, the Schwab Foundation for Social Entrepreneurship, and the Skoll Foundation. It is appropriate, therefore, to use the definitions of social entrepreneurship as given by these three organizations as a starting point for our examination of the concept and its practical application as a tool for addressing social issues.

Ashoka, founded by Bill Drayton in 1980, was the first platform for social entrepreneurs and today boasts the largest network of social entrepreneurs worldwide, supporting more than 3,000 Ashoka Fellows across the globe. In fact, it was Bill Drayton who coined the term "social entrepreneurship". According to Ashoka:

> Social entrepreneurs are individuals with innovative solutions to society's most pressing social problems. They are ambitious and persistent, tackling major social issues and offering new ideas for wide-scale change. Rather than leaving societal needs to the government or business sectors, social entrepreneurs find what is not working and solve the problem by changing the system, spreading the solution, and persuading entire societies to move in different directions.

> Social entrepreneurs often seem to be possessed by their ideas, committing their lives to changing the direction of their field. They are visionaries, but also realists, and are ultimately concerned with the practical implementation of their vision above all else.

Social entrepreneurs present user-friendly, understandable, and ethical ideas that engage widespread support in order to maximize the number of citizens that will stand up, seize their idea, and implement it.[1]

The Schwab Foundation for Social Entrepreneurship was founded in 1998 by Klaus and Hilde Schwab. The foundation is a non-profit and politically neutral organization that exists with the aim of advancing social entrepreneurship and supporting existing social entrepreneurs to transform society. They describe social entrepreneurs as the drivers of social innovation and transformation in various fields, seeking to

pursue poverty alleviation goals with entrepreneurial zeal, business methods and the courage to innovate and overcome traditional practices. A social entrepreneur, similar to a business entrepreneur, builds strong and sustainable organizations, which are either set up as not-for-profits or companies.[2]

The Skoll Foundation was founded in 1999 by Jeff Skoll, the first full-time employee of eBay, who later became the company's first president. Skoll created the foundation with the vision of establishing a more sustainable and peaceful world. The best way to do this, he thought, was to invest in the innovative and creative people who were already positively transforming their own communities: social entrepreneurs.

The Skoll Foundation describes social entrepreneurs as "society's change agents, creators of innovations that disrupt the status quo and transform our world for the better".[3] Furthermore, according to their understanding, social entrepreneurs possess similar personality traits; they are "ambitious, mission driven, strategic, resourceful, and results oriented".[4]

To understand the original meaning of the term "social entrepreneurship", as coined by Bill Drayton 30 years ago, it is important to understand what led to Bill's decision to start Ashoka and the historical context in which this initiative took place.

In the late 1970s, the social sector was growing in size and scope, more than any other sector. However, innovation and creative thinking were not encouraged in the social sector; on the contrary, government donors dominated and controlled the scene and imposed their own solutions to basic, structural social problems for NGOs everywhere. They used a "one-size-fits-all" approach, attempting to employ the same solutions for poverty, women's empowerment, and environmental challenges, and this was generally promoted and accepted. NGOs had to adapt their proposals and their needs to whichever priority or "fad" large, international, multinational and bilateral government donors wanted to address. Thus the policies, strategic development and approaches employed by the social sector were donor-centred rather than problem-centred or beneficiary-centred; they also often lacked cohesion or clear direction and were not based on the experience and priorities of experts working in the sector or of the beneficiaries themselves. The overall approach was nowhere near as effective as it needed to be, largely because it was tailored to the priorities of the donors, who did not have expert or in-depth knowledge of how to eradicate social problems.

Within this context, Bill Drayton saw a vastly different mindset in the business sector. Risk takers and innovative ideas were promoted, and people working in the sector were encouraged to expand markets and offered technical and financial support to scale and grow their initiatives. Bill Drayton identified the quality catalysing the growth of the business sector as "entrepreneurship", which was celebrated in a business context. Innovation was not frowned upon. He, therefore, decided to create the first platform to seek out innovative and entrepreneurial souls in the social sector and to support them to enable the effective growth of their ideas and initiatives. He called these people social entrepreneurs: risk takers committed to solving the social challenges they have identified as a priority in their countries and communities through the implementation of system-changing solutions, which address and tackle the root causes of these challenges.

In Bill's own words:

> Whenever society is stuck or has an opportunity to seize a new opportunity, it needs an entrepreneur to see the opportunity and then to turn that vision into a realistic idea and then a reality and then, indeed, the new pattern all across society. We need such entrepreneurial leadership at least as much in education and human rights as we do in communications and hotels. This is the work of social entrepreneurs.[5]

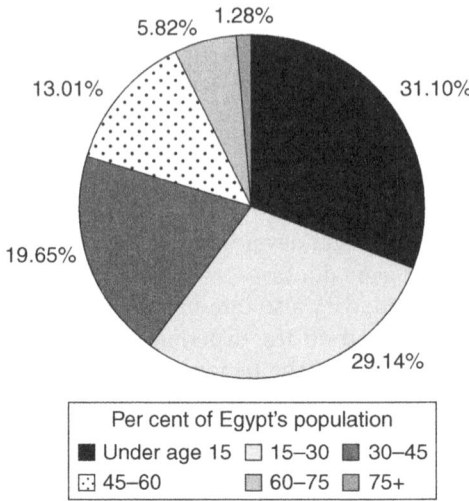

*Figure 1.1*  Pie chart highlighting Egypt's youth bulge
*Note*: Over 60 per cent of Egypt's population are aged 30 or below.
*Source*: CAPMAS – The official statistics agency of Egypt.

Understanding the historical context in which terms such as "entrepreneur" and "social entrepreneur" and their original and historical meanings developed is very important, especially given the recent emphasis on promoting social entrepreneurship as a means of rebuilding Egypt and the whole Arab region in the aftermath of the Arab Awakening (aka Arab Spring) (Figure 1.1).

Bill Drayton and Ashoka's definition of social entrepreneurship crucially includes the idea that its distinguishing characteristic, and its value, lies in using innovative approaches to create systemic change, tackling the root causes of problems to permanently solve them, regardless of the particular techniques and operational models implemented, business or otherwise. Ashoka and social entrepreneurs, therefore, have a long-term vision for sustainable change by eradicating problems in an effective way.

According to this vision, not only is financial profit not the primary objective of a social entrepreneur, but also social entrepreneurs do not necessarily seek financial sustainability. The sustainability of investing in a social entrepreneur comes from the long-term social and economic returns of the benefits their initiatives offer. Social entrepreneurship is, therefore, very different from social enterprise, inclusive business, and business with a heart. And these differences are vital and important when we examine the current situation and future prospects in Egypt and the whole Arab region.

Therefore, notions of affecting change and disrupting and transforming the status quo, for the benefit of certain sectors of society, are the defining aspects of social entrepreneurship. However, there is still an underlying implication within the business world and certain emerging branches of the social sector that financial sustainability, if not outright profit, is an important criterion for the initiative of a social entrepreneur. This assumption that social entrepreneurship means a business with a social cause or an inclusive business stems from how the term "entrepreneur" became associated with profit and business.

However, the term "business entrepreneur" does not describe someone who makes only money; it describes a person who innovates, thinks out of the box and expands his or her market. The word "entrepreneur" is derived from French and describes an adventurer, one who dares to take risks in pursuit of his or her goal and thinks and acts against the current. This is a person who sees an opportunity and seizes it and, in doing so, creates new value and wealth.

If entrepreneurs are successful in the business sector, they earn money. Their innovative and disruptive ideas shift economic resources from less productive areas to more productive areas and hence make a profit.[6] Importantly, the profit is derived from the innovation and the opening up of new markets. Profit-making alone does not describe an entrepreneur.

The entrepreneurial character trait has become strongly associated with business ventures because the people who exhibited this quality were pioneers and achieved high levels of success. Ford, Microsoft, Apple, Google, Facebook, and Twitter are all examples of entrepreneurial endeavours in the sense that they carved a new industry and created a new market because the pioneers behind them saw an opportunity and seized it. The fact that they made money – and lots of it – resulted in the term "entrepreneur" becoming closely affiliated with the business sector.

For social entrepreneurs, profit-making and financial sustainability are secondary concerns. Their defining character traits lie in their innovative, system-changing, and sustainable solutions to society's most pressing problems. Financial sustainability is achieved through the long-term social benefits accrued through the social entrepreneur's work; a more cohesive society, less crime, more women involved in social and economic life, improved education, increased employment meaning more tax revenues, more people with disposable incomes to spend on products and services – this is the long-term sustainability of social entrepreneurs. These economic and social returns allow societies to prosper and produce thriving markets and economic growth. Of course, social entrepreneurs can make profit and use business methods in their strategies, but such criteria are not their defining aspects; sustainable solutions to social problems, achieved in the most effective manner regardless of the technique or model, define social entrepreneurship.

Having said this, Egypt and the entire Arab World do need all types of investment in addition to empowering every innovative person and encouraging every idea that could address the social and economic challenges that we are facing, which have increased in the past three years since the Arab Awakening.

One such challenge is youth unemployment, and Figure 1.2 demonstrates the scope of the problem in Egypt, particularly female youth unemployment. Moreover, of the total unemployed women,

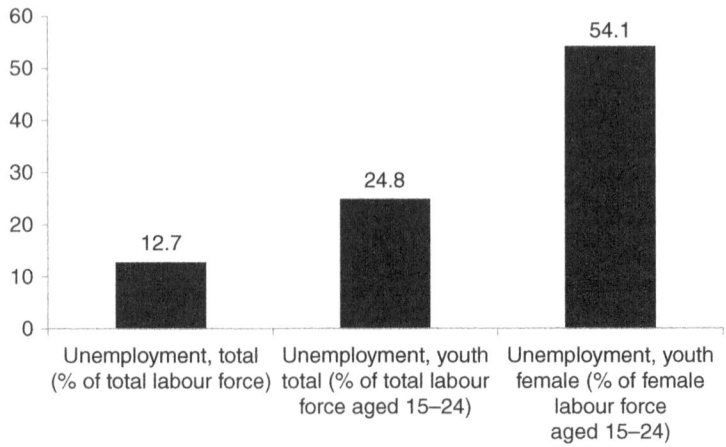

*Figure 1.2*   Egyptian unemployment figures
Source: World Bank Data Bank.

41.2 per cent have a university degree. This is a huge waste of talent and potential.

In addition to youth unemployment, the Arab World experiences a myriad of social and economic problems. There are women's rights issues, poverty issues, lack of quality education for all citizens, sectarian and ethnic strife, and many more challenges that are extensively researched and studied via numerous academic institutions, governments, and NGOs, and so do not need more details here.

There is, therefore, a very real need to create and promote social enterprises (social ventures that are financially sustainable) and social businesses (businesses that aim to do social good) alongside social entrepreneurs and their initiatives. We do need a responsible business sector, and we do need sustainable and economically viable solutions to the many challenges we currently face in the region. All of these approaches are extremely important; we just need to be clear and realistic about what is needed to facilitate each approach and identify where each one is most effective.

## Why is it important to invest in social entrepreneurship?

Investing in social entrepreneurs constitutes a long-term investment to solve the root causes and underlying phenomena of social and economic issues that will eventually create thriving, solution-focused communities, leading to long-term social and economic returns.

Investments should not be made out of vague notions of benevolence or even compassion; rather, like any other investment, it should be made for practical purposes. Self-interest, in the long term, coheres with the interests of society at large; a thriving society benefits your country's economy, your investment and yourself. Stable and productive societies produce better results; it is, therefore, in everyone's interests to invest in the people who solve the biggest social problems and create stable societies. We should be asking ourselves what the economic costs of social problems are and how we can reduce them.

For example, what are the benefits to society as a whole if we address problems in our education systems? There have been many studies showing that investments in education, particularly, in early education and quality of education, have a profound impact on society and the economy. Social problems, such as crime, are reduced and an increasingly skilled labour force is more able to compete in a 21st-century technological business world.

In a World Bank Policy Paper from 2007 on the role played by education quality in economic growth, three main findings were reported:

> First, educational quality has great effects on individual earnings, on income distribution and on economic growth. Furthermore, the paper found that individual earnings are "systematically related to cognitive skills" and economic growth is strongly affected by the skills of workers. The existing evidence suggests that as quality of education improves, economic performance improves and that the more skilled a population is, the better that nation will perform economically.[7]
>
> The second finding highlights the fact that current poor economic productivity and performance in developing countries are far worse than generally accepted and that poor rates of school enrolment and attainment are the main causes of failing to realize potential and create economic growth or development.
>
> Finally, the third finding of the paper posits that simply increasing resources in an attempt to quickly improve education will be insufficient, as structural and institutional changes are necessary in developing countries, highlighting growing evidence that the main objective should be to improve the quality of teachers and teaching. This supports the idea that the change needed is systemic and that increasing funds to existing projects will be insufficient.[8]

To further argue that investing in education is a financially sound investment, detailed quantitative research conducted in 2000 found that a difference of one standard deviation on test performance in mathematics and the sciences was related to a 1.4 per cent difference in annual growth rates of GDP per capita.[9] Not only does such growth directly impact on economic productivity, but greater incomes result in poverty reduction, healthier populations, and a wide variety of other added benefits leading to improved economic and social well-being. The research paper concluded that "labour force quality has a consistent, stable, and strong relationship with economic growth" and that there was mounting and clear evidence that differences in productivity between nations were related to international test performances and that these differences were caused by differences in the quality of schooling as opposed to any other cultural or familial factors.[10]

The effects of improvements in education on economic growth are far wider than simply producing a more skilled workforce. The cumulative benefits to society and the economy are manifold and include an overall reduction in crime and a healthier environment with more effective civil institutions; all sectors and stakeholders benefit from this, including the business sector. Characteristics such as persistence, problem-solving skills, and analytical thought are all developed and nurtured through a high-quality education, and well-educated citizens are more likely to be adaptable to change and responsive to alternative points of view. These are all important qualities in employees and the citizens of nation states.

In Egypt and the Arab World, the main issue with the education system is that it does not meet the demands of the jobs market. There is a gap between the skills acquired through the education system and skills demanded by employers. Evidence for this mismatch between education and employment is found in the growing numbers of unemployed youth. Worryingly, most unemployed youth are university graduates. Society invests significant amounts of time and resources to allow young people a university-level education; so when they graduate and do not find employment, it is not just their lost potential productivity that harms economic growth but also the wasted resources and energy spent on their earlier education. The only actors who can bridge this gap are social entrepreneurs.

*Raghda El Ebrashi*, an Ashoka Arab World Fellow, is creating employment opportunities for marginalized youth in Egypt by bridging the gap between the social sector and the business sector, training and matching prospective employees from communities without access to the labour market with corporations. Her organization, Alashanek Ya Balady (AYB), focuses on skills provision to potential employees, based on the needs of the business sector, as well as creating income generation opportunities in the informal sector. As such, she is helping to create a cadre of prospective employees trained in the skills they need to find work – which is more practical, more viable, and more cost effective than attempting to reform the entire education sector (Figure 1.3).

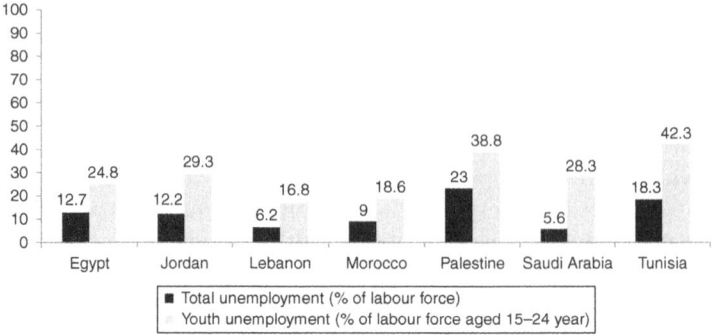

*Figure 1.3*  Comparison of per cent of total unemployment with per cent of youth unemployment

*Source*: World Bank Data Bank.

Another Ashoka Fellow, *Mohammed Abbad Andaloussi*, is likewise helping to bridge the gap between the education system and the business sector in Morocco, facilitating collaborations between the two to provide students with higher quality, market-relevant education to maximize their professional success. By ensuring that business organizations partner with schools, providing their expertise and tools to enhance the education and services provided to students, Mohammed is creating a market in which business leaders see the value of a true investment in the education system, undertaken for practical rather than charitable or philanthropic purposes. At the same time, he is catalysing a change within educational bodies, so that they focus on equipping students with the skills they need to be professional leaders in an increasingly globalized world.

Social entrepreneurs, such as Raghda and Mohammed, identify gaps and missing links at various stages of the value chain. Without them, these problems would go unsolved and the economic benefits associated with improved education and skills development of young people would be lost. An investment in El Ebrashi or Andaloussi, therefore, should be viewed as a sound financial decision as the long-term prospects for you, your business, your community, and your nation are improved with their success.

Another social issue obstructing economic and social development is the role and status of women in society. Again on this issue, investing in increasing women's rights, safety, and employment is not merely a social cause to be fought for by feminists. The economic benefits, both direct and indirect, associated with investing in women are enormous and will lead to financial returns on those investments. According to the UN Entity for Gender Equality and the Empowerment of Women (UN Women), by empowering women to participate fully in economic life across all sectors, we will "build strong economies, establish stable and just societies, achieve sustainability and human rights, improve the quality of life for women, men, families and communities and propel business operations and goals".[11]

According to USAID, any investment made in women is multiplied by the extension of benefits to the world around them, building stronger communities and increasing prospects of progress in a whole host of areas. Studies have shown that in the developing world, women reinvest 90 per cent of their earnings into their families whereas men reinvest only 40 per cent.[12]

Moreover, increasing education for girls has a number of important benefits.[13] Studies have shown that when an additional 10 per cent of a nation's girls attend school, extraordinary results follow: the GDP of that nation will increase by 3 per cent on average; fewer girls will fall victim to health issues, such as female genital mutilation and HIV; girls will have more control over their reproductive lives as an educated woman has a greater chance of surviving labour and is more likely to have fewer and healthier children, who themselves are more likely to receive a better education. Educating girls and women also increases agricultural productivity and combats malnutrition.[14]

The role of women in agriculture is another important issue, as they comprise 43 per cent of the global agricultural labour force. Many households and families worldwide rely on the productivity of these women, providing more proof that a woman's importance is not simply confined to family support and roles as caregivers. Despite these facts, women are the victims of all types of discrimination and receive very little support, a failure to recognize their important position in society.

According to the UN Food and Agriculture Organization (FAO), women struggle to access land and financial resources as well as experience wage discrimination, particularly in rural labour markets. This not only affects their own productivity, whereby agricultural production and quality is compromised, but further harms society

and the economy, as insecure jobs and low wages make it more difficult to provide sufficient support for the education, health, and development of their children. Investing in solving these structural issues
has the potential to lift many people out of poverty and hunger and
allow them to become productive and effective members of society
and contribute to the growth and development of the economy.[15]

Ashoka Arab World Fellow *Zeinab Al-Momani* founded the first
agricultural union operated by and for women in the Arab World
in Jordan, following the principle that women must demand and
instigate their own full economic, social and political participation.
Zeinab is providing women traditionally impeded by prevailing gender norms, a lack of access to education and training and a lack
of support from institutional and legal frameworks with a means
of organizing their work and collectively building their capacity.
Through these unions, Jordanian women in agriculture achieve economic independence, allowing greater investments in their families
and communities, and can take advantage of a supportive framework
in which the additional gains of employment – increased confidence,
knowledge, and collective social participation – can increase. Her
approach is adapted to the needs of a marginalized group, unemployed women in urban and rural areas of the Levant, by developing
a means of economic empowerment from within the targeted community. In this regard, it has the potential for long-term sustainability
as well as being replicable and scalable (Figure 1.4).

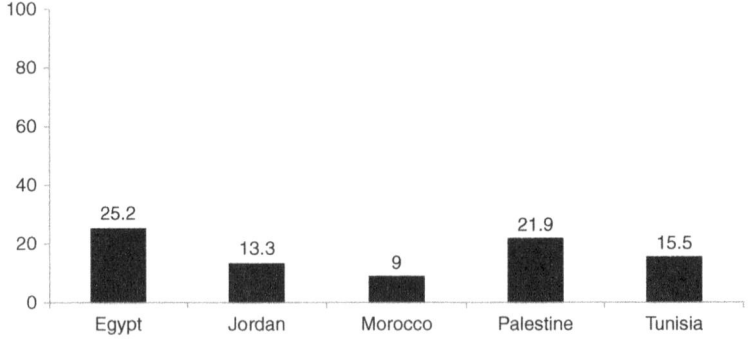

*Figure 1.4*   Poverty headcount ratio at national poverty line (per cent of
population)
*Source*: World Bank Data Bank.

Zeinab, as a social entrepreneur, identifies where markets and government interventions fail and fixes the problem. Through fixing these problems, in Zeinab's case creating agricultural unions for women, social and economic benefits are accrued and felt across all sectors of society. Investing in Zeinab not only benefits the women she works with and their families, but also increases agricultural productivity providing more food for the community and more food to be sold in markets. Improving health and local economies in this manner benefits everyone, including the investor who will see a return beyond a nice philanthropic feeling of "doing good".

Furthermore, many studies have shown that greater economic independence for females, in the form of higher earnings and greater bargaining power, results in increased investment in children's education, health, and nutrition, translating into future economic growth. For example, it has been predicted that GDP in India could increase by 8 per cent if the female-to-male ratio of workers increased by 10 per cent, and in Africa, increasing women's access to agricultural resources to similar levels of access enjoyed by men could see agricultural productivity increase by 20 per cent. Additionally, as has been seen all over the world, when the number of women-owned businesses increases, greater economic growth and poverty reduction are witnessed. Investing in women is a successful investment.[16]

As stated in a World Bank Group Gender Action Plan from 2006:

Gains in women's economic opportunities lag behind those in women's capabilities. This is inefficient, since increased women's labor force participation and earnings are associated with reduced poverty and faster growth; women will benefit from their economic empowerment, but so too will men, children and society as a whole. Women's lack of economic empowerment, on the other hand, not only imperils growth and poverty reduction, but also has a host of other negative impacts, including less favorable education and health outcomes for children and a more rapid spread of HIV/AIDS. In sum, the business case for expanding women's economic opportunities is becoming increasingly evident; *this is nothing more than smart economics.*[17]

(emphasis added)

Elected to Ashoka Arab World fellowship in 2013, *Khalid al Khudair* is working to enhance the role of women in Saudi Arabia and the

Gulf by carving out new professional work opportunities for Saudi women and leading their integration into the workforce. Khalid's organization "Glowork" uses a three-pronged approach: advocating at the government level for policy change to make it easier (and in some cases, a mandatory requirement) for companies to hire women; establishing a platform to connect Saudi women jobseekers to companies that are ready to hire them; and launching marketing campaigns that stimulate the Saudi populace as a whole to question their ideas about the role of women in the workplace.

The unemployed population in Saudi Arabia is estimated to be 1.6 million, with women constituting a huge majority of 1.2 million. Additionally, through research conducted by Khalid himself, he discovered that only 30 per cent of the Saudi population owns their own home and the Saudi middle class is not as affluent as most people assume. His conclusion was that most families were surviving on one income only. Allowing wives and working-age females to earn an income and be economically productive increases living standards across the Saudi middle class, producing healthier families with more resources to devote to their children's education.

During Khalid's first year of operations, he created over 6,000 employment opportunities for women by establishing partnerships with both Saudi and international corporations. That is 6,000 more incomes, 6,000 more economically productive members of society and 6,000 more economically secure families. It took a social entrepreneur to identify this market failure and increase economic growth for everyone.

Another Ashoka Arab World Fellow supporting women's economic empowerment is *Fidaa Abu Turky*. Fidaa is enabling women in rural areas of Palestine and elsewhere in the Levant to become increasingly independent and to contribute to the socio-economic development of their countries. Fidaa employs a grassroots venture capitalist model, providing marginalized women with seed funding to start small business enterprises, along with expert technical assistance and marketing services to ensure that the ventures are successful and economically viable. Fidaa's approach, which is unique to the region, is both transferrable and replicable, and she has ensured that her organization "Erada" is financially sustainable by reinvesting 20 per cent of all profits back into covering its operations.

According to the UNDP, 90.5 per cent of women in Palestine remain outside the formal labour force, working as unpaid family members or in the informal sector, where they do not enjoy the benefits and protections provided by the Labour Law. Neighbouring countries in the Levant, such as Jordan, Syria, and Lebanon, fare slightly better, but their numbers remain high at 85.8 per cent, 85.1 per cent, and 70 per cent, respectively.

Through Fidaa's initiative, women beneficiaries are active members of society and productive members of the economy. They have more disposable income to buy goods and services, will employ others who will also see their disposable incomes rise and can also provide better opportunities for their children, the future workforce of the country. Once more, an investment in a social entrepreneur is a financially sound investment that makes perfect business sense.

Other social challenges that social entrepreneurs solve for the benefit of both society and the economy are crime and social cohesion. There are huge direct costs associated with violent crime and even bigger indirect costs. Direct costs include the associated costs of police, courts, and correctional institutions, out-of-pocket medical expenses borne by victims and lost earnings by both victims and perpetrators arrested and convicted. In 2010, these direct costs amounted to more than $42 billion in the United States. Indirect costs include the pain and suffering of victims, a reduced quality of life for everyone and lower investment levels and property values. While these intangible costs are difficult to calculate with precision, analysts agree they greatly exceed the direct costs. In their study on eight American cities, Robert J. Shapiro and Kevin A. Hassett showed that reducing levels of violent crime generates significant savings for municipal budgets and large benefits for residents, apart from increases in their housing values.[18]

There are many other reasons why maintaining social order and cohesion results in overall improvements to the economy. When there is a lack of trust or cooperation between different groups in society, along ethnic, religious or other forms of identity lines, economic costs are increased and economic activity is reduced. If certain groups in society refuse to engage in economic transactions with other groups, productivity and allocation of resources are inefficient. Employers may hire less skilled staff out of loyalty to a particular ethnicity or religious group, eventually harming productivity. Moreover, if certain groups or minorities are prevented from accessing infrastructure or transport services, they will not fulfil their human potential or be economically productive.[19]

In societies where interaction between different groups goes beyond a lack of trust and enters into violence, economic costs, and risks must incorporate policing, security, and protection services. These extra costs deter investors, which stifle economic growth. Furthermore, when violence exists within society, capital is lost, through either property and infrastructure damage or loss of human capital, referring both to loss of life and emigration to more stable societies, commonly known as the "brain drain". Empirical studies have demonstrated the massive economic costs associated with civil war, whereby annual growth rate is reduced by 2.2 per cent and a 15-year civil war can reduce GDP per capita by nearly 30 per cent.[20]

Conversely, when society is harmonious and groups within society work together and are happy to do so, collective action improves public infrastructure, schooling, health, and a whole range of other public services. These improvements feed into creating safer and more prosperous economic and social environments.[21]

A lack of social cohesion and increased violence has been prominent in Arab countries experiencing political transition in recent years. In Cairo, we have witnessed economic stagnation over the last three years. Of course, we all desire stable and inclusive political systems but, unfortunately, the effect on the economy and livelihoods of many people as a result of recent turmoil means priorities are now focused on ensuring basic necessities for their families rather than affecting political change.

It is at times such as these that we rely on social entrepreneurs more than ever to solve our vicious social divisions threatening to tear the region apart. We need innovative, entrepreneurial solutions to revive the region socially, politically, and economically, and we need to invest in our greatest method to achieve this; we need social entrepreneurs.

*Sami Hourani*, one of our newest Ashoka Arab World Fellows elected in 2014, is working to prevent and alleviate the apathy and sense of hopelessness increasingly prevalent among Arab youth and decrease social tensions by bringing together all groups in society to discuss commonalities.

Sami is increasing opportunities for personal, educational, economic, and civic engagement among young Jordanians, altering the predominant mindset that dictates such opportunities should only be available to the wealthy and privileged. By using techniques such as role play, Sami is developing the confidence and skills of young people, as well as organizing capacity-building training sessions and creative public speaking forums. Sami is instigating a cultural shift to develop and empower Arab youth so as to capitalize on the "youth bulge" across the region to effect better social conditions and economic benefits for all citizens and stakeholders. The main goal is to promote a culture of sharing and build an active, aware, and engaged citizenship, permeating all levels and identity groups of society.

Another Fellow concerned with social cohesion is *Kamal Mouzawak*. Through promoting good health practices and supporting local farmers, Kamal is creating a unified Lebanese heritage and identity based on shared cuisine, by establishing a movement to promote organic, locally grown food.

Lebanon's long history of civil war, political conflict, and social tensions has resulted in low agricultural production, massive internal migration, inadequate agricultural policies, and ethnic divisions. Kamal's comprehensive and multifaceted approach addresses each of these problems, organizing a farmers' visit and exchange program, and a cultural tourism program, establishing a producer restaurant, pioneering educational programming for youth, and founding inclusive national festivals to promote reconciliation among the different religious and ethnic groups in Lebanon.

Through addressing social issues and challenges ignored by everyone else, these social entrepreneurs are bringing Arabs together to realize there are more commonalities than differences and to recognize the value of working together. Through their work, they are not only promoting peace and social cohesion but positively affecting the economy and allowing millions of people to realize their full potential.

These economic benefits, while not necessarily immediately obvious, are very real as proved by countless reports and researches. Whichever social challenge you wish to discuss, solving it – addressing the root causes of the issue in a system-changing manner – will bring about economic growth in a variety of ways. Therefore, investing in social entrepreneurs, the set of people able to implement these system-changing solutions, is not only a social duty but, moreover, an investment that will see significant financial returns.

## Creating a social entrepreneurship ecosystem in the region

Investing in social entrepreneurs constitutes a long-term investment in the solution of the above issues and in thriving, solution-focused communities, leading to long-term social and economic returns.

This investment is not charity; like any other investment, it should be made for reasons that benefit the investor. In the long term, a stable and thriving society benefits the country's economy by producing better results; it is, therefore, in everyone's interests to invest in the people who solve the biggest social problems and create stable societies.

In recent years, innovative members of the corporate and business sectors have become ever more amenable to the idea of investing to address and solve the root causes of social problems for the sake of long-term economic and social returns. They see the value in social investment to create harmonious, stable societies, in which their businesses can thrive. But often they still define social investment as related exclusively to social enterprise (business) when in fact it is still great and worthwhile – for practical, economic reasons, and not purely moral ones – to invest in not-for-profit social entrepreneurs who address the root causes of social problems to bring about long-term economic and social returns.

Academics and practitioners alike have identified a new terminology, "shared value", to denote a deep and comprehensive investment in addressing social challenges for the sake of generating long-term returns.

In an oft-cited essay in the *Harvard Business Review* from January 2011, Michael Porter and Mark Kramer set forth the argument for why creating shared value is good for both society and business. According to them,

> Solving social problems has been ceded to governments and to NGOs. Corporate responsibility programs – a reaction to external pressure – have emerged largely to improve firms' reputations and are treated as a necessary expense. Anything more is seen by many as an irresponsible use of shareholders' money...

> The concept of shared value, in contrast, recognizes that societal needs, not just conventional economic needs, define markets. It also recognizes that social harms or weaknesses frequently create

internal costs for firms – such as wasted energy or raw materials, costly accidents, and the need for remedial training to compensate for inadequacies in education. And addressing societal harms and constraints does not necessarily raise costs for firms, because they can innovate through using new technologies, operating methods, and management approaches – and as a result, increase their productivity and expand their markets.[22]

Solving social problems is an essential factor in economic growth and development and should not be viewed in charitable or even philanthropic terms, but in a highly pragmatic way as essential to improving outputs and creating an ecosystem that is conducive to sustained economic growth.

One of the ways to achieve this is through strategic social investment, such as investing in social entrepreneurs – who, after all, are driving impactful change through implementing innovative and contextualized solutions to endemic challenges.

In the Arab World, it is widely recognized by political and social scientists that social issues are impeding progress. The cost of inaction exceeds the cost of action and everyone loses; it is a race to the bottom. If we could tap into the unrealized potential of Arab populations, things could dramatically improve. Arab investors, unfortunately, seem unable to see this and are only interested in immediate financial returns even if such investments may harm long-term business.

The entrepreneurial ecosystem in the Arab World has not realized the potential of solving social problems. If we could build the enabling environment for social entrepreneurship in the Arab World – through financial investment in social entrepreneurs; through establishing effective networks and collaboration between different stakeholders (the social sector, the business sector, government bodies, educational institutions), partnerships with the media, and exchange, dissemination and documentation of best practices – we would have at our disposal a truly useful and adaptable tool to maximize our existing resources and empower our populations for the good of all.

More specifically, we need each of the aforementioned stakeholders to perform different yet complementary roles to establish and strengthen an enabling environment for social entrepreneurship.

Government bodies need to work to create a legal and policy framework that enables social entrepreneurs to start and grow their initiatives. Not only should legal obstructions that make it difficult for actors outside the government sector to build their own independent initiatives be removed, but policies should be established to facilitate the inception and growth of social ventures.

Educational institutions need to focus on nurturing entrepreneurial drive and the entrepreneurial, innovative, and creative skill set in students. This is tantamount to education reform in the sense that it involves teaching students to think analytically about the root causes of problems and how to change systems in order to solve these problems. This is far removed from our existing education system, which is very focused on rote learning, repetition, and memorization, with a notable absence of critical – or interrogative – thought. Our education systems need to shift from those in which sole authority and responsibility for knowledge transmission rests on the teacher as an arbiter of learning to those where students are encouraged or even required to proactively seek knowledge from a variety of sources, question concepts, and examine multiple viewpoints.

Ashoka has identified the need to recognize and cultivate change-making skills as being absolutely integral to establishing societies populated by individuals with the motivation and ability to address key challenges. To create an Everyone a Changemaker™ society, in which every citizen has a deep conviction of his or her ability to effect meaningful change and is able to translate this into action, we must start at an early age and operate through a sound education system. Valuing changemaking skills as a fundamental part of a young person's education and development and integrating such skills into educational curricula are important parts in nurturing changemakers – the social entrepreneurs of the future and those who support them.

By fostering the creativity and innovation of students – either overtly, through teaching more courses on social entrepreneurship, or covertly, through encouraging them to be active and engaged learners, critically examining what they are taught – educational institutions can provide substantial assistance in building an ecosystem conducive to addressing social issues and comprehensive economic and community development.

Given the impact of the Arab Awakening – the increased risks in security, the economic stagnation that has resulted from social and political instability, the increase in poverty, and the widening gap between rich and poor that is a natural consequence of a sluggish economy – being risk averse is no longer an option. We feel the impact very acutely in Egypt, where the last three years have been exceptionally tumultuous, but its echoes also reverberate across the Arab World. Civil society organizations and the business sector need to be willing to engage in creative partnerships to generate new ideas and explore ways of finding and supporting social entrepreneurs to tackle the root causes of social problems. We need to find committed media partners who will champion social innovation in the public sphere, just as we need to advocate for it at the government level. It is essential to forge new links between different stakeholders and help them all to understand the vital roles they each play in carving out a new market for positive change.

If we look at the recent past, the present and the future, it becomes very clear that the Arab Awakening was started by changemakers and that if the changemaking skills exhibited at this time could be nurtured and extended to the whole population through an effective and systematic approach and by the creation of an enabling environment for social entrepreneurship, substantial growth and development in the region would result. However, by failing to prioritize the cultivation of changemaking skills and empathy in our youth through educational and governmental initiatives and by not providing adequate support to the social entrepreneurs who are driving deep systemic change, we have collectively failed to capitalize on the promise of the Arab Awakening. Opportunities for social development and advancement still abound, but there is no question that the short-term impact of the Arab Awakening has been the exacerbation of social challenges and the deterioration of many issues key to the social framework of the region – including economic and social stability.

It is natural to conclude, when we see the evidence of how leading social entrepreneurs are effectively addressing the social challenges that impede development and advancement, creating real economic and social returns, that supporting these individuals and creating an enabling environment to cultivate the key changemaking skills and qualities that allow them to succeed in effecting meaningful change is the most practical, efficient, and worthwhile way to drive development in the region. The political and social turbulence that has resulted from the Arab Awakening, and its cumulative impact in reducing the quality of life for a large majority, should make it an ever more urgent priority for those who truly want to see progress to invest in the long-term well-being of the region, by supporting the change-making individuals who can drive positive, systemic improvements and create a broad range of opportunities for all.

## Acknowledgement

Omar al-Amin and Lucy Marx were essential to my writing this chapter; their research skills, review, and hard work were remarkable.

## Notes

1. Ashoka. *What Is a Social Entrepreneur?*, available at https://www.ashoka. org/social_entrepreneur (Accessed 10 February 2014).
2. Schwab Foundation for Social Entrepreneurship. *What Is a Social Entrepreneur?*, available at Schwab Foundation http://www.schwabfound. org/content/what-social-entrepreneur (Accessed 10 February 2014).
3. Skoll Foundation. *About Section*, available at Skoll Foundation http:// www.skollfoundation.org/about/ (Accessed 10 February 2014).
4. Skoll World Forum. *What Is Social Entrepreneurship?*, available at Skoll World Forum http://skollworldforum.org/about/what-is-social-entrepreneurship/ (Accessed 10 February 2014).
5. *GOOD Magazine* (28 November 2007). Interview with Bill Drayton, *GOOD Q&A: Bill Drayton*, available at http://magazine.good.is/articles/good_qa_bill_drayton; (Accessed 11 February 2014).
6. Say, Jean-Baptiste (1803). *A Treatise on Political Economy*, C. R. Prinsep, trans. and Clement C. Biddle, ed. 1855. Library of Economics and Liberty, available at http://www.econlib.org/library/Say/sayT.html (Accessed 10 February 2014).
7. Hanushek, Eric A. and Wößmann, Ludger (February 2007). "The Role of Education Quality in Economic Growth", World Bank Policy Research Working Paper 4122, p. 76.
8. Hanushek and Wößmann (February 2007). *The Role of Education Quality in Economic Growth.*
9. Hanushek, Eric A. and Kimco, Dennis D. (December 2000). "Schooling, Labor Force Quality, and the Growth of Nations", *American Economic Review*, 90(5), p. 1190.
10. Hanushek and Kimco (2000). "Schooling, Labor Force Quality, and the Growth of Nations", p. 1203.

11. UN Women. *7 Women's Empowerment Principles*, available at http://weprinciples.org/Site/.
12. USAID. *Why Invest in Women?* Infographic, available at http://50.usaid.gov/infographic-why-invest-in-women/usaid-women/?size=infographic Medium.
13. Global Campaign for Education (2012). *Women and Girls Education Policy Brief*, available at http://www.globalcampaignforeducation.nl/l/nl/library/download/584078.
14. All information on the benefits of women's empowerment taken from USAID Infographic *Why Invest in Women?*, and Global Campaign For Education (2012) *Women and Girls Education Policy Brief.*
15. UN Food and Agriculture Organization (FAO) (2012). *FAO POLICY ON GENDER EQUALITY: Attaining Food Security Goals in Agriculture and Rural Development*, available at http://www.fao.org/fileadmin/templates/gender/docs/FAO_FinalGender_Policy_2012.pdf.
16. All percentages on effects of greater economic independence of women taken from Department for International Development (DFID) (March 2010). *Agenda 2010 – The Turning Point on Poverty: Background Paper on Gender*, DFID, London, a Background Paper submitted at the MDG Conference on 11 March 2010.
17. World Bank (September 2006). *Gender Equality as Smart Economics: A World Bank Group Gender Action Plan (Fiscal years 2007–10)*, p. 2, available at http://siteresources.worldbank.org/INTGENDER/Resources/GAPNov2.pdf.
18. Hassett, Kevin A. and Shapiro, Robert J. (June 2012). "The Economic Benefits of Reducing Violent Crime: A Case Study of 8 American Cities", *Center for American Progress.*
19. Foa, Robert (2011). "The Economic Rationale for Social Cohesion – The Cross-Country Evidence", *OECD International Conference on Social Cohesion and Development (20–21 January 2011).*
20. Collier, P. (1999). "On the Economic Consequences of Civil War", *Oxford Economic Papers*, 51(1).
21. Foa, R. "The Economic Rationale for Social Cohesion – The Cross-Country Evidence".
22. Kramer, Mark R. and Porter, Michael E. (January 2011). "Creating Shared Value", *Harvard Business Review*, available at http://hbr.org/2011/01/the-big-idea-creating-shared-value/ar/1.

## References

Ashoka. *What Is a Social Entrepreneur?*, available at https://www.ashoka.org/social_entrepreneur (Accessed 10 February 2014).

Collier, P. (1999). "On the Economic Consequences of Civil War", *Oxford Economic Papers*, 51(1), 168–183.

Department for International Development (DFID) (March 2010). *Agenda 2010 – The Turning Point on Poverty: Background Paper on Gender*, DFID,

London, A Background Paper submitted at the MDG Conference on 11 March 2010

Foa, Robert (20–21 January 2011). "The Economic Rationale for Social Cohesion – The Cross-Country Evidence", *OECD International Conference on Social Cohesion and Development.*

Global Campaign for Education (2012). *Women and Girls Education Policy Brief,* available at http://www.globalcampaignforeducation.nl/l/nl/library/download/584078.

*GOOD Magazine* (28 November 2007). Interview with Bill Drayton, *GOOD Q&A: Bill Drayton,* available at http://magazine.good.is/articles/good_qa_bill_drayton (Accessed 11 February 2014).

Hanushek, Eric A. and Kimco, Dennis D. (December 2000). "Schooling, Labor Force Quality, and the Growth of Nations", *American Economic Review,* 90(5), 1184–1208.

Hanushek, Eric A. and Wößmann, Ludger (February 2007). *The Role of Education Quality in Economic Growth,* World Bank Policy Research Working Paper 4122.

Hassett, Kevin A. and Shapiro, Robert J. (June 2012). "The Economic Benefits of Reducing Violent Crime: A Case Study of 8 American Cities", *Center for American Progress.*

Kramer, Mark R. and Porter, Michael E. (January 2011). "Creating Shared Value", *Harvard Business Review,* available at http://hbr.org/2011/01/the-big-idea-creating-shared-value/ar/1.

Say, Jean-Baptiste (1803). *A Treatise on Political Economy,* C. R. Prinsep, trans. and Clement C. Biddle, ed. 1855. Library of Economics and Liberty, available at http://www.econlib.org/library/Say/sayT.html (Accessed 10 February 2014).

Schwab Foundation for Social Entrepreneurship. *What Is a Social Entrepreneur?,* from Schwab Foundation, available at http://www.schwabfound.org/content/what-social-entrepreneur (Accessed 10 February 2014).

Skoll Foundation. *About Section,* from Skoll Foundation, available at http://www.skollfoundation.org/about/ (Accessed 10 February 2014).

Skoll World Forum. *What Is Social Entrepreneurship?,* from Skoll World Forum, available at http://skollworldforum.org/about/what-is-social-entrepreneurship/ (Accessed 10 February 2014).

UN Food and Agriculture Organization (FAO) (2012). *FAO Policy on Gender Equality: Attaining Food Security Goals in Agriculture and Rural Development,* available at http://www.fao.org/fileadmin/templates/gender/docs/FAO_FinalGender_Policy_2012.pdf.

UN Women. *7 Women's Empowerment Principles,* available at http://weprinciples.org/Site/

USAID. *Why Invest in Women?* Infographic, available at http://50.usaid.gov/infographic-why-invest-in-women/usaid-women/?size=infographicMedium.

World Bank (September 2006). *Gender Equality As Smart Economics: A World Bank Group Gender Action Plan (Fiscal years 2007–10),* available at http://siteresources.worldbank.org/INTGENDER/Resources/GAPNov2.pdf.

# 2
# The Context for Social Entrepreneurship in the Middle East

*Diana Greenwald and Samantha Constant*

## Introduction

Since the popularization of the term in the 1980s and 1990s, the concept of "social entrepreneurship" (SE) has continued to attract a significant amount of attention from a diverse set of actors. The community includes entrepreneurs, investors, educators, and policy-makers who share a commitment to achieving positive social impact using innovative and financially sustainable methods. In parallel, theoretical and empirical research in this area has proliferated, engaging scholars across fields such as business and management, social sciences, organizational studies, and public policy.[1]

It is likely that many entrepreneurs and organizations in the Middle East and North Africa (MENA) have been adopting the principles of SE for some time. However, efforts to recognize SE as such did not begin in the region until the early 2000s.[2] Individuals are increasingly identifying themselves as social entrepreneurs, and organizations and businesses are marketing themselves as social enterprises. While the concept – and even the precise terminology to be used in Arabic – is still contested, there is a growing interest in models that seek to achieve positive social impact by blending traditional non-profit and for-profit approaches. While many of these efforts are focused locally, there is an ongoing discussion in the SE community of whether, and how, the strategies pursued by social entrepreneurs might tackle some of the region's long-standing development priorities. These include reducing high unemployment among young people, addressing resource and environmental challenges, achieving more equitable service delivery, and promoting good governance.

This chapter assesses the institutional and macroeconomic environment for SE in the MENA region.[3] In the following section, we begin by providing some background on the region's social and economic landscape, including what have been identified by citizens of MENA and international observers as some of the most prominent development challenges. We discuss how the tumultuous events of the "Arab Spring" likely arose in part from, and subsequently interacted with, these pre-existing challenges. This is followed by a definitional discussion of the core principles of SE in the third section. Next, in the fourth section, we focus on three sets of institutional actors – governments, investors and support organizations, and educational institutions – and evaluate their respective roles in shaping the environment for SE in the Middle East. Following this institutional overview, the fifth section highlights the environment for SE by exploring three country case studies in depth. The aim of this chapter is primarily descriptive; however, in the last section, we conclude by outlining some broad principles for those who seek to support the growth of the sector.

The findings presented in this chapter rely on an in-depth literature review, including academic research on entrepreneurship and SE; reports from think tanks, civil society organizations, and social investment actors; and finally, a number of interviews and informal conversations with key actors in focus countries.

## New and persistent development challenges in the Middle East

The MENA region comprises a diverse set of countries: the estimated income per capita of Qatar, considered the highest in the region, is over 30 times that of Yemen, among the poorest in the world. Egypt, with a population of over 80 million, contains more than 60 times as many people as the least populous country in the region, Bahrain (The World Bank, 2013).[4] While the Gulf economies are strongly oriented towards natural resource production and export, the non-oil-exporting countries – including Lebanon, Syria, Palestine, Jordan, Egypt, Tunisia, and Morocco – rely on a mix of services, agriculture, and industry to sustain growth.

Despite this diversity, certain broad, shared characteristics have influenced patterns of development across countries. First, the MENA region is young and growing fast. Annual population growth rates in the Arab World have consistently exceeded the global average in recent years (The World Bank, 2013). With a total population of 310 million, roughly 60 per cent of the population is under the age of 30 (WDI, 2013; DESA, 2012). While estimates project that this will decrease to about 55 per cent by 2020, more than 65 per cent of the population of Iraq, Yemen, and the Palestinian Territories is still predicted to remain under 30 at this time (DESA, 2012). Scholars have previously written about the region's "youth bulge", the large share of its population in the 15–24 or 15–29 range, and its low dependency ratio (Dhillon and Yousef, 2009). While the demographics of each country vary, it is clear that both the social needs and the future high potential of the region will be driven by this young generation.

Progress has been made in educational attainment across all MENA countries, with close to universal access at the primary level. Net secondary enrolment levels in most countries across the region exceed the global average – 63 per cent in 2011 – with some countries still lagging behind (WDI, 2013). Further, educational attainment among the poor, those living in rural areas, and among young women is often lower than that suggested by the national-level data. As access to education continues to improve across the region, the focus of policymakers has shifted towards the quality of education and school-to-work transitions.

Indeed, the mismatch between education and labour markets complicates the transition to stable employment for many young people across the region. In general, unemployment and vulnerable employment have been persistent problems throughout much of the MENA. In particular, the region has among the highest youth unemployment rates and the lowest labour force participation rates by women in the world (Table 2.1). It is important to note that a large portion of women not participating in the formal labour market are likely engaged in unpaid family work or irregular wage employment (Assaad and El Hamidi, 2001). Reasons for female non-participation vary depending on the individual and her context; these reasons range from access issues, societal and cultural factors, and personal choice.

*Table 2.1*   Youth unemployment and female labour force (LF) participation in the MENA region, 2013

| Country | Youth unemployment (%) | Female LF participation (%) |
|---|---|---|
| Algeria | 24.0 | 15.2 |
| Bahrain | 27.9 | 39.2 |
| Egypt | 38.9 | 23.7 |
| Iraq | 34.1 | 14.9 |
| Jordan | 33.7 | 15.6 |
| Kuwait | 19.6 | 43.6 |
| Lebanon | 20.6 | 23.3 |
| Libya | 51.2 | 30.0 |
| Morocco | 18.5 | 26.5 |
| Oman | 20.5 | 29.0 |
| Palestinian Territories | 38.3 | 15.4 |
| Qatar | 1.5 | 50.8 |
| Saudi Arabia | 28.7 | 20.2 |
| Syria | 29.8 | 13.5 |
| Tunisia | 31.2 | 25.1 |
| United Arab Emirates | 9.9 | 46.5 |
| Yemen | 29.8 | 25.4 |

Youth unemployment is the per cent of the 15–24-year-old labour force that is without work, has sought work in a recent past period, and is currently available for work. Female labour force participation is the proportion of the female population ages 15 and older that is economically active.
*Source*: ILO Key Indicators of the Labour Market, accessed through World Development Indicators (2013).

## The "Arab Spring": Preliminary lessons

The effects of the "Arab Spring" – the wave of popular movements that began in Tunisia in December 2010, and subsequently swept through the region – continue to be felt to varying degrees across countries. There are various theories about what caused the series of uprisings. From the chants heard in the streets of Tunis, Cairo, Damascus, Sana'a, and Manama, it is clear that political change was a universal demand of protesters. Yet, there was an economic side to many of these frustrations: high unemployment rates, especially among youth, high food prices, and an unfair playing field have resulted in economic exclusion. The story of Mohamed Bouazizi, the 26-year-old produce vendor who set himself on fire in Sidi Bouzid,

Tunisia, sparking the massive protests and revolution that followed, exemplifies the frustrations of many young people who have been denied access to decent livelihoods.

More generally, moderate to high inequality, combined with low levels of social and economic mobility, has characterized much of the region. While economic inequality is a long-term condition of many of the region's economies, some suggest that it played a role in precipitating the unrest (Ncube and Anyawu, 2012). On the other hand, a brief review of Gini coefficients using a data set that standardizes estimates across surveys does not appear to show any relation between inequality and a country's centrality in the Arab Spring uprisings.[5] Note, however, that missing data is a concern: a number of MENA countries are missing from large, cross-country datasets on inequality, thus complicating any attempt to draw inferences about the relationship between inequality and unrest in the region.

At the time of writing, many countries in the region are still experiencing political instability or are in the midst of post-conflict transitions, while Libya, Iraq, Syria, and Yemen remain immersed in violent conflict. The scale of the conflict in Syria has been immense, with refugee flows placing great pressure on neighbouring countries. As of May 2015, there were 3.98 million registered Syrian refugees (UNHCR, 2015). Getting funding and humanitarian support to Syrians inside the country has also been an enormous challenge. While a growing number of recognized SE initiatives are specifically targeting the refugee population as beneficiaries, the needs – from basic humanitarian relief, to legal services, education, employment, and health services – remain massive. As the conflict inside Syria continues, it is clear that local knowledge will be needed to help engage in the massive effort to rebuild the country, along with the combined efforts of bilateral and multilateral donors, humanitarian organizations, non-governmental organizations (NGOs), and entrepreneurs alike.

### The importance of expectations

How, if at all, have recent events in the region affected individual expectations? Here, we refer not only to expectations of economic opportunities that will be available to individuals in the future, but

> *"For us, looking for system change is more important than making money. Our focus is on the sustainability of the idea, the spread of the idea, the tipping of the sector. In the Middle East, very few of us were really able to tip the sector because there isn't the kind of policy support or large scale funding required to make this happen."*
>
> (Interview with authors, 20 February 2014)

also to the relative roles of the government and private sectors in providing those opportunities. In countries that experience revolution or political transition, we may expect popular expectations for individual and economic prosperity to be heightened in the period immediately following the change. Did popular opinion experience such a "honeymoon" period after large-scale transitions took place in Tunisia, Libya, Egypt, and Yemen between 2011 and 2012? If so, have those expectations already begun to readjust to new realities?

A series of recent surveys by the Pew Global Attitudes project provides some suggestive evidence towards answering these questions (Pew Research Center, 2014).[6] When asked "Over the next 12 months do you expect the economic situation in our country to improve a lot, improve a little, remain the same, worsen a little, or worsen a lot?", the share of Egyptian respondents answering either "improve a lot" or "improve a little" increased from 25 per cent in Spring 2010 to 56 per cent in Spring 2011, just after the former president, Gamal Mubarak, had resigned in February. Subsequently, in Spring 2012, the share dropped to 50 per cent, then to 29 per cent in Spring 2013. In Tunisia, the poll was conducted in Spring 2012 and Spring 2013, and the share of positive responses decreased from 75 to 50 per cent over this time. Even in countries where large-scale popular uprisings and regime transitions did not take place, we observe similar trends. In Lebanon, positive responses were less common, but peaked in Spring 2011 at 25 per cent before declining to 19 per cent by Spring 2013. Finally, in the Palestinian Territories, only three surveys were conducted, but those thinking the economy would improve a lot or a little comprised 33 per cent of respondents in 2009, 39 per cent in 2011, and just 27 per cent in 2013.

Further, in the 2013 Pew survey, lack of employment opportunities was identified as a "very big" problem by 60 per cent of respondents in Egypt, 56 per cent in Jordan, 91 per cent in Lebanon, 86 per cent in the Palestinian Territories, and 90 per cent in Tunisia. In an earlier edition of the same survey, 75 per cent or more of respondents in Egypt, Jordan, Lebanon, and Tunisia say that it is "somewhat" or "very" difficult for "a young person to get a better job and to become wealthier than his or her parents".

These are snapshots of public opinion over a small window of time and do not necessarily reveal long-term trends. However, we do find preliminary support for the idea that expectations in a number of countries appeared to be most optimistic in the time closely following the uprisings. Many of the problems that existed in the region prior to the Arab Spring remain unaddressed in the few years that have followed, which has perhaps had an effect of moderating or reducing positive sentiment. In general, individuals' hopes for inclusiveness, both in government policies and in economic development, seem to have persisted in the period following the uprisings, as have their frustrations with the barriers they continue to experience.

Of course, large-scale investments are necessary to address the region's core development challenges. While governments, foreign donors, and international financial institutions (IFIs) have made tangible progress, foreign aid volatility is likely to continue so long as the region, and donor priorities, remains in flux.[7] Below, we define SE and begin to address how it can fit into this landscape. Social entrepreneurs certainly have a role in filling in the gaps that are left unaddressed by foreign aid and domestic government spending. Further, they may be a source of experimentation with new technologies and locally driven solutions that can then be encouraged or replicated by other national and international actors. Yet, SE cannot be understood to be a cure-all for these numerous challenges. Effective local models need to be identified and scaled up to better connect this emerging sector with larger regional development priorities. While the sector blends the principles of non-profit, commercial business, and public policy, how, and under what conditions, can these linkages materialize into something transformational? At this stage, there is an increased awareness of the potential of SE in the public and private sectors, yet our discussions with key stakeholders show that challenges remain in how to translate the discourse and activities labelled as "social entrepreneurship" into practical connections to national-level priorities (Interviews with authors, 10 February 2014, 13 February 2014).

## What is social entrepreneurship?

> *"One of the Achilles' heels, or disadvantages, of social entrepreneurship [investment] programs is that you tend to attract people who are good at filling out applications, good at presenting their projects ... but we are missing out a whole segment of the population that may not be plugged in to this type of communication or this type of application process, but they are doing exceptional work. It is just more costly to reach those communities."*
>
> (Interview with authors, 13 February 2014)

We define *social entrepreneurship* as engaging in an initiative *whose primary aim is to achieve positive social impact and to do so using financially sustainable methods.* In this context, we refer to the individual as a social entrepreneur and the entity as a social enterprise. In keeping with the criteria that many SE support organizations use in practice, we allow for a range of organizational structures to be considered social enterprises. The key elements are a primary aim of achieving social impact and the adoption of a strategy for achieving financial sustainability. This rules out "pure" for-profit enterprises and "pure" non-profits in the traditional sense, but leaves essentially everything in between. Adopting the framework proposed by Abdou et al. (2010), social enterprises may be organized as one of the following: (i) a leveraged non-profit (a financially sustainable non-profit that relies entirely on strategic partnerships for sustainability); (ii) an enterprising non-profit (a financially sustainable non-profit that generates some of its own income); (iii) a social business (a company legally registered as for-profit but whose mission is to achieve social impact, reinvesting a large share of its revenues back into funding its core social impact activities); or (iv) a hybrid model that combines features of the above three categories.

The aforementioned definition leaves much room for interpretation. What, exactly, is "positive social impact"? Individuals who identify as social entrepreneurs and the numerous organizations and investors supporting them have various perspectives on what makes an entrepreneurial initiative "social". Here, we focus on efforts to *benefit marginalized or overlooked communities*, in addition to those who seek to *increase the provision of non-excludable "public goods" that are underprovided in the existing marketplace.* Thus, initiatives which focus on environmental conservation or rehabilitation of public spaces, for example, may not be specifically targeting marginalized subsets of the population; however, they are aiming to improve public goods provision for a broader community. These goods are defined as "non-excludable" because their use and consumption is not restricted to particular individuals or groups. Beneficiaries, in this context, should also be understood broadly: they may include those who are employed by the social enterprise or those who consume its products or services.

The ways of evaluating social impact may vary to some degree, depending on the mission of the enterprise and local context. Still, there have been a number of efforts globally and regionally to create universal benchmarks for social and environmental impact investing.[8]

The term "financially sustainable methods" means that social enterprises should seek to recoup at least some of their costs through their regular operations. This means they do not rely exclusively on grants and donations, but instead rely on market-driven approaches. Just as the phrase "social impact" is the subject of much debate in this field, so is the concept of financial sustainability. However, despite the number of distinct criteria employed by different actors in the field, these twin pillars of SE are a common theme.

The specific operational structure, financing strategies, and methods for achieving social impact will clearly vary depending on the local context. Thus, while the basic definition of the population of potential social entrepreneurs may be clear, the specific relationships the social entrepreneur or enterprise forges to reach their goal are often unique. An individual in the social enterprise support sector in Tunisia notes that, while identifying social enterprises may be relatively straightforward, "the real innovation is in the way we support them" (Interview with authors, 24 February 2014).

## Fostering social entrepreneurship: The institutional environment

This section aims to describe the institutional landscape of SE. Because social entrepreneurs and enterprises are often establishing new business models, processes, financing strategies, and/or organizational structures, the ecosystem of actors with which they come into contact is large and diverse.

Such constraints manifest explicitly as formal rules (i.e. laws, constitutions, established regulations) and as informal constructs (i.e. customs, traditions, and organizational behaviour). Globally, institutions play an important role in supporting the emergence of SE and in shaping its outcomes. It is outside the scope of this chapter to provide a comprehensive overview of all of the formal and informal institutional actors who have the potential to shape the incentives and behaviour of social entrepreneurs and enterprises. Further, the roles of these actors and their interactions with each other vary across geographic and socio-economic contexts within the MENA region. Below, we focus on three sets of formal institutional actors: governments, educational institutions, and social investors and support organizations. Each set of actors has an important role to play – independently and interdependently – in encouraging SE in the Middle East. Further, we do not devote much attention to informal institutions – i.e. customs, traditions, and organizational behaviour – which may contribute substantively to understanding SE in the region (North, 1991). This becomes especially important in a region where even formal institutions may be built on personal networks such as local or familial affiliations. In some cases, entrepreneurs and social entrepreneurs achieve initial success while operating informally within their communities (see Box 2.1 for a snapshot of the informal sector).

A look at the role of institutional actors as well as *how* each interacts is important to understand what makes a conducive environment for innovation to develop and be scaled up. Figure 2.1 provides a stylized illustration of how the convergence of formal and informal spheres can enable and constrain social entrepreneurs. In the best cases, these spheres can come together to enable SE to flourish: building its credibility, sustaining its growth, and harnessing a supportive culture specific to the communities where it emerges. The following subsections characterize some aspects of the existing formal institutional environment in the MENA region. The next section discusses three country cases that demonstrate different SE landscapes resulting, in part, from variation in the institutional climates.

---

**Box 2.1  The Nexus of Informality and Social Entrepreneurship**

The challenge of informality in MENA is a new yet growing subject of importance in development literature. In most countries across the region, it is estimated that 27 percent of their GDP is produced informally and 67 percent of their labor force exists in the informal sector (Angel-Urdinola et al., 2012). Despite these staggering statistics, there is a significant knowledge gap in capturing the potential impact of the informal sector, and how it relates to emerging areas such as entrepreneurship and social enterprise development.

Traditionally, the informal sector has been defined according to three main factors: i) the actual registration of any given firm or enterprise, ii) policies and regulations being practiced by entities (i.e. taxes paid, business fees incurred), and/or iii) provision of safety nets and social security (Angel-Urdinola et al., 2012; Ishengoma et al., 2006; Williams et al., 2010). While the first two factors frame the issue in the context of business ethics and conduct, the latter issue triggers a fundamental concern of informal activities in economic development, mostly related to improved livelihoods, adequate social protection and human development progress.

In countries where data is available, it is estimated that 57 percent of firms in MENA are competing against unregistered or informal firms (IFC Enterprise Survey Tool). Yet, there is large variation across countries. In Egypt, only 18 percent of firms had formally registered when they started operations in 2007 and the average number of years firms operate without formal registration is approximately 17 years (IFC Enterprise Survey Tool, 2007). In Lebanon, the situation is quite different:

Box 2.1   (Continued)

close to 98 percent of firms had formally registered when they started operations in 2009 and average time to register is measured in months rather than years (IFC Enterprise Survey Tool, 2009).

In the context of SE in MENA, informality need not only be defined under the aforementioned traditional economic rubric. Much of the social innovation (whether it survives or not) starts informally and is able to succeed to some extent because of the flexibility such informal spaces afford it. In countries such as Egypt, many organizations that operate in the informal sector do so to avoid political obstacles rather than for financial reasons. Hence informality plays a substantive role in influencing outcomes of social entrepreneurship along with formal institutional actors.

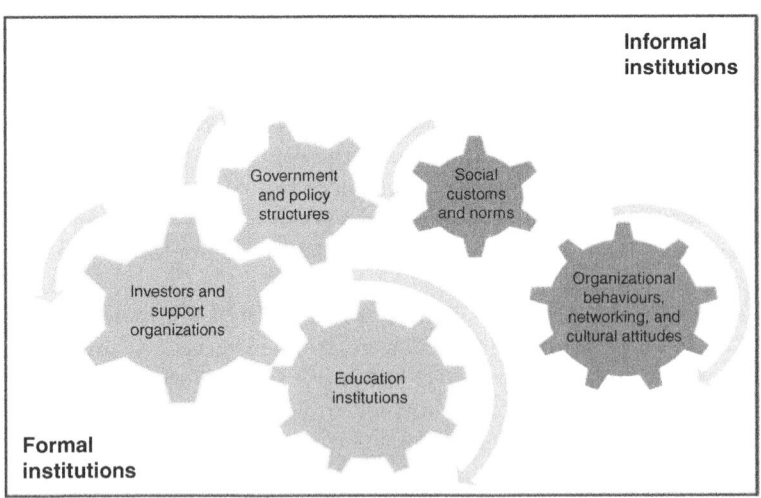

*Figure 2.1*   Institutional interactions and SE outcomes
*Source*: Authors (2014).

## Governments

Public policy has a significant role to play in shaping the incentives and opportunities for social entrepreneurs. Policies affecting the informal sector, small- and medium-size businesses, as well as NGOs all have the potential to affect social entrepreneurs. In addition, laws regulating financial institutions are relevant for the supply of SE financing. Governments can play a variety of roles in encouraging SE – here, we focus mainly on their ability to shape the regulatory environment.[9]

To get a sense of how the business climate has evolved in the Middle East, we turn to the International Finance Corporation (IFC) and World Bank *Doing Business* reports. These reports have been published annually since 2005 and assess the regulatory environment for businesses across 189 countries. While these reports capture a number of indicators of interest to entrepreneurs, one that we focus on in particular is the cost of starting

> *"In Arab culture, there is a different relationship between entrepreneurship and failure than in the US. In the US, people understand and celebrate failure as a necessary path to success. People fail, learn from failure and continue, and try something else. When you look at the enabling environment in the region, failure is not accepted that way. Policy-wise, institutions make it hard to fail. The common denominator among SE people we work with is their higher risk tolerance and acceptance of failure despite the risk-averse environment they operate in. This is what makes them so exceptional."*
>
> (Interview with author, 13 February 2014)

one's own business as a share of income per capita (Figure 2.2). A number of countries in the region – such as Egypt, Saudi Arabia, Jordan, Tunisia, and Yemen – have seen a fairly steady decrease in the cost of starting a new business. Others, such as Algeria, Morocco, the Palestinian Territories, and Syria, have had a more uneven trajectory.

Laws governing NGOs and associations are especially relevant for social entrepreneurs who want to establish their enterprise with that structure. Some reforms are underway, but for most countries in the region, NGOs are forbidden from engaging in profit-seeking

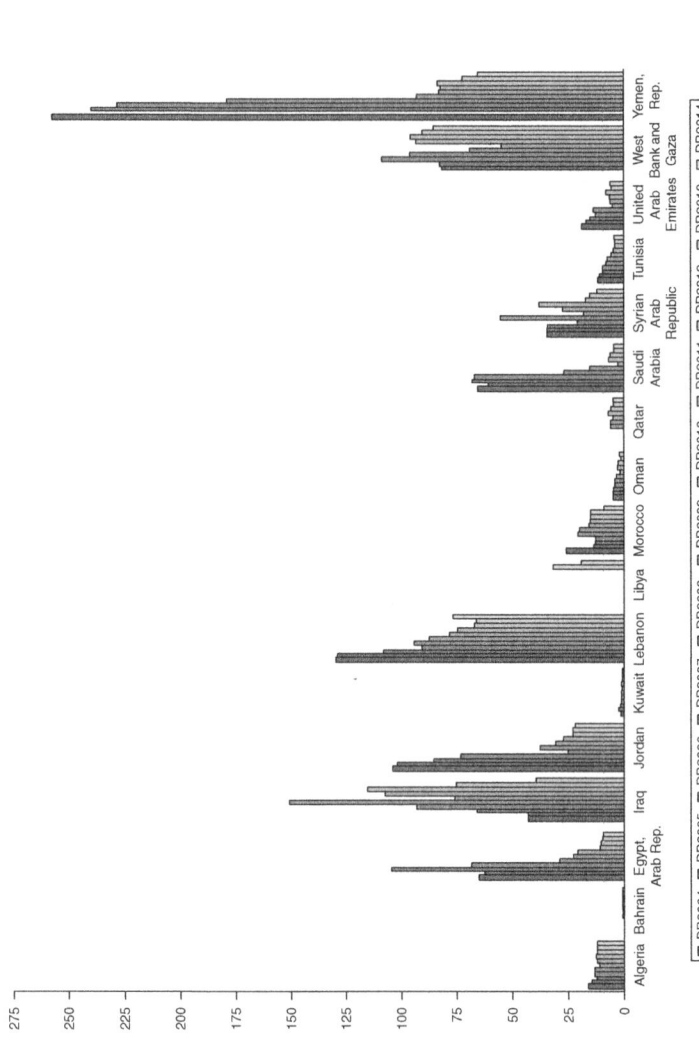

*Figure 2.2* Cost of starting a business (per cent of GDP/capita)

*Source:* IFC and World Bank, *Doing Business* Reports 2005–2014. Note that the 2014 report was published in September 2014 and covers regulations from June 2012 to May 2013. Previous reports cover a similar temporal frame.

activities. While new, hybrid organizational models that allow NGOs to pursue earned income strategies have been discussed, such opportunities are very limited.

Tax laws and incentives are another area where policy can encourage existing enterprises to take on more social benefit activities. Abdou et al. (2010) provide a brief discussion of how tax legislation can affect the incentives of both for- and non-profit organizations to engage in "public benefit" activities. While taking the costs of enforcement into consideration and distinguishing how different types of profits are taxed, organizations such as the Nonprofit Enterprise and Self-sustainability Team (NESsT) have developed legal guides for social enterprises in Latin America and Central Europe (Mazzeo and Etchart, 2009). Similar reviews of relevant legislation for social enterprises operating in the Middle East would be welcomed by entrepreneurs and policymakers alike.

To fulfil its roles in regulation and oversight of social enterprises, governments may require new skills and technical expertise. For example, there will be increased demand for regulation and oversight of the microfinance industry in some countries in the region where that sector is poised to grow.

In some ways, MENA countries find themselves in a paradox. On the one hand, governments are becoming more aware of the potential impact of SE and the need to build on the growing interest of their citizens to engage in community-level efforts; and, on the other hand, governments are increasing public sector wages, sending mixed messages about the need for creating a balanced public–private playing field.[10] The incentives for entrepreneurship, risk-taking, and innovation depend on a conducive institutional environment, as well as a commitment by governments to allow a competitive private sector to flourish.

### Investors and support organizations

The landscape of international organizations explicitly supporting SE in the Middle East is easily captured by a few major players: that is, Ashoka, Synergos, the Schwab Foundation, and the Skoll Foundation. Many of these international organizations have developed, or are developing, a strong presence in the MENA region. There are also a number of country-specific efforts to support SE locally, such as Yunus Social Business in Tunisia, the Egyptian Enterprise Initiative (a partnership between Nahdet El-Mahrousa and M4D), C3 (Consult & Coach for a Cause) in UAE, and others. An even broader range of organizations and financial institutions are supporting general entrepreneurship – too many to capture here. Additionally, there are regional competitions, many of which are sponsored by Gulf countries in partnership with internationally recognized institutions, to support young social entrepreneurs from around the Middle East. The "impact investing" community has tentatively penetrated some MENA markets, but risk and uncertainty seem to deter many of the larger funds.

Through our conversations with individuals in some of the leading international and regional organizations supporting SE, there appears to be unmet demand for local intermediaries – individuals and organizations – who can connect these larger organizations to efforts getting underway on the ground. In an interview with the authors, a senior staff member of one of the support organizations noted the shallow pool of quality entrepreneurs from the region (Interview with authors, 21 February 2014). Another noted the challenges of recruiting outside of existing networks, explaining that alumni of the programme are a primary connection used to recruit new potential entrepreneurs (Interview with authors, 13 February 2014). Reducing uncertainty by increasing intermediation efforts between entrepreneurs and international investors, thus reducing transaction and information costs, may assist in increasing the supply of both entrepreneurship and investment.

### Educational institutions

One area of particular promise in the MENA region is educational curriculum development around the ideas of SE. A number of universities and business schools have begun offering courses and holding workshops on the subject, and some have even established special concentrations or degree programmes (see Box 2.2). Much of this trend appears to be focused in the private universities, though, increasingly, new partnerships are emerging between governments and internationally recognized SE outfits to carry out special SE initiatives.[11] The status of SE education in public universities is less developed.

---

**Box 2.2   Educational Initiatives in the Middle East**

The study of social entrepreneurship is increasing in popularity, especially in higher education curriculums. Students are seeking more meaning in programs that can successfully translate theory into practice. At the same time, the international SE community is generating greater opportunities for linking to local education institutions in order to foster an innovation culture indigenous to the region.

Over the last five years, educational institutions have begun to teach or provide workshops related to social entrepreneurship as part of business and management tracks at graduate or pre-professional levels. The Entrepreneurship and Innovation Initiative at the School of Business, American University in Cairo has partnered with the George Washington University School of Business to provide an integrated MBA course on the principles and practical application of emerging business concepts, such as corporate social responsibility, social entrepreneurship and sustainability management. Similarly, American University of Beirut's Olayan School of Business offers social entrepreneurship workshops and seminars with a vision to create a culture of innovation and leadership among students seeking to make a difference in the everyday lives of citizens while building practical, business skills for their transition to the workforce.

Other private universities have embedded curricula adapted from SE programs carried out by their US-based sister institutions. For example, The New York University in Abu Dhabi provides a pre-professional track for its undergraduate students "to study the dynamics of social innovation, organizational change, and transformative leadership – with a particular focus on the not-for-profit and government sectors."

---

## The context for social entrepreneurship in the Middle East: Country cases

Below, we briefly evaluate the economic and institutional context for SE in three countries – Tunisia, Libya, and the West Bank and Gaza.

These illustrative examples demonstrate some of the country-specific priorities and challenges facing the sector.

We selected these countries for several reasons. First, social entrepreneurial activities in these countries have gained different amounts of recognition by international organizations: while many Palestinian initiatives have been recognized by the global SE support sector, only one social enterprise from Tunisia has been recognized by one of the international support organizations identified above and none have been recognized from Libya so far (see Figure 2.3).[12] Thus, we have selected one country – Palestine – that has been well represented in the global SE ecosystem and two others – Tunisia and Libya – that have not been given as much attention.

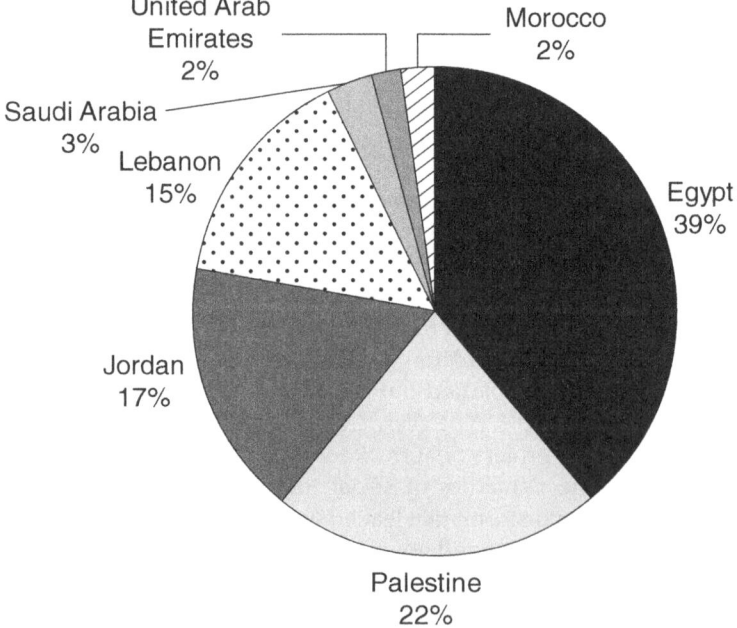

*Figure 2.3*  Globally recognized social entrepreneurs in the Middle East by country, 2011–2014

*Sources*: Ashoka, Synergos Arab Social Innovators, Skoll, and Schwab Foundation websites.

While we do not leverage comparisons between these cases to make any strong causal claims, we do note that the SE sector in Tunisia, Libya, and Palestine exhibits a range of outcomes worth noting. SE in Tunisia is at an exciting crossroads after the revolution, with concentrated gains in microfinance and growth in the number of SE efforts being organized as cooperatives. The environment for entrepreneurship and SE in Libya is still nascent but, as the country's private sector continues to develop, presents an opportunity for rapid growth. Still, ongoing conflict in Libya has generated extremely difficult conditions for service delivery organizations in many parts of the country. Finally, as described below, some have suggested that the SE sector in Palestine is more developed and has succeeded due to its role in complementing or even replacing the existing, weak governance structures.

## Tunisia

Tunisia has fostered an export-oriented market economy over the past several decades. Economic growth was consistent in Tunisia throughout the 1990s and 2000s; yet the most profitable forms of private enterprise under the old regime were controlled by a small

> "There are real advantages to informality. You can be more agile, more flexible, evolve like an amoeba when the situation changes. Sometimes formality brings with it rigidity. For me, [the relationship of informality and formality] is a process issue and it is emergent.... Like-minded people come together, get excited about an idea and come to work on it. It may or may not survive. But those who do have early success, and who can feed back into that group a sense of efficacy ... nearly get to the point where they want more structure. They want to be able to accept donations, or they want to be able to lobby more effectively at local council. For a variety of reasons, they wish to move toward formality but it is dangerous. There were a lot of organizations that were determinedly informal because to be formal and visible would have meant to be crushed."
>
> (Interview with author, 20 February 2014)

ruling clique. The regulatory environment favoured enterprises with personal connections to the Ben Ali family (Rijkers et al., 2014). The country is currently undergoing a transition from authoritarian political rule to democracy. This has had effects on overall economic stability. While average GDP growth from 2000 to 2009 was about 4.7 per cent, growth slowed in 2010 and contracted by 2 per cent in 2011 (The World Bank, 2013). The economy has since rebounded in 2012 and 2013, but growth is slower than the earlier part of the 2000s.

Following the revolution and the toppling of the Ben Ali regime, Tunisians "were allowed to demonstrate, express themselves, and form parties and associations to an extent unmatched since independence in 1956" (Human Rights Watch, 2012). Estimates vary, but it seems that thousands of new associations were registered in the wake of the revolution (Freedom House, 2012). A new decree-law passed following the revolution (Decree Number 88, 2011) grants associations a number of rights not previously permitted. However, according to the legislation, associations are not permitted to realize profit, drawing a stark line between non-profit and for-profit enterprise in Tunisia.

It is clear that expectations for employment generation and inclusive growth have been high among Tunisians in the wake of the revolution. SE has been an area of growth in the post-revolutionary era. Enterprises have focused on addressing rural–urban inequality, microfinance, and environmental and waste management issues, and cooperatives have emerged as a means of livelihood generation for marginalized populations.

While cooperatives represent an interesting organizational structure for social enterprises, it is important to note that both positive assets and negative liabilities are often shared between members (Interview with authors, 24 February 2014). Entrepreneurship programmes, in general, have sprouted up. For example, the Women's Enterprise for Sustainability (WES) provides training and support to eight partner centres throughout Tunisia, in turn delivering a curriculum of entrepreneurship, e-commerce, home-based business, and leadership to women. Some of these women are working in more traditional sectors (i.e. fashion design, textiles, food production), while others are pushing into new frontiers for women in SE (i.e. robotics for disabled services).

Microfinance is an area where observers of Tunisia predict future growth. The co-founder of one of the country's largest and earliest microfinance institutions, enda inter-arabe, was recognized as a leading social entrepreneur in the region by the Schwab Foundation in 2010. The sector is still not extremely competitive, but some predict it will continue to grow, while pointing to the importance that the sector is properly regulated. Islamic finance and Islamic microfinance are also developing areas of interest for social entrepreneurs. Based on secondary sources, the Consultative Group to Assist the Poor (CGAP) notes there may be as many as "2.5–3 million potential clients for microfinance services, including 1.2 to 1.4 million for microcredit" in the country (Kallel and Negre, 2011). Microfinance was hit by the revolution – strikes, instability in neighbouring Libya (a trading partner), and acts of crime/looting all took their toll, according to one account by enda co-founder and secretary general, Michael Cracknell (2011). He notes, in financial terms, enda's Portfolio at Risk greater than 30 Days (PAR30) ratio, a standard portfolio quality measure, "stood at 0.33% at end-December 2010", and as of December 2011, it was approximately 6 per cent. Now, as Tunisia consolidates its democracy and achieves greater political stability, the climate for risk-taking and entrepreneurial activities can only be expected to improve.

## Libya

The 2011 uprising in Libya resulted in international intervention to support the opposition to the regime of Muammar Qaddafi. By October 2011, Qaddafi had been captured, killed, and a new transitional government took over. In July 2012, elections were held and authority was transferred to the General National Congress, which was replaced by a Council of Deputies in 2014. However, an increase in militant fighting and increased activity by groups loyal to the self-proclaimed Islamic State in the west of the country have marshalled in severe instability once again. The Council of Deputies has since fled to Tobruk, in the eastern part of the country, while a separate militia operates a self-proclaimed government from Tripoli. In addition to the ongoing conflict, the country is facing considerable infrastructure- and security-related challenges. Over 60,000 Libyans were estimated to be internally displaced as of July 2014 (UNHCR, 2014). Prior to the most recent upsurge in conflict, a nascent domestic private sector was emerging in an environment where private sector development was previously discouraged.

The concept of entrepreneurship is somewhat new in Libya. Drawing on interviews with individuals in the entrepreneurship support sector, the precedent that many young Libyans are accustomed to is government employment or working for a family business (Interview with authors, 3 March 2014). Many young people still see government employment as, if not a guarantee, then, a strong possibility. Some of these expectations stem from the incentive structure in an oil-rich economy where the public sector share of the economy has traditionally been large.

Access to start-up capital for aspiring entrepreneurs in Libya can pose a challenge. According to one individual working with entrepreneurs, initial investments are often obtained through family and personal connections. Indeed, additional accounts point to the fact that informal finance is common for new enterprises in Libya, a situation that has carried over, to some extent, from the pre-revolutionary environment (ElTaweel, 2012). Beginning in 2013, banks were mandated to be Shariah-compliant, resulting in a difficult transitional phase where lending dried up. "Access to finance is a challenge in Libya. Both for NGOs that want to support [entrepreneurs] and for the entrepreneurs themselves that want to start businesses," points out one of our interview subjects (Interview with authors, 3 March 2014).

The post-Qaddafi government seemed to recognize the importance of supporting entrepreneurship. "Libya Enterprise" was a branch of the Ministry of Economy that was launched in 2012 to promote entrepreneurship and small and medium enterprise (SME) development. Yet, some in the sector have pointed to the "loss of confidence between the banks, the state and the private sector" during the pre-revolution period, a confidence that is difficult to now rebuild (Zaptia, 2014).

What about the skill set of young people seeking to start their own enterprises? Many NGOs have emerged in Libya since the revolution. Since there was no space for a developed and diverse civil society under the previous regime, many have taken advantage of the opening. Some note the trend of the return of an educated and entrepreneurial class of Libyans who had been living outside the country. This population brings important skills and business acumen which, combined with local knowledge, could be a great asset in the development of the private sector.

Absent from much of the conversation in Libya is a focus on the "social" aspect of SE. In some ways, this is unsurprising: the immediate priorities of Libyans are to fuel growth and job creation. New NGO creation has, no doubt, been fuelled in part by the considerable flows of international aid entering the country following the 2011 conflict. To date, no Libyan social entrepreneurs have been recognized by any of the major SE support organizations. There is reason to push for that to change in the coming years, as the country hopefully overcomes its all-encompassing conflict and begins to rebuild.

### West Bank and Gaza

Ashoka recognized its first Palestinian social entrepreneur in 2006: Abdelfattah Abusrour. Abusrour founded the Al Rowwad Community Center, which seeks to empower Palestinian youth and women, in particular, with creative and educational means of peaceful resistance. In the past seven years, Palestinians have come to comprise a large share of the social entrepreneurs supported by the major international and regional organizations (22 per cent, see Figure 2.3).

It has been suggested that life in the West Bank and Gaza – life under occupation, with governments whose capacities are limited – may encourage some of the qualities conducive for entrepreneurship. These include an appetite for risk, a willingness to work with contingencies (Interview with authors, 13 February 2014). Because there are many gaps in development unfilled by the government or donors, there is actually quite a bit of room for grass-roots-led businesses. The service sector dominates the local Palestinian economy, with telecom and technology on the rise.

> *"We need champions in the business sector and government to believe in what we are saying [about the need for social impact]. The majority of funding for most of the NGOs in Egypt and [Ashoka] in the Arab World is not from Arabs. There are lots of partnerships but in reality 95 percent of all funding to the social sector is not from Arabs."*
>
> (Interview with Authors, 20 February 2014)

Some of the prototypical examples of SEs that have been globally recognized include Canaan Fair Trade, which sells olive oil and other produce from a network of farmers represented by the Palestine Fair Trade Association, and Souktel, which provides job-matching services for employers and applicants using mobile phone technology. Unsurprisingly, the context of occupation has placed hard constraints on economic development in the Territories. By focusing on export markets and the use of technology to over-come transportation and communication barriers, these enterprises are demand-driven solutions for the Palestinian context.

## Conclusion

Why support SE? The counter-argument holds that the traditional private sector – from small, local businesses to large corporations – and the traditional non-profit space arose separately and operate in separate spheres for a reason. SE suggests new organizational struc-tures, new operating procedures, and thus uncharted territory in public policy discourse.

Importantly, promotion of SE should not be confused with seeking to substitute the traditional private sector or non-profit sector with social enterprises. Not all entrepreneurs are equipped to transform into social enterprises, yet their efforts may be just as impactful and built on some of the same principles. Further, the adoption of SE in educational institutions may demonstrate that SE has potential not only as an tool for employment generation, but also as a means to build leadership, social awareness, and business skills.

Our analysis shows that there is increased awareness and grow-ing interest in engaging in social entrepreneurship in the region. However, the policy environment and funding mechanisms remain constrained. As one of our informants argued, one area that deserves additional thinking how SE can be better 'socialized' into gover-nance and policymaking, so that policies are tailored to enable the success and growth of creative, demand-driven, and successful ini-tiatives (Interview with authors, 20 February 2014). Socialization can result in better mainstreaming of SE in existing priorities and enable stakeholders to utilize it in a more, constructive, streamlined fash-ion. The informal sector is also an area that needs greater attention, since it is often in the informal sphere where we will witness innova-tions among marginalized groups and those whose entrepreneurship goes largely unnoticed by regional and global organizations. In summary, while social entrepreneurship is not a "one size fits all" policy for the diverse range of social and economic development challenges confronting populations across the MENA region, it is nonetheless likely that effective innovation at the intersection of the traditional non-profit and for-profit spheres will be able to address critical gaps at the local, national, and perhaps even regional levels.

## Notes

The authors would like to thank, in alphabetical order, Iman Bibers, Asem Haggiagi, Barbara Ibrahim, Mazen Al Kassem, George Khalaf, Fares Mabrouk, Katherine Milligan, and Jamil Wyne for their input during the writing of this chapter. All errors and omissions are the authors' own.

1. There are many studies of social entrepreneurship, but for some recent examples of both conceptual and evaluative work, see: Nicholls, 2006; Dacin et al., 2011; Kerlin, 2013; Brock and Steiner, 2009.
2. The first international organization officially dedicated to supporting social entrepreneurs, Ashoka inducted its first fellows from the Arab World in 2003, with seven fellows from Egypt ("Ashoka Fellows", Ashoka.org).
3. While definitions vary, the MENA region as referred to here comprises Algeria, Bahrain, Egypt, Iraq, Jordan, Kuwait, Lebanon, Libya, Morocco, Oman, the Palestinian Territories, Qatar, Saudi Arabia, Syria, Tunisia, the United Arab Emirates, and Yemen.
4. 2012 GDP per capita based on purchasing power parity.
5. Among eight countries covered – Algeria, Egypt, Iraq, Lebanon, Morocco, Syria, Tunisia, and Yemen, with data ranging from 2004 to 2010 – Lebanon appears to have the highest pre- and post-tax-and-transfer levels of inequality (Standardized World Income Inequality Database, Version 4.0).
6. Sample sizes for the countries mentioned in the following sections ranged from 800 to 1,000. Multi-stage cluster and/or stratified sampling was used. For more information, see www.pewglobal.org.
7. Trends in international development assistance show sharp increases in net ODA to Egypt and Syria from 2011 to 2012, while aid disbursements to the West Bank and Gaza have stagnated, and aid to Iraq has dramatically decreased (OECD DAC). Libya saw a temporary spike in 2011, but fell again in 2012 back to pre-revolution levels.
8. These efforts include the Impact Reporting & Investment Standard (IRIS). IRIS provides suggested metrics that are both sector-specific (i.e. health; education; and environment, water, and energy) and multi-sectoral (i.e. financial performance; environmental performance; and beneficiaries, including suppliers, distributors, and clients). See www.iris.thegiin.org.

9. Other areas of potential interest for additional research include procurement policies and public–private partnerships, for example.
10. In 2011, Qatar increased public sector wages for all national employees by 60 per cent.
11. "البحرين في الثاني «الاجتماعية الأعمال رِيادة» أسبوع فعاليات انطلاق" Asharq al-Awsat (25 October 2013), available at http://www.aawsat.com/details.asp?section=6&issueno=12754&article=748282.
12. Note that the Tunisian social entrepreneur, Essma Ben Hamida, was recognized by Schwab Foundation in 2010 and thus does not appear in Figure 2.3.

# Bibliography

Abdou, Ehaab (2010). "A Practitioner's Guide for Social Entrepreneurs in Egypt and the Arab Region", John D. Gerhart Center for Philanthropy and Civic Engagement, The American University in Cairo.

Angel-Urdinola, Diego F. and Tanabe, Kimie (January 2012). "Micro-Determinants of Informal Employment in the Middle East and North Africa Region". Social Protection Paper No. 1201, Social Protection and Labor, World Bank.

Assaad, Ragui and El-Hamidi, Fatma (2001). "Is All Work the Same? A Comparison of the Determinants of Female Participation and Hours of Work in Various Employment States in Egypt", *Research in Middle East Economics*, 4, 117–150.

Bibars, Iman (6 February 2013). "Why the Arab Awakening Depends on Social Entrepreneurs", *The Guardian Professional*, available at http://www.theguardian.com/social-enterprise-network/2013/feb/06/social-entrepreneurship-shaping-egypt.

Brock, Debbi and Steiner, Susan (2009). "Social Entrepreneurship Education: Is It Achieving Its Aims?" Social Science Research Network Working Paper Series, available at http://ssrn.com/abstract=1344419.

Boss, Suzie (Fall 2013). "An Arab Spring for Entrepreneurs?" *Stanford Social Innovation Review*, available at http://www.ssireview.org/articles/entry/an_arab_spring_for_entrepreneurs.

Buckner, Elizabeth, Beges, Sarina and Khatib, Lina (March 2012). "Social Entrepreneurship: Why Is It Important Post Arab Spring? Online Survey Report", available at http://iis-db.stanford.edu/pubs/23656/White_Paper_Social_Entrepreneurship.pdf.

Convergences (2012, 2015). *Barometer of Social Entrepreneurship*, 2nd Edition, available at www.convergences2015.org.

Cracknell, Michael (4 December 2011). "Measures to Overcome Revolution-Induced Problems", *The Consultative Group to Assist the Poor (CGAP)*, available at http://www.cgap.org/blog/measures-overcome-revolution-induced-problems.

Dacin, M. Tina, Dacin, Peter A. and Tracey, Paul (2011). "Social Entrepreneurship: A Critique and Future Directions", *Organization Science*, 22(5), 1203–1213.

Deane, Shelley (2013). "Transforming Tunisia: The Role of Civil Society in Tunisia's Transition", *International Alert*.

Dhillon, Navtej and Yousef, Tarek (Eds.) (2009). *Generation in Waiting: The Unfulfilled Promise of Young People in the Middle East*. Washington, DC: Brooking Institution Press.

Eltaweel, Mukthar E. (18–19 December 2012). "How Are Small Businesses in Libya Financed?" *International Conference on Business, Finance and Geography*, Phuket, Thailand.

Fahmy, Amina, Greenwald, Diana, Abdou, Ehaab, and Nelson, Jane (2010). "Social Entrepreneurship in the Middle East: Toward Sustainable Development for the Next Generation", *Middle East Youth Initiative*.

Freedom House (2012). "Tunisia", available at http://www.freedomhouse.org/report/countries-crossroads/2012/tunisia#_edn16.

Gatti, Roberta, Angel-Urdinola, Diego F., Silva, Joanna and Bodor, Andras (December 2011). Striving for Better Jobs: The Challenge of Informality in the Middle East and North Africa. MENA Knowledge and Learning Quick Notes Series. Number 49.

Human Rights Watch. "World Report 2012: Tunisia", available at http://www.hrw.org/world-report-2012/world-report-2012-tunisia.

Institute for Integrated Transitions (2013). "Supporting Countries in Transition: A Framework Guide for Foundation Engagement", John D. Gerhart Center for Philanthropy and Civic Engagement, The American University in Cairo.

International Finance Corporation (2010). *The SME Banking Knowledge Guide*. IFC Advisory Services: Access to Finance, 2nd Edition.

International Labor Organization (2013). *Women and Men in the Informal Economy: A Statistical Landscape*. 2nd Edition.

Ishengoma, Esther K. and Kappel, Robert (April 2006). Economic Growth and Poverty: Does Formalisation of the Informal Enterprises Matter? GIGA Research Program: Transformation in the Process of Globalization, GIGA Working Papers No. 20.

Kallel, Emna and Negre, Alice (23 October 2011). "From Microcredit to Microfinance: Ambitions for Tunisia", *The Consultative Group to Assist the Poor (CGAP)*, available at http://www.cgap.org/blog/microcredit-microfinance-ambitions-tunisia.

Kerlin, Janelle A. (2013). "Defining Social Enterprise across Different Contexts: A Conceptual Framework Based on Institutional Factors", *Nonprofit and Voluntary Sector Quarterly*, 42(1), 84–108.

Martin, Roger L. and Osberg, Sally (2007). "Social Entrepreneurship: The Case for Definition", *Stanford Social Innovation Review*, 5(2).

Mazzeo, Santiago and Etchart, Nicole (2009). *The Legal and Regulatory Framework for CSO Self-Financing in Argentina*, Santiago, Chile: NESsT Legal Series.

Monitor Institute (2009). *Investing for Social and Environmental Impact: A Design for Catalyzing an Emerging Industry*. Monitor Institute.

Ncube, Mthuli and Anyanwu, John C. (2012). "Inequality and Arab Spring Revolutions in North Africa and the Middle East", Africa Economic Brief 3(7). African Development Bank.

Nicholls, Alex (2006). *Social Entrepreneurship: New Models of Sustainable Social Change*. New York: Oxford University Press.

North, Douglass C. (1991). "Institutions", *The Journal of Economic Perspectives*, 5(1), 97–112.

The Organization for Economic Co-operation and Development (OECD), Development Co-operation Directorate (DCD-DAC) Annual Aggregates Database, available at http://www.oecd.org/dac/stats/idsonline.htm.

Pew Research Global Attitudes Project, Datasets, available at http://www.pewglobal.org/category/datasets/.

Rijkers, Bob, Freund, Caroline and Nucifora, Antonio (2014). "All in the Family: State Capture in Tunisia", World Bank Policy Research Working Paper 6810.

Saleem, Qamer. Overcoming Constraints to SME Development in MENA Countries and Enhancing Access to Finance (May 2013). *IFC Advisory Services in the Middle East and North Africa*. International Finance Corporation.

Sabha, Muhanad (12 November 2013). "تدريبية تعليمية مبادرات تنتج الاجتماعية الريادة. السوريين", Wamda, available at http://ar.wamda.com/.

Schroeder, Christopher M. (2013). *Startup Rising: The Entrepreneurial Revolution Remaking the Middle East*. New York: Palgrave Macmillan.

The World Bank and the International Finance Corporation (2013). "Doing Business 2014 Regional Profile: Middle East and North Africa (MENA)", Doing Business 2005–2014.

United Nations Development Programme (UNDP) (2011). *Arab Development Challenges Report 2011: Toward the Developmental State in the Arab Region*. Cairo: UNDP.

United Nations High Commissioner for Refugees (UNHCR) (2015). "Syria Regional Refugee Response", available at http://data.unhcr.org/syrianrefugees/regional.php.

—— (2014). "2015 UNHCR Subregional Operations Profile – North Africa", available at http://www.unhcr.org/cgi-bin/texis/vtx/page?page=49e485f36.

United Nations, Department of Economic and Social Affairs (DESA) (2012). World Population Prospects, The 2012 Revision, available at http://esa.un.org/unpd/wpp/index.htm.

Williams, Colin C. and Nadin, Sara (2010). "Entrepreneurship and the Informal Economy: An Overview", *Journal of Developmental Entrepreneurship*, 15(4), 361–378.

World Bank. World Development Indicators (WDI) (2013). Available at http://data.worldbank.org/data-catalog/world-development-indicators.

Zaptia, Sami (1 April 2014). "SMEs Central to Development of Libyan Economy – says Libya Enterprise", *Libya Herald*, available at http://www.libyaherald.com/2014/04/01/smes-central-to-development-of-libyan-economy-says-libya-enterprise/#axzz2xedABE00.

# 3
# The Rise of Social Entrepreneurship in the Middle East: A Pathway for Inclusive Growth or an Alluring Mirage?

*Soushiant Zanganehpour*

## Introduction

Many communities and nations across the Arab World face compounding social and environmental challenges. The rising levels of unemployment, illiteracy, poverty, corruption, and inequality coupled with increasing resource dependency, high rates of pollution, water shortages, and ensuing conflicts have sown many seeds of disenchantment across the region. More importantly, those trying to usher in positive change on any single one of these challenges appear to be faced with superhuman barriers; the underlying complexities and structural considerations make direct action with scalable results a near impossibility.

That said, many believe that the Arab World is at an important socio-political and economic inflection point. They take comfort in Henry Ford's espoused wisdom that "when everything seems to be going against you, remember that the airplane takes off against the wind, not with it".[1] Following the Arab Spring, the region has witnessed a renewed sense of optimism about its future. Scanning the horizon and global landscape for ideas, some enlightened activists have turned to social entrepreneurship as one possible solution set to respond directly to the rising regional challenges. From impact investing conferences to social venture pitch competitions, the region's budding social entrepreneurship ecosystem espouses confidence about the future and in the model for helping realize future prosperity. They do not complain about lightening their burden of challenges, but instead look to broadening their shoulders[2] and realizing positive impact by using enterprise models, efficiency, and other concepts borrowed from the private sector's lexicon to turn complex social and environmental challenges into self-sustaining business and community solutions.

Enthusiasm for the concept is undeniable, and parts of the Middle East and North Africa (MENA) region appear to be on the right trajectory to realize positive change. This chapter explores the extent to which social entrepreneurship as a concept can help facilitate change in the near term while considering how the concept might aid in the region's broader and more long-term transition to prosperity.

## The tale of two Arab Worlds

Across the Arab World, demands to curb the swelling youth unemployment and job crisis are urgent. According to the International Labour Organization (ILO), the unemployment rate in the MENA region is twice the rate of the global average. Its latest 2013 Global Employment Trends for Youth Report found that unemployment rates in the MENA, currently at 28.3 per cent and 23.7 per cent, respectively, are rising and are expected to reach 30 per cent in the Middle East and 24 per cent in North Africa by 2018.[3] Among the MENA countries, more than 50 per cent of the population is younger than 25. Within this demographic group, the unemployment rate averages about 40 per cent – four times that for adults – the largest youth-to-adult unemployment ratio in the world. Women in the Middle East suffer a 42.6 per cent unemployment rate while their labour participation rate is the lowest in the world, sitting at only 13.2 per cent in 2012.[4] Youth and women continue to bear the brunt of joblessness across the region.

Regional analysts predict that the Middle East will require around 100 million new jobs by 2020, a doubling of the current level of employment – a tall order for even those regional markets with healthy growth rates such as the Gulf countries.[5] According to the World Bank and the IMF, MENA public sectors employ between 14 per cent and 40 per cent of all workers in the region.[6] Historically, the public sector served as a political solution to the economic problem of unemployment.

Equally urgent is the need for effective and meaningful responses to root issues that catalysed the 2010 "Arab Spring". Despite early positive achievements, the Arab Spring and ensuing initiatives by business, policy, or social movements have failed to drive forward systemic changes across the region. Endemic corruption, rising costs of living and inequality, policy dysfunctionality, and inequitable growth still persist. The civil unrests have led to severely disrupted economic activity in most countries, forestalling foreign direct investment and causing bank liquidations, shut down of stock exchanges, and declining tourism.[7] This is particularly pronounced in Egypt, where the country has seen a 30 per cent drop in visitors so far in 2014, and tourism revenue is down by an enormous 43 per cent.[8] Until 2011, Egypt's tourism industry employed 3.7 million people, many of them indirectly, representing 15.5 per cent of the country's work force.[9] But between 2010 and 2013, the number of visitors dropped from 14 million to nine million, and tourism revenues more than halved to US$5.8 billion.[10] Some report that Egypt's continued unrest has starved Bedouins in the Sinai desert of tourist revenue, forcing them instead into illegal opium production to sustain themselves, where death penalty is the price one pays if caught.[11]

These harsh realities are further contorted by the region's relatively high illiteracy rates, whereby the MENA region still lags behind other regions of the world. Literacy generally increases more rapidly in urban areas, and therefore countries with very significant rural populations (Egypt, Morocco, and Yemen) have lower adult literacy rates – around and above 50 per cent. Moreover, literacy rates in the region are about 20 per cent lower among women – females in predominantly rural countries, such as Morocco and Yemen, are at a distinct disadvantage: only one in ten rural women can read and write in Morocco, and only one in nine can in Yemen.[12]

Frustration, anger, and impatience dominate psyches across the region. The sheer scale of the problems seems insurmountable, and the necessity for demonstrating economic growth in the short term is inescapable.

Following the Arab Spring however, a more hopeful and optimistic narrative is espousing the region's potential for self-improvement and prosperity. Countries across the Middle East witnessed an increase in community spirit and a budding awareness of the need for citizens to take responsibility for their own socio-economic and political futures. This shift has manifested into greater calls for regional entrepreneurship, as youth have become more fatigued with the prospects of social change resulting from movements and protests and look less and less to the public sector for employment. Some reports even share that despite civil strife and political instability, more and more people want to start their own businesses: the 2012 Global Entrepreneurship Monitor reported that in the midst of political turmoil, 88 per cent of Tunisians viewed entrepreneurship as a desirable career choice.[13]

Also, across the MENA region, over 100 million people are under the age of 15, and around 93 per cent of the young and tech-savvy population have mobile devices.[14] Smartphone penetration in the region is projected to grow up to 39 per cent by 2015.[15] Looking at historical trends, advances in technology and communications have provided opportunities for the average citizen to demand more accountability from prominent social institutions, particularly voicing their concerns about how public affairs and welfare provision are managed. If theory holds true, the rise of the Internet and increased mobile penetration rates should provide a means for the average citizen to express dissent online and mobilize support to hold large organizations, including states, accountable for their actions. Increased socio-economic and cultural participation will also create spillover opportunities for consumers to have greater participation in shaping the overall system.[16] Many are hopeful that the Middle East, despite its challenges, is a region endowed with a unique set of positive macroeconomic and demographic attributes that position it for rapid growth and prosperity. Some even go as far to believe that the cultural, technological, and paradigmatic shifts resulting from these macroeconomic and demographic trends will help transform the average citizen from a passive recipient of services into an active consumer and agent, demanding more, better, and faster from governments and business alike. Arif Naqvi, Abraaj Group's founder and a private equity investor, who sees the MENA region as "global growth markets", has a different take. He sees the magnitude of challenges facing the region to inspire more selflessness as a result of enlightened self-interest: "Inclusiveness doesn't come naturally to human beings, but in a storm when the waves are up all boats must rise, not just the strong ones."[17]

Though the MENA appears to be on the right trajectory for some important shifts, how quickly these changes materialize is the crux of the concern. History reminds us that irreversible social change takes decades to come to fruition and institutionalize. Can the MENA region afford that kind of patience?

## The rise of social entrepreneurship across the MENA

As countries in the region have begun transitioning from decades of autocratic leadership to the beginnings of more democratic forms of representation, some believe the spread of "social entrepreneurship" is essential to help meet concurrent demands of driving more equitable economic growth while protecting fragile ecologies and excluded societies.

Around the world, the concept has emerged against a turbulent and complex backdrop. With the proliferation of government failures, civil society actors began raising concerns that government authorities and states are increasingly unable or unwilling to fulfil their duty to protect citizens, solve social problems, and ensure equitable distribution of resources and wealth. Many believe corporations and the private sector have the powers and capabilities to respond adequately to the scale of social and environmental problems in the world. Unfortunately, corporations are only legally accountable to their shareholders, even though the scale of their activities, footprint, and associated obligations far outstrips those expressed in legal instruments. Change needs to be driven by different actors.

The global non-profit sector – which has traditionally been responsible for the delivery of public services as a counterpoint to the private market – has also lost much credibility in dealing with new problems effectively. The sector has begun facing intensifying demands for improved effectiveness, efficiency, and sustainability, as traditional sources of funding have diminished and competition for scarce resources has significantly increased.

Consequently, many believe that traditional social institutions – public bureaucracies, corporations, churches, non-profit organizations – are either unwilling to accept responsibility for addressing the complexity of society's contemporary problems or incapable of doing so with the transformational qualities necessary to address them adequately.

Enter "social entrepreneurship", a concept promising innovative approaches for dealing with today's complex social needs. With an emphasis on market-based approaches to social and environmental problems, social entrepreneurship blurs the traditional boundaries between the public, private, and non-profit sectors and pursues social change through hybrid models of for-profit and non-profit activities.[18]

Its advocates argue that social entrepreneurship seeks to transform society through revolutionary and disruptive experiments in ownership, human/user-centred design, open-sourced operating platforms, equitable decision-making and governance structures, fair incentives, and distributed responsibilities traditionally at the heart of the activities in either the public or private realm.

In the fight against poverty, social enterprises and market-based solutions promise to create sustainable social impact by providing the poor with beneficial products and services, while creating improved livelihood opportunities.[19] From health care to education, sanitation to housing, these innovative models already span various industries in many parts of the world. The excitement around them is heightened by the belief that they will achieve scale by tapping investment capital.[20]

The concept is inspiring a passionate following, especially across the MENA region. Some believe it is a new, innovative model for harnessing the potential of the "youth bulge" to fuel economic and social growth and addressing the systemic roots of poverty and inequality in Arab societies. They believe the factors driving the Arab Spring – namely, lost dignity, social justice, the need for job creation, and a heightened sense of citizenship and social engagement – indicate the birth of a socio-economic environment amenable to social entrepreneurship, drawing young people towards this emerging sector out of both opportunity and necessity. Many also believe that social entrepreneurship is particularly well suited to youth since it not only taps into the desire for independence and self-actualization, but is also relevant for a generation whose worldview incorporates a sense of responsibility that goes significantly beyond immediate family and self. Already the region is seeing the proliferation of numerous social impact meet-ups, social business plan competitions, accelerators, and social angel venture capitalist networks.[21] According to Lina Hourani, director of Al-Ahli

Groups CSR Division and co-lead of the UAE Social Enterprise Task Group (SETG),

> Social entrepreneurship is needed for both economic and social development as it creates new jobs and sources of income, while at the same time encouraging innovation. It can also bring new unconventional products and services to market that can contribute to solving societal problems such as illiteracy, health and poverty.[22]

With transitions underway in post-Arab Spring countries, is "social entrepreneurship" an appropriate response to the scale of the MENA's existing problems? And if so, can it achieve scale soon enough to respond to regional demands?

## The promise versus realities of social entrepreneurship globally

Drawing on data from the United Kingdom, one of the most advanced countries for the development and institutionalization of social entrepreneurship, the results are mixed.

According to the UK Cabinet Office's 2013 Social Enterprise Market Trends report, 6 per cent of all SME employers conform to the definition of a social enterprise,[23] totalling nearly 70,000 organizations in the United Kingdom.[24] Of these SME social enterprises, the report estimates they employ nearly one million people in the United Kingdom.[25] According to Matter&Co,[26] a prominent UK social enterprise advocacy intermediary responsible for tabulating a yearly index of the top 100 high-performing social enterprises, the total combined annual turnover of the 508 registered high-performing social enterprises on their index is £12.4 billion GBP.[27] When comparing that figure to the size of the United Kingdom's economy, the sixth largest in the world, which stands at a towering £2.3–2.4 trillion GBP, one can see that the aggregate economic contribution of the high-performing segment of the United Kingdom's social enterprise sector is approximately 0.5 of 1 per cent of GDP. Though the concept has come a long way, these figures help convey how large the disparity is between the promise and reality of social enterprise today, even in a country where the concept has had decades to penetrate and bloom.

While the proliferation of social entrepreneurship is encouraging, it is still early days for the movement, and the concept is far from having a strong economic impact on the scale of pressing national or global challenges.

When benchmarking performance across the globe, one quickly realizes that only a small percentage of social enterprises globally have made a significant dent on the problems they are trying to address. When colleagues at the Monitor Institute studied 439 market-based solutions in Africa, they found that 13 per cent of them had achieved significant scale, and by doing so have been able to improve the lives of millions of people.[28]

Putting these insights into the context of global macroeconomic trends for the social enterprise investment market, the findings are equally sobering. According to Boston Consulting Group's (BCG) latest Global Wealth report, total aggregate global financial wealth stands at US$135 trillion.[29] Of this, the total size of global capital markets is valued at US$62.3 trillion.[30] Compared to this, the total size of "socially responsible investments" across the world, which are effectively investments that are negatively screened to ensure funds are not used to support the arms trade, tobacco, or junk companies and the like, sits at US$13 trillion (approximately 21 per cent of the market size).[31] From this, the total current market sizing for the global "impact investing" movement, which is the asset class most supportive of "social enterprises", is estimated by various sources to be between US$40 billion and 60 billion in terms of current assets under management.[32] This figure (US$40–60 billion) translates into less than 1 per cent of global investments so far, which are strongly socially oriented (e.g. intending to be "catalytic impact investments" and meant to support social enterprises to reach scale) when compared against the size of global capital markets (valued at US$62.3 trillion); the bulk of responsible investing looks at social issues rather passively. It appears we have a long way yet to go.

Though progress has been impressive in the many short years the concept has come to bloom, enthusiasm around the concept's promise demands some restraint, especially given social entrepreneurship's track record for driving scalable and systemic change forward in other parts of the world.

## The prospects of social entrepreneurship in the MENA

To what extent might social entrepreneurship contribute positively to broader economic growth requirement in the MENA in the near to mid-term? The Moroccan Centre for Innovation and Social Entrepreneurship's (MCISE) first published report on social entrepreneurship provides some insights into the challenges ahead.

According to MCISE, awareness of social enterprise is extremely low in Morocco, the concept is as trendy in certain circles as it is unknown to the vast majority of people, and those who have heard the term "social enterprise" are likely to have first come across the term for sometime in the past four years.[33] Social entrepreneurship appears to be driven by a relatively small circle of people who share common characteristics (e.g. those with advanced degrees and exposure to international ideas and experiences).[34] Personal funds, membership fees, and government funding are the three most common sources of funding for the surveyed organizations, but challenges other than the lack of funding hinder the concepts' fruition, including the lack of appropriate technical support, lack of finance and funding, the limitations of the legal framework, the lack of an enterprise culture and mindset, and barriers around language.[35]

In addition to regional- and country-specific challenges, colleagues at the Monitor Institute, Acumen Fund, and Shell Foundation offer an approximate timescale required to grow a social enterprise to significant scale. After studying the development trajectory of hundreds of social enterprises, they conclude in their seminal "From Blueprint to Scale" report that five to ten years is the typical time horizon required to grow a social enterprise sustainably to significant scale from the start-up phase.[36]

Other findings point out that social entrepreneurs need an ecosystem of support, including involvement of multiple sectors, if they are to be successful. The constellation of a supportive ecosystem usually includes stakeholders, such as government, and the education sectors.[37] Collaboration with the private sector is vital because social entrepreneurs borrow so much of their principles from successful businesses.[38]

There are many positive indicators in the MENA region that make for a compelling case, signalling an accelerated development pace for social entrepreneurship across the region. Building any kind of business or organization (whether socially oriented or traditional) is, however, an extremely difficult task. Establishing a social enterprise is even more challenging than a conventional enterprise, due in part to the need to embed a social or environmental dimension to the DNA of the venture, while building strong governance and operational systems that can achieve social outcomes on the ground in a competitive and efficient manner.[39] Building a double- or triple-bottom line business does not make any founder's life easier.

Since the MENA region also faces unique institutional barriers and idiosyncrasies that constrain both social and traditional entrepreneurs, advocates must spend some energy lobbying to overcome these challenges if the concept stands a chance to live up to its promise.

For example, most countries across the MENA region do not have a standard legal definition or model that reflects the intentions and unique aspirations of social enterprises. This causes unnecessary miscommunication, obstacles, and delays for gaining the right business licenses and legitimacy to operate, in order to attempt to demonstrate a proof-of-concept.

Also, according to the World Bank and International Finance Corporation's (IFC) *2011 Doing Business* report, they found it takes an average of 20 days and 38 per cent of per capita income to start a business in the MENA region.[40] Subsequent updates to this report do not reflect any improvements to this situation in most countries. In practical terms, such high capitalization requirements and business licensing delays significantly reduce the likelihood of letting thousands of social enterprises bloom and scale.

Research from the World Economic Forum reinforces this narrative. The research found that entrepreneurial initiatives in the Arab World face higher rates of failure as compared to initiatives seeded elsewhere, mostly due to the absence of structural factors in Arab countries – namely, finance, policy, cultural norms, infrastructure, human capital, and networks – which allow an entrepreneurial environment to fully thrive.[41] Other research points to different barriers – corruption, indecipherable customs regulations, cultural resistance to investing in start-ups, poor address systems, lack of secure online payment options, and restrictive Internet laws – that currently prevent the development of a fully functional ecosystem for social entrepreneurs.[42]

Thankfully over the course of history, activists, entrepreneurs, and intermediaries took on the responsibility of driving forward the social entrepreneurship ecosystem long before any government got on the band wagon. Reflecting on the development journeys of certain advanced countries, however, one will see that social entrepreneurship really flourishes when key institutions and economic actors actively engage in creating a conducive environment that supports and cultivates new, indigenous ideas and innovative practices.

To accelerate the process, colleagues across the Arab World should reflect on what supportive institutions are needed to unleash this movement, and what the sequence of interventions needs to be at the policy level before engaging government institutions.

These challenges are not unique to the region; they mirror the development narrative of the concept in almost every new city and region social entrepreneurship has grown in. Still, to this day, in large parts of the United Kingdom, Europe, and North America, social entrepreneurship remains a misnomer and an opaque concept to many. Concepts take significant time to penetrate the mainstream conceptual framework, though social entrepreneurship appears to be making headway faster than expected.

## Conclusions: Social entrepreneurship unleashed

Can social entrepreneurship and social enterprises solve for the scale of challenges facing the MENA region?

Indeed, it may be misleading to extrapolate and correlate the limited results achieved by social entrepreneurship globally to mirror the expected impact of the concept in the MENA region. On the contrary, what appears most interesting to advocates and the budding social entrepreneurship ecosystem across the region is not the "level" of the results achieved so far, but its "trajectory". For example, the number of problems now being solved through social entrepreneurship than other tools as compared to the past is most promising. Some may argue that social entrepreneurship is probably also solving regional challenges faster or in a more appealing and satisfactory manner than alternative approaches (e.g. microfinance, traditional aid, and development). Most importantly, the concept may be able to make headway on solving problems that other approaches have not been able to even address.

At its current stage of development, the concept is nascent and confronted by many obstacles and dangers, which, if left unaddressed, could undermine its future potential and ability to drive forward change.

One of the principal symbolic assets of social entrepreneurship is its normative power: what it promises, not necessarily what it delivers. Since social entrepreneurship is increasingly, and often impatiently, being acknowledged as an effective source of solutions for a variety of social problems, without strong empirical evidence about its ability to realize change at scale, it risks being framed as a self-fulfilling prophecy, potentially triggering its premature dismissal. If discursive framing and ideology, rather than empirical evidence, become the primary means fuelling the growth and uptake of social entrepreneurship across the region, the concept may soon be expected to provide comprehensive solutions to social problems that it currently lacks the ability, legitimacy, or scope to adequately address.

More fundamentally, if social entrepreneurs are to stand a chance at solving systemic problems at their roots, other necessary stakeholders must begin aligning institutional support to help build out ecosystems that help accelerate social entrepreneurial solutions for change.

Despite these challenges, social entrepreneurship holds great promise for driving continued social transformation and has so far made positive contributions to socio-economic and socio-political evolution around the world.

Social entrepreneurship is a disruptive social movement framing citizen/human-centred and rights-based demands within a market rationale, in order to legitimize their inclusion into a dominant paradigm and contest the conventional understanding of that paradigm. Social entrepreneurs are social architects, aiming to alter unjust circumstances that cause the marginalization of a segment of humanity that lacks either the financial means or political clout to address these issues themselves by designing new systems all together. Social entrepreneurs are also innovators who defy the traditional boundaries that constrain and categorize innovation and help reconfigure accepted value creation boundaries (blurring between public, private, for-profit, not-for-profit models) by building market-based solutions in order to fundamentally challenge the status quo.[43]

Our trajectory on this earth is fast approaching an important inflection point. Every day, collective awareness expands about the planet's resource constraints. As commodity prices rise disproportionately to economic trends and as a new global middle class emerges (doubling in size to nearly five billion by 2030 and demanding more resources to consume), evidence about the dangers of mismanaged climate change becomes ever more incontrovertible.[44] We have already surpassed many of the planet's natural thresholds and carrying capacities and are on pace for surpassing thresholds of irreversible change.

Demands for social entrepreneurship reflect wider aspirations of seeing fundamental change to how economic value is generated, externalities are accounted for, and economies and societies are structured. Social entrepreneurship can be more fully appreciated if seen as a smaller part of a larger outcry for a more equitable and sustainable normal, for economies to grow within the confines of the earth's carrying capacity, and for businesses and political institutions to facilitate every citizen's upward mobility. In that light, social enterprises that have been able to scale and demonstrate new organizational, economic, and social dynamics are possible. They act as micro proofs-of-concept in themselves, showing that economic and social advancement do not necessarily conflict and need to be trade-offs, but they can be integrated and managed under the right circumstances, operating contexts, and frameworks.

If we are to realize a more equitable world, profound structural changes are necessary. Our dominant social institutions need to reconfigure how they engage the public, how they make decisions, and how they remain accountable for their activities. We need new leaders who challenge the status quo and have the interests of the majority in mind. In our current world context and across the MENA region, the rise of social entrepreneurship helps maintain a level of pressure necessary for continued reform on both fronts, while continuing to inspire new forms of leadership for positive social, economic, and political transformation. The rise of social entrepreneurship in the MENA region should not be considered a panacea for all social ills; however, in an era of rising social and environmental problems and catastrophic market and government failures, social entrepreneurship is a source of innovative solutions to reconcile systemic and institutional failures contributing to a distorted world.

## Notes

1. Quote by Henry Ford, available at http://www.goodreads.com/quotes/ 107178-when-everything-seem-to-be-going-against-you-remember-that.
2. *Popular Jewish Proverb*, available at http://www.quotegarden.com/ adversity.html.
3. International Labour Organization. "Global Employment Trends for Youth 2013", available at http://www.ilo.org/wcmsp5/groups/public/— dgreports/—dcomm/documents/publication/wcms_212423.pdf.
4. Ibid.
5. *The Guardian*. "Youth Employment: Generation Jobless – Overcoming the Challenge of Unemployment and Skills Mismatch Requires Participation from All Members of Society", available at http://www.theguardian.com/ global-development-professionals-network/emirates-foundation- partner-zone/youth-employment-generation-jobless.
6. Ibid.
7. Economist Intelligence Unit. "Political Unrest Hits Economic Prospects in the Middle East", available at http://digitalresearch.eiu.com/searchfor growth/reports/the-search-for-growth/section/political-unrest-hits- economic-prospects-in-the-middle-east.
8. *The Daily Mail*. "Egypt Tourism Continues to Plummet as Thomas Cook Loses Quarter of a Million Holidaymakers due to Turmoil", available at http://www.dailymail.co.uk/travel/article-2605863/Egypts- tourism-revenue-drop-nearly-50-holidaymakers-avoid-troubled-coast. html.
9. Christian Science Monitor. "Poppies Replace Tourists in Egypt's Sinai Desert", available at http://www.csmonitor.com/World/Middle- East/2014/0427/Poppies-replace-tourists-in-Egypt-s-Sinai-desert.
10. Ibid.
11. Ibid.
12. The World Bank, Human Development Network. "Education in the Middle East & North Africa: A Strategy towards Learning for Development", available at http://www.worldbank.org/education/strategy/MENA-E.pdf (p. 10); see also, UN Experts Meeting on Adolescents, Youth and Development – Population Division, Department of Economic and Social Affairs, United Nations Secretariat New York, 21–22 July 2011. "Youth Population and Employment in the Middle East and North Africa: Opportunity or Challenge?", available at http://www.un.org/esa/population/ meetings/egm-adolescents/p06_roudi.pdf; see also, International Monetary Fund. "Youth Unemployment in the MENA Region: Determinants and Challenges", available at https://www.imf.org/external/np/vc/2012/ 061312.htm.

13. Centre for International Private Enterprise (CIPE). "Startup Rising: Entrepreneurship Ecosystems in the Middle East & North Africa", available at http://www.cipe.org/blog/2014/04/24/startup-rising-entrepreneurship-ecosystems-in-the-middle-east-north-africa/.
14. Insight MENA. "Mobile Ownership Rates", available at http://www.insightsmena.com/en/#!place=category&cat=Mobile&qid=Mobile+Ownership&filter=2011.
15. Go-Gulf. "Smartphone Usage in the Middle East – Statistics and Trends", available at http://www.go-gulf.ae/blog/smartphone-middle-east/.
16. Mair, J. (2010). "Social Entrepreneurship: Taking Stock and Looking Ahead", IESE Business School, University of Navarra, Working Paper WP-888, 1–11, available at http://www.iese.edu/research/pdfs/DI-0888-E.pdf; Mair, J. and Marti, I. (2006). "Social Entrepreneurship: A Source of Explanation, Prediction, and Delight", *Journal of World Business*, 41(1), 36–44; Mair, J., Seelos, C. and Borwankar, A. (2005). "Social Entrepreneurial Initiatives Within the Sustainable Development Landscape", *International Journal of Entrepreneurship Education*, 2(4), 431–452; Mair, P. (2006). "Ruling the Void?", *New Left Review*, 42, 25–51.
17. Centre for International Private Enterprise (CIPE). "Startup Rising: Entrepreneurship Ecosystems in the Middle East & North Africa", available at http://www.cipe.org/blog/2014/04/24/startup-rising-entrepreneurship-ecosystems-in-the-middle-east-north-africa/.
18. Light, P. (2008). *The Search for Social Entrepreneurship*, New York: Brookings Institution.
19. Skoll World Forum (2014). "Can Social Enterprises Really Solve Poverty?", available at http://skollworldforum.org/2014/04/06/can-social-enterprises-really-solve-poverty/.
20. Ibid.
21. Available at http://www.wamda.com/2014/04/nahdet-el-mahrousa-and-barclays-bank-egypt-fight-unemployment-by-supporting-startups-
22. *The Guardian*. "Catalysing Social Enterprises in the UAE", available at http://www.theguardian.com/global-development-professionals-network/emirates-foundation-partner-zone/catalysing-social-enterprise-uae.
23. Social enterprise is defined as follows:

    i. Considers itself to be a social enterprise
    ii. Not pays more than 50 per cent of profit or surplus to owners or shareholders
    iii. Not generates more than 75 per cent of income from grants and donations
    iv. Not generates less than 25 per cent of income from trading
    v. Agrees that it is "a business with primarily social/environmental objectives, whose surpluses are principally reinvested for that purpose in the business or community rather than mainly being paid to shareholders and owners"

    UK Cabinet Office. "Social Enterprise: Market Trends – Based upon the BIS Small Business Survey 2012", pp. 1–2, available at https://www.gov.

uk/government/uploads/system/uploads/attachment_data/file/205291/ Social_Enterprises_Market_Trends_-_report_v1.pdf.

24. Actual figures reported were 973,700 jobs. See: UK Cabinet Office, "Social Enterprise: Market Trends – Based upon the BIS Small Business Survey 2012", p. 2, available at https://www.gov.uk/government/uploads/ system/uploads/attachment_data/file/205291/Social_Enterprises_Market_ Trends_-_report_v1.pdf.

25. Ibid.

26. Matter&Co, available at http://matterandco.com.

27. RBS Social Enterprise 100 Index, available at https://se100.net/data?

28. See Monitor Deloitte's Monitor Institute. "From Blueprint to Scale: The Case for Philanthropy in Impact Investing," available at http://www. mim.monitor.com/downloads/Blueprint_To_Scale/From%20Blueprint% 20to%20Scale%20-%20Case%20for%20Philanthropy%20in%20Impact %20Investing_Full%20report.pdf – p. 53

   Acumen Fund's investing experience reflects this reality: it has considered more than 5,000 companies in the past ten years and has invested in just 65 of those. Recent Monitor studies of inclusive businesses on the ground paint a similarly challenging picture. In 2009–10, a team led by Mike Kubzansky conducted an ambitious 16-month study of inclusive businesses across nine countries in sub-Saharan Africa. Their aim was to gain a better understanding of when, where and how market-based approaches in Africa succeed. The team looked at 439 promising inclusive businesses and found that only 32 percent were commercially viable and had potential to achieve significant scale. Only 13 percent were actually operating at scale.

   See also the website http://skollworldforum.org/2014/04/06/can-social-enterprises-really-solve-poverty/.

29. The Boston Consulting Group. "Global Asset Management 2013 – Capitalizing on the Recovery", available at http://www.bcg.de/documents/ file135355.pdf.

30. Ibid.

31. Global Sustainable Investing Alliance. "2012: Global Sustainable Investment Review", available at http://gsiareview2012.gsi-alliance.org/ pubData/source/Global%20Sustainable%20Investement%20Alliance.pdf.

32. Ibid.

33. Ibid.

34. Ibid.

35. Ibid.

36. Monitor Deloitte Monitor Institute. "From Blueprint to Scale: The Case for Philanthropy in Impact Investing", available at http://www.mim. monitor.com/downloads/Blueprint_To_Scale/From%20Blueprint%20to %20Scale%20-%20Case%20for%20Philanthropy%20in%20Impact%20 Investing_Full%20report.pdf – "Monitor's research suggests that it is not

uncommon for the firm's journey to viability and scale to take five to ten years." p. 53.

37. *The Guardian.* "Catalysing social enterprises in the UAE", available at http://www.theguardian.com/global-development-professionals-network/emirates-foundation-partner-zone/catalysing-social-enterprise-uae.
38. Ibid.
39. Ibid.
40. The International Finance Corporation (IFC). "Doing Business 2011", available at http://www.doingbusiness.org/~/media/GIAWB/Doing%20Business/Documents/Annual-Reports/English/DB11-FullReport.pdf.
41. World Economic Forum, Special Meeting. "Economic Growth and Job Creation in the Arab World", Dead Sea, Jordan 21–23 October 2011, available at http://www3.weforum.org/docs/ME11/WEF_ME11_Report.pdf.
42. Centre for International Private Enterprise (CIPE). "Startup Rising: Entrepreneurship Ecosystems in the Middle East & North Africa", available at http://www.cipe.org/blog/2014/04/24/startup-rising-entrepreneurship-ecosystems-in-the-middle-east-north-africa/.
43. Nicholls, A. (2010). "The Legitimacy of Social Entrepreneurship: Reflexive Isomorphism in a Pre-Paradigmatic Field", *Entrepreneurship Theory and Practice*, 34(4), 611–633.
44. The Ellen MacArthur Foundation. "Towards the Circular Economy Vol. 2 2013", available at http://www.ellenmacarthurfoundation.org/business/reports/ce2013#.

# 4
# Social Enterprise in the MENA Region: False Hope or New Dawn?

*Rebecca Hill and Medea Nocentini*

## Introduction and approach

As active members of Middle East and North Africa's (MENA) emerging social enterprise community, our beliefs regarding the potential of social enterprise in the MENA region are optimistic based on empirical observation of the convergence of different stakeholder efforts (such as strategic philanthropy, corporate social responsibility (CSR), public–private partnerships) towards social enterprise models. Not only do we believe social enterprise is necessary to create sustainable social impact (in particular where philanthropy or economic development has failed to do so), but we also appreciate its business potential and its resilience to market volatility. Nonetheless, through our work at C3 – Consult and Coach for a Cause[1] – we have experienced, first hand, some of the challenges that social entrepreneurs encounter when launching and growing their organizations.

In this chapter, we assess the social enterprise potential in the MENA region by

1. identifying likely drivers for social enterprise prosperity, such as

   a. the presence of social issues requiring sustainable solutions,
   b. a favourable demographic structure as well as youth interests,
   c. stakeholders' focus on entrepreneurship,
   d. technology infrastructure development and social media consumption;

2. recognizing existing *"social good" initiatives*, such as

   a. regional philanthropy and international support,
   b. government efforts and investment,
   c. CSR initiatives;

3. briefly touching on such initiatives' current achievements by

   a. acknowledging *limitations of existing efforts*,
   b. analysing their convergence towards models that are, in essence, social enterprises;

4. providing an overview of the MENA social enterprise sector status quo by

   a. identifying *emerging social entrepreneurs' challenges*,
   b. celebrating the initial success of social enterprise efforts;

5. describing the *"ideal" ecosystem* able to serve social entrepreneurs' needs and help them overcome obstacles to growth and social impact, while identifying the ecosystem's enablers that already exist, the ones that need additional development, and the ones that are missing, such as

   a. personal enablers,
   b. financial enablers,
   c. business enablers,
   d. environmental enablers,
   e. social impact and ecosystem enablers;

6. discussing a collaboration framework and providing *actionable recommendations* for stakeholders;

7. and ending the chapter with an optimistic view of social enterprise bringing a *new dawn* for the MENA region.

Given the limited literature on social enterprise in the region and the need for some conceptual framing, the bulk of the materials we cite is not from academic journals; instead, it is taken directly from practice – from market-leading consulting companies, government agencies, and funding organizations – that are shaping the debate on social enterprises. Additionally, our analysis relies significantly on our personal experience as key representatives of C3.

---

### Social Enterprise Definition

*At Consult and Coach for A Cause, we define social enterprise as an organization (for profit or non profit) whose mandate is social and/or environmental impact: at least 50% of the enterprise's turnover comes from commercial undertakings and at least 50% of the profit is invested back into the business' social mandate. Social and/or environmental impact needs to be measurable, tracked and proven.*

---

## Drivers of social enterprise growth in MENA

In our opinion, social enterprise growth drivers are different in nature than those of for-profit. In the following section, we identify a few that are likely to create a favourable environment for the creation, launch, and development of social enterprises.

### Abundance of social issues requiring sustainable solutions

The challenges the MENA region faces are daunting despite the significant wealth created by the petro-industry. Underinvestment and political instability has led to weak infrastructure, primarily in housing, health care, education, unemployment, and environmental conservation.

Table 4.1 illustrates some of the challenges facing MENA governments that seem to be growing even more pressing each day, in addition to the emerging political and regional issues leaders have to deal with.

Most social issues, such as poverty and unemployment, can be associated with economic underdevelopment (and a lack of investment); but some issues such as diabetes, water shortage, and waste are paradoxically due to "consumerism" associated with economic success.

### Young population driving social consciousness and entrepreneurial spirit

Today, with half of the population under the age of 25, MENA has the second youngest population after sub-Saharan Africa. One in five

*Table 4.1* MENA region's social issues

| Issues | Key data points |
|---|---|
| Population growth | Since the 1970s, the MENA population almost tripled from 128 million to 359 million people in all Arab countries (Mirking, 2010). By 2015, this region is expected to have a population of 692 million (Roudi-Fahimi, 2007) |
| Poverty | While 14% of the MENA region (less than 50 million people) are below the $2 a day poverty line in 2008, the number increases to 53% when using the $4 a day benchmark (Viswanath, 2012) |
| Unemployment | Every MENA country suffers from high unemployment that mostly affects the young, the educated, and women. Coupled with a rapid labour force growth, around 100 million new jobs are needed by 2020, double the current level of employment (World Bank, 2004) |
| Climate change | The MENA region is threatened by desertification and degradation of ecosystems due to global warming and overuse of natural resources (Mostafa, 2009; Saab, 2012). Desertification is expected to threaten 14% of Algeria's and 52% of Morocco's land base, while in Egypt, 30–40% of total irrigated land is affected by saline water (Varis, 1997; Chenoweth, 2011) |
| Waste | The waste management sector lacks funding and innovation. For instance, 57% of waste water from MENA countries is partially treated or not treated at all (Kfouri, 2009); due to a lack of financial resources, municipalities rely on traditional "waste mobilization ponds": effluent from plants is sometimes mixed with freshwater sources and used for irrigation, causing serious contamination problems from the high concentration of chloride and nitrate |
| Water scarcity | According to the United Nations (UNDP, 2011), the total renewable water per capita decreased from 3035 $m^3$ in 1958–1962 to 1000 $m^3$ in 2003–2007, making this the most water-stressed region. Some countries are below the scarcity level, with 12 other countries in a state of water crisis (less than 500 $m^3$) and, of these, nine are in a state of absolute scarcity (less than 165 $m^3$). The MENA region is expected to be drier with higher near-surface temperature with threatening consequences on all vital sectors. For example, Jordan's annual per capita water resources are expected to decrease from 110 $m^3$ to 56 $m^3$ by 2050 (Ammary, 2007) |

*Table 4.1*   (Continued)

| Issues | Key data points |
| --- | --- |
| Food security | Food production in MENA is limited due to a shortage of arable land and water. In addition to the water issues described above, only 3.9% of the total land area in the region is under cultivation. Consequently, the region meets about 50% of its food requirements through imports. In 2008, the food import bill for the MENA region was US$61.4 billion and is expected to reach US$92.4 billion by 2020 (Al Masah Capital Limited, 2011) |
| Health care | People in the GCC are widely recognized as one of the most obese in the world, with close to two-thirds of the entire adult population being overweight. Recent studies suggest that obesity is more expensive to the healthcare system than smoking, with obese patients tending to spend 2–3 times as much as the average patient on health care. Saudi Arabia has the fourth highest rate of diabetes globally at about 22%, while Kuwait and UAE are also in the top 20. In the UAE, chronic lifestyle diseases and injuries cause almost 90% of all deaths (Informa, 2012) |
| Education | As per the World Economic Forum's Global Competitiveness Report 2013–2014, except for Qatar, Lebanon, and UAE, most countries in the region scored low on various parameters related to the quality of the educational system, including primary education, higher education and training, enrolment rates, level of access to the Internet in schools, and availability of specialized research and training services (Al Masah Capital Limited, 2014) |

people living in MENA is aged between 15 and 24 years – nearly 90 million in 2010 (Roudi, 2011).

This age group (otherwise known as Generation Y – people born between 1981 and 2000) seems to be more sensitized to ethical consumerism, workplace values, and social and environmental issues (VanMeter, 2012); and the fact that youth consists a large proportion of the population in the region is a significant driver of social enterprise development.

A 2011 survey of MENA youth run by YouGov in collaboration with Stanford University and Bayt.com demonstrated a strong culture of volunteerism and interest in improving communities, in particular after the uprisings. The same study also shows that MENA youth is very keen on starting businesses or NGOs, promising great potential for social enterprise in the region (Buckner, 2012).

### Entrepreneur-focused initiatives

MENA governments are increasingly focusing on entrepreneur-focused initiatives driven by the realization that one of the most significant social and economic challenges in MENA is youth unemployment. As shown in Table 4.1, around 100 million jobs are needed by 2020, forcing MENA governments to assess entrepreneurship as a potential solution to job creation. Significant effort has been made to develop a broad-based systems-thinking approach to underpin an ecosystem in which entrepreneurs can thrive, such as educational reform, business regulation and licensing, financing (credit rating, investor protection, bankruptcy support, etc.), seed funding (angels, incubators, accelerators, etc.), knowledge sharing, culture change, and numerous other current initiatives.

In the World Bank's *Doing Business 2014* report, 11 elements of business regulations are measured with particular scrutiny of reforms that either hinder or help business. Due to the significant effort made by GCC governments, the UAE is now the most competitive (23rd on the ranking), followed by KSA (26th), Bahrain (46th), Oman (47th), and Qatar (48th). These efforts will continue to stimulate the SME sector, including social enterprise (World Bank, 2013).

### Technology infrastructure development

ICT infrastructures in MENA still require sizeable investments and development initiatives (El-Darwiche, 2011). Some countries have realized how technology is key for economic and social development (Gelvanovska, 2014) and have started focusing on the ICT sector (such as Jordan) and as a result, penetration of mobile, Internet, and broadband platforms is on the rise across the region: more than 135 million individuals use the Internet in the 22 Arab countries; this is coupled with a mobile penetration rate at around 110 per cent on a regional level.

Broadband is still underpenetrated in most Arab countries, and in the era of "smart cities" and "smart government", expanding broadband penetration is becoming a pressing developmental issue, as increased broadband connectivity promises several opportunities, such as driving economic growth, increasing educational and skills development, and enhancing job opportunities (Mohammed Bin Rashid School of Government and Bayt.com, 2014), all critical elements for social enterprise development and success.

MENA has more than 71 million active users of social networks. As a recent study by CONE Communications & Echo Research (Global CSR Study, 2013) suggests, social media usage, especially in developing countries such as China, India, and Brazil (where more than eight in ten consumers use social channels to engage with companies around social and environmental issues), is a critical factor in driving socially responsible business practices. Citizens are universally taking to social channels to learn more about issues, share information, and influence their personal networks. Companies (including SMEs) must recognize social media as a powerful tool with equal ability to give an advantage or peril.

## Existing regional "social good" initiatives

The MENA region is not lacking in initiatives to achieve positive social impact, from individual generosity to government efforts as well as international support and corporate philanthropy – there are many examples of impactful initiatives across MENA countries.

### Philanthropy and official development assistance

Regionally based philanthropists motivated by religious beliefs and personal values play a huge part in addressing social issues. In its annual survey, Coutts (The Million $ Donors Report, 2014) found that $727 million was donated by GCC-based donors. While a relatively small sum compared to other economies ($14 billion in the United States), we have to assume it is the tip of an iceberg given cultural reticence to publicize charity (zagat) donations.

Numerous non-profit organizations ranging from large zagat houses and government-funded entities like the UAE's Khalifa Fund, to microfinance institutions such as Saudi-based Grameen-Jameel and smaller "single-cause" non-profits are also at work.

Official Development Assistance funds are sizeable both to and from Arab countries, although not always social in purpose. According to a Reality of Aid report (Mahjoub, 2013), official financial assistance to 22 Arab countries from 2000 to 2006 was $82.5 billion (18.9 per cent of all the assistance given to developing countries), although 46 per cent went towards the Iraq invasion and occupation.

### Government initiatives and regional aid

Many government initiatives focused on reducing unemployment by stimulating entrepreneurship and technology innovation have been mentioned in previous sections. The region annually invests an estimated $40–50 billion, or approximately 5–7 per cent of GDP, in new infrastructure projects including health care, education, and renewable energy (Shediac, 2008). For instance, MENA countries on average spend one-fifth of total public expenditures on education (World Bank, 2007).

Also, the GCC states took the lead in responding to the unprecedented political and economic changes triggered by the Arab Spring. Saudi Arabia announced generous financial aid packages to Bahrain, Oman, Egypt, and Jordan, pledging $10 billion aid packages to the former two countries, $5 billion to Jordan, and significant bilateral assistance to Morocco (Ulrichsen, 2013). In addition, GCC assistance mushroomed at a time when austerity packages and cost-cutting measures in western states have reduced their capacity to engage at anything like the same level; this is especially the case of southern European states where the "(in-)ability to take the lead in addressing the transitions underway in their immediate 'strategic neighborhood' in North Africa or the Levant" has had a profound impact (Ulrichsen, 2013). A combination of the GCC states' abundant resources, linguistic and cultural connection, and geographical proximity has propelled them to the forefront of regional engagement, requiring western actors, whether governmental, humanitarian, or civil society organizations, to become familiar with a frequently diverging set of operational procedures or broader objectives.

### Corporate social responsibility

There are clear signs that CSR in the region is gaining momentum: for example, the list of signatories to the UN's Global Compact[2] from the MENA region has grown from three in 2003 to 262 by the end of 2012 (Shehadi, 2013). Regional CSR is practiced at national and local levels. State-owned enterprises, such as Saudi Telecom Company (STC), have launched CSR programmes in health care, education, training, and employment. SMEs, such as Saudi's Rumman Company, recruit and invest in local talent. Multinational companies, such as HP, HSBC, Pepsi, Microsoft, and many others, have launched multiple initiatives across the region.

## Limitations of existing efforts and convergence towards social enterprise models

All mentioned "social good" initiatives are important drivers of positive social and environmental change. Nonetheless, they all present several limitations that social enterprise models could help overcome.

### Limitations of existing efforts

Non-profit organizations often experience challenges in terms of scalability (W. Clement and Jessie V. Stone Foundation, 2009) as well as donors' trust due to a variety of reasons, such as lack of transparency or proven social impact (Ebrahim, 2010). Government budgets and efforts are unsustainable and inefficient (Shediac, 2008) and often affected by corruption.

The Social Progress Index (SPI)[3] is a recently developed tool that measures the extent to which countries provide for the social and environmental needs of their citizens. At a disaggregated level, it shows areas of underperformance and success for countries at all income levels. Many rich nations, for example, perform poorly on some measures – the United States (which spends the most per capita on health care globally) ranks 11th in terms of health and wellness; Australia (7th on the index, 6th in terms of GDP) ranks 22nd for shelter; Spain (10th overall, and 11th in terms of GDP) ranks 22nd for personal freedom and choice. In contrast, many poorer nations perform better than expected, based on their level of income. Rwanda is 46th overall and 48th in terms of GDP but ranks 9th in terms of primary school enrolment; Mozambique is 47th overall and bottom (50th) in terms of GDP, but ranks 14th in terms of equality and inclusion.

Just focusing on job creation does not address other more intractable social problems within the broader economic system. Moreover, CSR initiatives, although a positive step towards social impact, rarely reach sizeable scale and sustainability, especially when not aligned with the core strategy of the business.

In summary, we should not expect the current "business as usual" approach to solve pressing social and environmental issues. While economic development is necessary for social progress, it is not sufficient.

### Convergence towards social enterprise business models

At C3 – Consult and Coach for a Cause, we believe in two basic principles:

- Business principles and practices can unlock the potential of "social good" organizations to make a sustainable impact on the community.
- "Strategic" social missions can improve long-term financial performance of businesses.

For both altruistic and commercial reasons, non-profits, governments, and business organizations alike are converging around social enterprise solutions for social and environmental issues. Our optimism for social enterprise comes from this convergence:

a. Philanthropic organizations are increasingly embracing revenue-generating and cost-optimizing activities to reach sustainability and maximize social impact; a great example is Water.org, increasingly providing microloans to underprivileged households to buy their water systems, instead of donating them.
b. Governments are increasingly achieving costs savings and efficiencies through private–public partnerships with private service providers (Shediac, 2008).
c. Businesses are increasingly influenced by consumers, in particular the youth, who are vocal advocates of social causes and empowered, often through social media, to take action (CONE Communications & Echo Research, 2013).

## Emerging MENA social entrepreneurs: Challenges and successes

A vibrant community of MENA social entrepreneurs is emerging. To date, Egypt has the most social ventures, followed by West

Bank/Gaza, Jordan, Lebanon, and Morocco (Shehadi, 2013). Even in the GCC, although specific numbers are not available, social entrepreneurship is on the rise: the growth of C3 – Consult and Coach for a Cause is a living example of the rising number of GCC-based social businesses.

Having said the above, while launching social enterprise makes great business sense, it certainly has its challenges, and based on findings in Africa, this is especially true if focusing on low-income segments (Kubzansky, 2011).

### Social entrepreneur types and their typical challenges

Social enterprises are socially driven businesses and combine the challenges of a business (e.g. gaining market share, reaching profitability and scale) with those of a non-profit (e.g. having sustainable impact, building lean yet efficient operations, greater transparency). They have the additional pressure of being positioned as world "saviours", so expectations for them are high. To balance this scrutiny, social enterprises need to be efficient, transparent, and data centric.

The combination of these simultaneous challenges (the triple-bottom line) creates additional levels of complexity that need to be tackled in a focused and targeted way: the support services and the emerging enablers dedicated to purely commercial entrepreneurs or to non-profits will not be enough to foster the growth and impact of social enterprises.

In our work at C3, we have observed hundreds of aspiring social entrepreneurs who typically fall into two main categories:

i. *The social mission-driven social entrepreneurs* have identified a social cause they are super passionate about and seek to solve it through a business idea. They often lack business acumen (few in our experience know how to write a business plan) and have weak analytical skills. What they have in abundance are high expectations of community support that, when they do not get it, leads to frustration and a loss of motivation.

ii. *The commercially driven social entrepreneurs*, while focused on their business idea's success, are also intrigued by the idea of doing something good at the same time. They often choose a social cause that they may or may not be passionate about and probably lack knowledge of. They do not have strong links with beneficiaries and NGOs and lack credibility. Their messages and marketing reflect this ambivalence.

The most successful social entrepreneurs are, of course, a combination of these two and run enterprises where the social mission is at the core of their business model. It is rare to see a perfect balance between social and business objectives at the beginning of the entrepreneurial journey, normally finding a balance along the way through experience and alignment efforts.

A common challenge for social entrepreneurs is choosing which business licence to go for – a non-profit or for-profit. Some MENA countries have made setting up a non-profit easier than a for-profit and vice versa. Because the business model fits neither, social entrepreneurs often find themselves in a bind – being cut off from donor fundraising or CSR funds because they are not a charity or not able to undertake any revenue generation activity because they are a registered non-profit. C3 often falls into this grey zone.

An additional challenge for social entrepreneurship has been the lack of a "term" not just in English, but also in Arabic and a widely shared definition.

### Success stories

Despite the above challenges, social enterprises in MENA are emerging. As pointed out by Jamil Wyne and Yehia Houry (Wyne, June 2013), 20–30 per cent of companies participating in regional business plan competitions are de facto social enterprises.

Socially driven entrepreneurs are using whatever resources they can get, working within existing systems and sometimes under the radar. Without any specific legal nomenclature around social business, either most end up with a standard for-profit license or they go the non-profit route if fund raising is core to their model.

What we have is an emerging white space for social entrepreneurs: many are already capitalizing on it. Just a few examples C3 has interacted with are *Palestyle* that has brought efficient water tanks to Palestinian homes as well as outlets for refugees selling traditional art objects and *Ustad Mobile* that developed a software to support learning programmes on very cheap mobile phones without Internet connection, targeting impoverished areas and refugee camps. And there are many more.

We believe regional social enterprises will not only help solve growing social and environmental issues, but also contribute to MENA economic growth. An analysis of the UK social enterprise market reveals that between 2012 and 2013, social enterprises outperformed SMEs in turnover growth (*The Financial Times*, 2013), while a paper from New Philanthropy Capital (Ogain, 2011) on the growth and development of United Kingdom-based social enterprises demonstrates that social enterprise are, on average, more likely to survive than the average UK business, especially in times of an economic downturn.

## The "ideal" social enterprise ecosystem

Given the growth in SME initiatives to develop business acumen, skill sets and access funding, is there a need for additional support for social entrepreneurs?

We strongly believe that to unlock the endless opportunities for social impact in the MENA region, social entrepreneurs need a specialized and social enterprise-focused ecosystem that supports the creation and growth of both individual enterprises and the sector. Ideally, the ecosystem includes the usual building blocks for start-ups – regulation, funding, education, mentoring, and so on – in addition to the social-oriented support functions that include cultural and religious values.

As each MENA country finds its own path, we believe there are some core structures that need to be in place to support social enterprise (Table 4.2).

### Personal enablers

Many founders have to convince themselves as well as their loved ones that the pros of a bootstrapped existence that characterize a start-up outweigh the cons of a "secure job". In the MENA region, a business failure can mean real hardship given the absence of a social safety net and limited finance options.

Friends and family of social entrepreneurs play a key role – in C3's experience, most of the social entrepreneurs we see survive only because of the encouragement and financial support of family

*Table 4.2* The social enterprise ecosystem's building blocks

| Category | Enabler | Current contribution |
| --- | --- | --- |
| a. Personal enablers | Formal education | Emerging |
| | Informal education | Emerging |
| | Mentors/advisors | Emerging |
| | Friends and family | Effective |
| b. Financial enablers | Micro/SME finance | Effective |
| | Banks | Limited |
| | Equity/angel investors | Limited |
| | Government programmes | Emerging |
| | Friends and family | Effective |
| c. Business enablers | Networking associations | Emerging |
| | Incubators | Emerging |
| | Professional services | Emerging |
| d. Environmental enablers | Infrastructure | Limited |
| | Regulatory framework | Limited |
| | Media/culture | Limited |
| | Lobbies/entrepreneur organizations | Emerging |
| e. Social impact and ecosystem enablers | Non-profits | Effective |
| | Government | Emerging |
| | Corporate | Emerging |
| | Data and research | Limited |
| | Technology infrastructure | Emerging |

*Source*: C3 – Consult and Coach for a Cause.

and friends. In a culture where extended family needs come first, this can be quite a fraught time for a budding entrepreneur so morale-boosting support is almost as critical as financial support.

Universities are vital incubators for social enterprise as they encourage students to venture into start-ups. Competitions that develop social consciousness are the most impactful, such as NYUAD's Hackathon and the MIT Enterprise Forum's Arab Startup Competition, now in its seventh year.

And a number of universities now have entrepreneurship in the curricula with "how to" courses on starting a business giving the much-needed technical knowledge for students seeking self-employment. For example, 277 students have gone through Abu

Dhabi University's Innovation and Entrepreneurship Centre since 2012 (more than 50 per cent Emirati, 190 male and 87 female), and the next phase is an incubator and research centre open to students and non-students.

Regional initiatives focusing on youth business skills development like Injaz, and the Middle East Youth Initiative, have gained traction as they successfully respond to the changing needs of young people and provide access to the private sector. However, while internships are relatively common, we do not see many companies providing structured (or paid) training for students, and opportunities for gaining experience in social impact (beyond volunteering initiatives, such as beach clean-ups) are limited.

### Financial enablers

Even though banks recognize that SMEs are a regional priority, they have not returned to the same level of lending seen before 2008. Burnt by the financial crisis and the lack of a credit rating system, regional banks lag social innovation for entrepreneurs in general, let alone social entrepreneurs (Rocha, 2010).

In this context, the emergence of incubators such as Oasis 500, in5, turn8, the Khalifa Fund, the Dubai Municipality (who are offering AED 1 billion private sector partnerships), Synergos, and other start-up platforms (often social enterprises themselves) is encouraging (The National, 2014).

Similarly, an increasing number of venture capitalists (often incubators as well) are operating in the region, mostly established by corporate organizations. However, while they are active, they are mainly interested in IT and technology investments (47 per cent of total) that are expensive, and not in small loans or investments.

Angel investors are more numerous, but are not organized in any official network and so they are difficult to find and approach. International patient capital funds, such as the Acumen Fund, are not yet investing in the GCC, while other non-profit organizations supporting social enterprise, such as Ashoka, have limited their presence to selected countries (e.g. Egypt).

Other forms of government financial support targeting nationals are available; Emirates Foundation, Mohammed Bin Rashid Establishment for Young Business Leaders, the aforementioned Khalifa Fund for Enterprise Development, and the Qatar Business Incubation

Center to name a few. Microfinance is well established in Morocco, Egypt, and Jordan.

While this is all encouraging, our optimism for the funding gap comes from the online crowdfunding and crowdinvesting platforms that provide a valuable alternative to traditional funding. We believe that platforms like Aflamnah and Eureeca will change the funding landscape and really enable start-ups to gain access to small amounts of funds.

### Business enablers

In addition to their CSR activities, large companies can make a difference through their procurement policies, possibly setting aside a portion of their budgets for social enterprises seeking to break into a market.

Business associations, such as the Dubai Chamber of Commerce's Centre for Responsible Business, provide huge networking opportunities for social businesses, but are limited to onshore companies and have high membership fees. Similarly "hot desk" *hubs*, such as the Cribb, the Impact Hub, Make, Altcity, are created to provide work space and networking, for a price; while start-up competitions held by Arabia 500 and MIT's Arab Business Plan Competition are making an impact, they again reach limited numbers.

Gathering momentum are mentoring platforms such as JeeranSME, WAMDA, REACH, and Baraka Advisors, as well as our own C3, that create networks of skilled individuals ready to coach and mentor young entrepreneurs. Whether sector-specific, such as Abu Dhabi's twofour54[4] or general, these platforms provide a critical service for entrepreneurs who often lack basic business skills and know-how.

### Environmental enablers

While we have already discussed regulatory issues and licensing, we believe other enablers are key for a successful sector.

Current media coverage for emerging social enterprises is limited, and the media community is often unable to explore social issues that have a political edge. This is a challenge as the media could provide an easy access for knowledge sharing and "reassurance" via online blogs, forums, and case studies. Some media platforms like WAMDA have spotted this as an opportunity, and other social enterprises are entering the market with positive social stories, like Baraka Bits.

The real environmental driver though is technology: the exponential growth of social media and digital platform consumption, together with investments in connectivity and Internet penetration, is helping entrepreneurs reach customers and stakeholders in the most cost-effective way.

While the number of Internet users has increased exponentially, the level of penetration differs quite widely within MENA from over 86 per cent in Qatar to less than 15 per cent in Yemen, Algeria, and Iraq. Penetration is highest in the GCC countries with over 53 per cent, compared to regional penetration rate just under 30 per cent (IMRG/MENAP, 2013). Facebook alone has seen a tripling in the last three years to 45 million users in the region. If we assume parity of penetration over the next ten years, then technology, and the use of social media, will be the number one driver for convergence around social issues.

## Social impact and ecosystem enablers

We already touched on the role of non-profits, corporate organizations, and government entities in fostering a social enterprise ecosystem. Their contribution will be pivotal for social enterprises' set-up, growth, and success.

In terms of underlying enablers, data (for both social issues and market potential) is a key component in building robust business plans. Currently, there is very little research done on the size and effects of social issues or on social consciousness in purchasing behaviour. Businesses, both for- and non-profit, are currently operating with limited knowledge on regional needs. The lack of data-driven decision processes results in misleading conclusions that could significantly reduce a social entrepreneur's chances of success. The only sources of social sector data are governments, a handful of universities, and international organizations such as the UN and World Bank.

If educational institutions and government bodies are able to produce and supply additional solid data on social issues, technology platforms can help spread knowledge and insights to the emerging social enterprise community, accelerating its growth and impact.

## Suggested collaboration framework and recommendations

We believe a collaborative approach among all players is a pre-requisite for social enterprise to make significant social impact: as suggested by the UN Global Compact (UNGC and The Rockefeller Foundation, 2012) philanthropy, governments, corporations, and investors all have an important role in promoting sustainable development, in particular through social enterprise development support. As already discussed in the earlier section (The "ideal" social enterprise ecosystem), academia and media can also propel aspiring social entrepreneurs through skills development and success stories and role models coverage.

Key priorities to be addressed as soon as possible are as follows:

a. A specific trade license and category for social enterprise – as in the United Kingdom and the United States. This critical government intervention would provide a legal structure for those seeking social impact using a for-profit business model. For countries with income tax like Lebanon and Jordan, tax breaks could be made available for social enterprises to ensure profits are properly reinvested back into the business.

   i. The official endorsement would place social enterprise within a commercial context with clear regulations for compliance.
   ii. The creation of a social enterprise category would address the issue of Arabic terminology and create a standard approach to its communication.

b. Data and research – successful stakeholder outreach, whether for a new product, service or a social issue campaign, requires robust market data and an informed understanding of consumer behaviour. This is often lacking or hard to find within the region making audience segmentation challenging.

   i. Ideally, research is a collaborative effort between educational institutions, government agencies, and the business community or non-profits, but regional initiatives are limited and often funded by international donors. To be effective, regional players need to step up with governments taking a lead. Innovation is often the result of research and, with an increasing amount of airtime being given to this region's need for innovation, we are hopeful that locally driven research will become more commonplace.

c. Funding options – although there are many emerging opportunities, they tend to be limited in terms of size and reach. Government funds targeting SMEs, such as the Emirates Fund in the UAE and the Kuwait SME fund, rightly target nationals. However, many social enterprise start-ups have non-national founders who have to find other sources of finance. Banks are still wary of lending to SMEs, especially high-risk start-ups, and are seen more of a growth option.

i. Personal capital, as well as friends and family, provide the initial seed money, but second round funding is limited and expensive (some financiers require 20 per cent or more equity) with little protection for either party.

ii. A more structured approach to SME evaluation and investment is required with more sizeable funds to invest in different sectors and different ROI targets. This requires a concerted and collaborative approach with local lenders taking a lead.

d. Raising general awareness of social enterprise and addressing the misconceptions of linking business with "doing good" will help underpin existing initiatives and provide reassurance and role models for aspiring social entrepreneurs. While regional-based English media have already covered such topics, this has yet to be seen in the Arabic media.

i. Religious and community leaders can also help the discussion, especially within the Islamic *waqf* context, and endorse the concept of making money by "doing good".

e. Existing social entrepreneurs need encouragement from the business and social impact community, while aspiring ones need to build their leadership skills and self-confidence through their educational and professional experiences.

i. This can best happen in forums, conferences, and events as well as informal networks such as created by the growing number of incubators and accelerators that organize pitch weekends. Mentoring platforms exist, and by all accounts getting mentors is not a challenge, it is finding the entrepreneurs!

   ii. Larger businesses could seek out social enterprises for procurement purposes, ensuring that purchasing dollars have a social impact as well as commercial.

f. While technology is enabling more communication, many organizations (private, governments, NGOs, etc.) still lack the confidence to have open and authentic communication where experiences (i.e. failures) are shared. While organizations remain hesitant to share "lessons learnt" especially in public forums, whether online or offline, building a collaborative and informed ecosystem to support social change will always be challenging.

## Conclusion

Social consciousness, enabled by technology and combined with converging philanthropic and business solutions, has the power to transform how we live, work, and give back today within our communities and broader societies. As consumers, we can spread greater well-being because we are more connected– we have a better understanding of what is needed, where the gaps are, what initiatives are being developed, and who is doing what and how well. As business owners or philanthropist, we can "do good" by converging towards sustainable solutions as well as towards transparency, integrity, and authenticity around intentions and purpose. Social issues can now be addressed in a collaborative environment, with each actor doing what it does best to deliver sustainable results.

   We see social enterprise as the missing agent of social impact bringing disruptive solutions and systemic changes to endemic issues. Our optimism for social enterprise in this region grows as a direct correlation with the increasing convergence of actors, events, and information that underpins social change and drives a convergence of solutions that, when added to a growing rejection of "business as usual", makes for a potent mix – a convergence of values embedded in the power of business as a force for good.

## Notes

1. Coach and Consult for a Cause is a UAE-based social enterprise mobilizing business professionals to support emerging social entrepreneurs on a volunteer basis.

2. United Nations Global Compact – A strategic policy initiative for businesses committed to aligning their operations and strategies with 10 principles on the areas of human rights, labour, the environment, and anticorruption.
3. The index, published by non-profit *Social Progress Imperative*, is based on the writings of Amartya Sen, Douglass North, and Joseph Stiglitz. The SPI measures the well-being of a society by observing social and environmental outcomes directly rather than the economic factors. Fifty-two indicators in the areas of basic human needs, foundations of well-being, and opportunity show the relative performance of nations. Social and environmental factors include personal safety, ecosystem sustainability, health and wellness, shelter, sanitation, equity and inclusion, and personal freedom and choice.
4. twofour54 is an Abu Dhabi government agency that funds and incubates production and content start-ups targeting Arabic content and local talent. MBC Ventures is another example set up by the MBC group.

# Bibliography

Al Masah Capital Management Limited (2014). *MENA Education Sector*, available at http://almasahcapital.com/uploads/report/pdf/report_110.pdf.
Al Masah Capital Management Limited. (2011). *MENA Food Security: Are We Doing Enough to Feed the Population?*, available at http://almasahcapital.com/uploads/report/pdf/report_20.pdf.
Ammary, B. (2007). "Wastewater Reuse in Jordan: Present Status and Future Plan", *Desalination*, 211(1–3), 164–176.
Atalla, G. A. (2010). *Joint Ownership – A New Approach in Public-Private Partnerships*. Strategy& (formerly Booz&Co).
Buckner, E. B. (2012). *Social Entrepreneurship: Why Is It Important Post Arab Spring?*. Dubai: YouGov Siraj, Stanford University, Bayt.com, available at http://fsi.stanford.edu/sites/default/files/White_Paper_Social_Entrepreneurship.pdf.
Chenoweth, J. H. (2011). "Impact of Climate Change on the Water Resources of the Eastern Mediterranean and Middle East Region: Modeled 21st Century Changes and Implications", *Water Resources Research*, 47(6), x–x.
CONE Communications & Echo Research (2013). *Global CSR Study*.
Coutts (2014). *The Million $ Donors Report 2014*
Ebrahim, A. R. (July 2010). "The Limits of Nonprofit Impact – A Contingency Framework for Measuring Social Performance". Harvard Business School, Working Paper, available at http://hbswk.hbs.edu/item/6439.html.
El-Darwiche, B. S. (2011). *Stimulating Innovation – Building the Digital Advantage for MENA Countries*. Strategy& (formerly Booz&Co), available at http://www.strategyand.pwc.com/media/uploads/Strategyand-Stimulating-Innovation-Digital-Advantage-MENA.pdf.
Gelvanovska, N. R. (2014). *Broadband Networks in the Middle East and North Africa: Accelerating High-Speed Internet Access Directions in Development*. World Bank.

Gleeson, T. W. (2012). "Water Balance of Global Aquifers Revealed by Groundwater Footprint", *Nature*, 488(7410), 197–200.

IMRG/MENAP (2013). *B2C e-Commerce Overview 2012 – Focus on Middle East.* North Africa and Pakistan.

IPCC (2007). *Fourth Assessment Report: Adaptation, Impacts, Adaptation and Vulnerability*. Intergovernmental Panel on Climate Change.

Kfouri, C. M. (2009). Water Reuse in MENA Region: Constraints, Experiences, and Policy Recommendations. In A. Jagannathan (ed.), *Water in the Arab World: Management Perspectives and Innovations* (pp. 447–477). The World Bank.

Kubzansky, M. C. (2011). *Promise and Progress: Market-Based Solutions to Poverty in Africa*. The Monitor Group.

Life Sciences – Informa Exhibition (2012). Healthcare in the GCC: A Snapshot.

Mahjoub, A. (2013). Official Development Assistance in Arab Countries. *Reality of Aid (Asia Pacific Network)*. Arab NGO Network for Development (ANND).

Mirking, B. (2010). *Population Levels, Trends and Policies in the Arab Region: Challenges and Opportunities*. Arab Human Development Report.

Mohammed Bin Rashid School of Government and Bayt.com (2014). *The Arab World Online 2014: Trends in Internet and Mobile Usage in the Arab Region*.

Mostafa, K. (2009). *Impact of Climate Change on Arab Countries*. Arab Forum for Environment and Development.

Ogain, E. (2011). *Are Social Enterprises More Resilient in Times of Limited Resources?* New Philanthropy Capital.

Power, G., Wilson, B., Brandenburg, M., Melia-Teevan, K., Lai, J., and Gowda, R. P. (2012). *A Framework For Action: Social Enterprise and Impact Investing*. UNGC and Rockefeller Foundation.

Rocha R. S. F. (2010). *The Status of Bank Lending to Smes in the Middle East and North Africa Region: The Results of a Joint Survey of the Union Of Arab Banks and the World Bank*. World Bank.

Roudi, F. (2011). *Youth Population and Employment in the Middle East and North Africa: Opportunity or Challenge?* United Nations: Population Reference Bureau.

Roudi-Fahimi, F. (2007). *Challenges and Opportunities – The Population of the Middle East and North Africa*. Population Reference Bureau.

Saab, N. (2012). *Arab Environment: Survival Options; Ecological Footprint of Arab Countries*. Beirut: Arab Forum for Environment and Development.

Shediac, R. A. (2008). *Public-Private Partnerships – A New Catalyst for Economic Growth*. Strategy& (formerly Booz&Co).

Shehadi, R. G. (2013). *The Rise of Corporate Social Responsibility – A Tool for Sustainable Development in the Middle East*. Strategy& (formerly Booz&Co).

*The Financial Times* (9 July 2013). Social Enterprises seen as driver for growth. *Financial Times. The Innovation Capabilities of Nations: Five Key Performance Measures*. INSEAD, Innovation and Policy Initiative. INSEAD.

*The National* (12 February 2014). Entrepreneurship will help UAE's Economy. *The National*.

Ulrichsen, K. (2013). *The Gulf Goes Global: The Evolving Role of Gulf Countries in the Middle East and North Africa and Beyond.* Fride and Hivos.

UNDP (2011). *Arab Development Challenges Report 2011: Towards the Developmental State in the Arab Region.* United Nations Development Programme.

UNGC and The Rockefeller Foundation (2012). *A Framework for Action: Social Enterprise & Impact Investing.*

VanMeter, R. G. (2012). *Generation Y's Ethical Ideology and Its Potential Workplace Implications.* Dordrecht: Springer Science+Business Media.

Varis, O. (1997). "Global Urbanization and Urban Water: Can Sustainability Be Afforded", *Water Science and Technology,* 35(9), 21–32.

Vishwanath, T. (2012). *Poverty in MENA: Advances and Challenges.* World Bank.

W. Clement and Jessie V. Stone Foundation (2009). *Challenges and Consideration in Scaling Nonprofit Organizations.*

World Bank (2007). *The Road Not Traveled – Education Reform in the Middle East and North Africa.* World Bank.

World Bank (2013). *Doing Business 2014: Understanding Regulations for Small and Medium-Size Enterprises.* World Bank.

World Bank, MENA Development Report (2004). *Unlocking the Employment Potential in the Middle East and North Africa: Toward a New Social Contract.* World Bank.

World Bank, MENA Development Report (2012). *Renewable Energy Desalination: An Emerging Solution to Close the Water Gap in the Middle East and North Africa.* World Bank.

Wyne, J. H. (June 2013). "Impact Investing in the Middle East – What Next?", *Stanford Social Innovation Review,* available at http://www.ssireview.org/blog/entry/impact_investing_in_the_middle_east_what_next.

Zyadin, A. (2013). "Water Shortage in the MENA Region: An Interdisciplinary Overview and a Suite of Practical Solutions", *Journal of Water Resources and Protection,* 5, 49–58.

# 5
## Social Enterprises: A Panacea for Engaging Youth and Inspiring Hope?

*Clare Woodcraft-Scott and Fatimah S. Baeshen*

### Introduction

This chapter looks at the combined regional curse of high unemployment and high levels of youth disengagement and seeks to establish the extent to which "enterprise" and specifically "social enterprise" can provide a common solution for both. While particularly entrenched in the Arab World, neither youth unemployment nor disengagement is unique to it, suggesting that we first need to look more broadly at what ails global socio-economic progress and how multiple failures to deliver equitable prosperity – partly, one could argue, due to the breakdown of modern capitalism – have fuelled and inspired the world of social innovation.

### People are our core asset

The issue of human capital is increasingly at the top of both corporate and government agendas, with a growing recognition that the oft-cited mantra "people are our most valuable asset" is actually more reality than spin. Unemployment and youth disengagement have never been such ubiquitous issues in the Middle East and North Africa (MENA), where damning statistics continue to reveal them as a key development challenge.

A recent Gallup poll that surveyed Arab employees in MENA countries noted that "actively disengaged workers make up more than a fourth of the employed population", adding that "this group includes

107

countries – Tunisia (54%), Algeria (53%) and Syria (45%) – with the highest percentage of actively disengaged employees in the world".[1]

But, worse than employee disengagement is, of course, unemployment. MENA reports some of the highest unemployment rates in the world, and according to a recent World Economic Forum (WEF) report, "youth unemployment in the Middle East and North Africa will remain at close to 30% until 2017". Clearly both high levels of disengagement and unemployment create a toxic union. The WEF report notes that long-term unemployment leads to the "discouragement and *loss of human capital* [emphasis added] ... [and] is associated with physical and mental ill-health, imposing continuing burdens on health and welfare systems and ultimately having a negative impact on growth".

The WEF also points out that youth unemployment has a particularly devastating effect by "increasing unemployment risks later in life and depressing lifetime earnings". Moreover, MENA's high rates of youth and adult unemployment also reveal another negative trait – particularly high rates of unemployment among women which skew the much more favourable rates for men.[2]

MENA's metrics are also less than competitive when it comes to the broader fundamentals, and notably education. While the level of enrolment in education across the region has progressed rapidly and positively over the past two decades, there remain consistent calls for a radical overhaul of the approach to education (encouraging a shift from didactic to cognitive) and for dramatic improvements in the quality.[3] School leavers in the Arab World continue to score lower than their global counterparts.[4] And industry continues to complain about the mismatch between educational output and the required industrial input.[5]

The lack of social and economic integration also holds back the region's potential for job creation and human capital absorption. The World Bank[6] noted in 2010 that things are improving with all but five MENA countries, now members of the WTO. However, in comparison to other regions, MENA remains "less globally and regionally integrated in terms of trade, investment and capital flows... [and] ... for most Arab countries, regional trade accounts for less than 10 percent of total trade". This not only leads to an estimated 1–2 per cent lower GDP growth according to the Bank, but also a high opportunity cost in terms of job creation. "Regional and global integration would go a long way in increasing productivity and economic growth through economies of scale and enhanced country specialization and thereby create jobs of the MENA youth," the Bank notes.

Creating relevant and meaningful jobs for MENA youth is perhaps the number one challenge that the region faces – in socio-economic and political terms. Estimates suggest that the region needs to create over 80 million jobs in the next 15 years.[7] And the "elephant in the room" of public sector dominance remains. Dr Tzannatos rightly notes that the regional private sector is innovation and risk averse, thus stymieing the ability to create job opportunities and attractive employment opportunities, noting that "The traditional social contract whereby the population exchanged political freedom in return for public sector jobs, free public services, low taxes and other hand-outs from the state creates increasing fiscal pressures on government and rising gaps in private sector productivity and competitiveness." This inevitably leads to an underinvestment in talent such that "the region has the highest skilled emigration rate in the world".[8]

This catalogue of underachievement has not only created huge social strain in the region – clearly manifest through the high level of regional social unrest – but has also pitched "enterprise" as a panacea for MENA's ails. Be it "social enterprise" or simply "enterprise", there is growing acknowledgement that without a greater sense of innovation, creativity, and drive in the private sector, MENA's prospects will diminish further.

And MENA is not alone. The WEF report points out that globally, "without decisive action, the cyclical unemployment that followed the [2007] crisis could very quickly become long-term, structural unemployment. That risk is now becoming a worrying reality for many [countries]".[9] Even the oil-rich economies of the Gulf Cooperation Council (GCC)[10] countries are not immune and face issues related to youth unemployment. Relatively buoyant oil revenues have not offset the challenge of ensuring youth have the right skills to support indigenous economic growth – the "paradox of plenty" prevails.[11]

## The failure of the capitalist model

At the WEF in Davos, January 2014, Oxfam released a report about the state of global socio-economic progress: that is to blame, and what can be done. Very disturbingly they noted that

Economic inequality is rapidly increasing in the majority of countries. The wealth of the world is divided in two: almost half going to the richest one percent; the other half to the remaining 99 percent...Extreme economic inequality and political capture are too often interdependent. Left unchecked, political institutions become undermined and governments overwhelmingly serve the interests of economic elites to the detriment of ordinary people. Extreme inequality is not inevitable, and it can and must be reversed quickly.[12]

These fiscal disparities call for a reassessment of the capitalist paradigm which, in the absence of effective regulation, could be held responsible as the impetus for the current socio-economic imbalances. The dialectical discourse surrounding capitalism, its evolution, and, most importantly, its effect on societies has raged on for centuries. However, in light of growing concerns about the global Gini coefficient (a statistical measure to gauge a country's income distribution), it is now of particular relevance. Despite capitalism's effectiveness in comparison to other economic doctrine, even today, some political economists argue that its negative externalities still require substantial assessment, particularly in terms of inclusion and stability.[13]

Classical economics posits a laissez-faire approach to market competition in terms of regulation, initially as relayed by Adam Smith in *An Inquiry into the Nature and Causes of the Wealth of Nations,* which asserted that the market would standardize in and of its own activity. In other words, it would be ruled by the "invisible hand". However, as markets have cyclically varied and the interpretation of Smith's free market vision evolved, sociologists and other academics have started to question the viability of the capitalist construct for today's world, given its excessive emphasis on output, monetary gains, and, ultimately, its role in contributing to many of the social imbalances we currently witness.

The 20th century sociologist, Anthony Giddens, known for his social theory on structuration (i.e. social, systemic analysis of the symbiotic relationships between structures and agents at both the macro and micro levels), explained capitalism's ability to thrive: through the commodification of time. "The advent of capitalism...produced a significant change in the social structuring of time."[14] He posits that within this framework, where space and time are bound, is the crux of social action established affecting the actors, be they institutional or individual. Ultimately, the actors' repetitive actions perpetually reinforce the structure. He simultaneously asserts, "The invisible hand of action coordination must then be found in the 'the practical consciousness' of the actors themselves."[15]

Other modern-day political economists, such as Edmund Phelps, have gone even further in questioning the current application of capitalism's original intent as propounded by classical economists. In his work, *A Strategy for Employment and Growth and the Failure of Statism Welfarism & Free Markets,* Phelps discusses this at length. "For two decades now the Western system has been failing. But I would argue that the decline of inclusion, and even some of the slow-down in economic growth, results from the neglect and infidelity shown by the core model."[16] Phelps opines that free market capitalism, as Smith described in the 18th century, intrinsically had an inclusionary element to it. Today, however, the system has evolved in a manner that goes beyond simply "weeding out the competition" to something much more exclusive. "This model, call it competitive capitalism," he argues, is not at all the 'free market' of recent decades... In contrast, the Scots [who later came to be known as the classical economists] advocated circumscribed government intervention to help enterprise and broaden opportunity.[17] Phelps goes on to explain that a "free market", in and of itself, is inclusionary: "For them it was a moral axiom that running the economy on the principle of free enterprise would lack legitimacy if the system left many people out."[18]

Today, the debate about capitalism and its effectiveness is no less complex and continues vociferously, notably around resource distribution. This is no doubt fed by the fact that despite 21st century where technology has driven greater connectivity and accountability and where ostensibly better living standards prevail, equality and sustainable growth are increasingly scarce commodities.

Frustration and disillusionment with prevailing socio-economic constructs have been particularly vocal in MENA societies despite the prevalence of an Islamic ethos in the MENA region in which equitable distribution of wealth is not an alien concept. Islamic principles inculcate messages of social equality, wealth (re)distribution, and giving.

However, youth dissatisfaction continues apace, nurtured by social media platforms, such as Facebook, Twitter, and YouTube, which have given people more direct access to leadership and a means of mobilizing popular discontent. Be it the loss of confidence in political leaders, distrust of the business sector, or the growing disenfranchisement of youth, many commentators are increasingly concluding that there is something fundamentally wrong with the system.[19]

Moreover, while the growth of corporate social responsibility (CSR) globally has suggested businesses are now interested in managing negative externalities and the social costs of their operations – something that Phelps and others might support – there is still much scepticism about how meaningful many of these investments really are.

"Corporate philanthropy for the purpose of reputation and PR does not create impact but risks and liabilities. Companies need to use their skills, brand and convening power and networks and use this for creating good," notes Chris West, director of Shell Foundation.[20] As John Bryant of Operation Hope – a US-based not-for-profit that aims to help young people become financially literate – says, the issue lies not "with capitalism *per se* but the model of capitalism that we have allowed to dominate".[21]

Herein lies perhaps the key to understanding the rapid, high-profile, and vocal birth and growth of social enterprise. In the past decade, the concept has gone from being relatively obscure jargon limited to select circles of social innovators to being one that even big business embraces. As the flaws of capitalism have become increasingly visible – through global recession, fraud, and corruption among once respected corporates and government inertia in the face of them – a global hunger for a more responsible and equitable model has emerged.

It is our belief that this hunger has led to what is essentially a coming together of developmental and social innovators who care deeply about the way the world works and the "wicked" problems that it still faces and yet endorse the practical and effective principles of business that allow for value creation at scale. This new mindset and approach to "making the world a better place" is surely a cultural and community response to the failure of traditional approaches to international development and perfectly reflects the philosophy of Gandhi: "be the change you wish to see". It is also an indictment of the insouciance of the global business community about their role in addressing issues related to global poverty and social equality. This goes some way to explaining the sudden and swift growth in the concept and existence of the social enterprise – essentially a hybrid of the international development community (IDC) and its business counterpart, or a more responsible capitalism.

Clearly, successful and equitable global development cannot happen in the isolation of the IDC, business, or government. However, there is growing recognition that the importance of other actors is gaining. Philanthropy is a case in point notably due to its sheer size.[22] The global philanthropic capital market is now a billion dollar one and, with this new found wealth, there is more pressure on philanthropists to be more innovative, more creative, more impactful, and more transparent. Philanthropists themselves are increasingly looking to the private sector and applying the principles of creating commercial value at scale to creating social value.[23] In so doing, they are redefining how third sector organizations can solve some of the world's most intractable social problems. Many are adopting wholesale the idea that "social enterprises" are the new, business-based form of tackling social issues.

The momentum is gaining with the number of social enterprises growing,[24] their influence on policy decisions increasing, and their importance in education bringing them centre stage: Harvard Business School alone had 607 cases and teaching notes in 2010–2011, up from the 45 it had in 1995–1996.[25]

Social enterprise is also gaining, as young people increasingly face tougher odds around employment opportunities than previous generations and become disillusioned with the status quo. They too are injecting a new energy into this movement. Youth now eschew high salaries for the chance of working for an organization that is responsible and that delivers social as well as commercial value.[26] The concept of social enterprise has never been so appealing.

While still nascent, in MENA, the concept is increasingly a topic of discussion for citizens, governments, and even the private sector, as calls for a more responsible world marry traditional profit-making aspirations. The convergence of business and social organizations – albeit a seemingly confusing alliance in the region more accustomed to a strong distinction between civil society and the business world – is attracting a diverse audience. Self-empowered citizens, many of whom are youth, are trying to leverage social entrepreneurship to proactively facilitate civic engagement that is impactful, meaningful, and yet still profitable. It is becoming increasingly apparent that while young Arabs clearly want to make a living, they also want to do it responsibly.[27]

## So, what is a social enterprise?

Any discourse around social enterprises inevitably entails a debate about the definition – all too often an overly long one. However, we would argue that there exist several that can serve their purpose effectively with little need for further deconstruction. Ashoka[28] (founded in the United States by Bill Drayton) argues effectively that social entrepreneurs are "individuals with innovative solutions to society's most pressing social problems... [adding further clarification that]... while a business entrepreneur might create entirely new industries, a social entrepreneur develops innovative solutions to social problems and then implements them on a large scale".[29]

The commonly referenced UK definition comes from Social Enterprise UK which refers to itself as the national body for social enterprises in the United Kingdom:

> A business driven by social and/or environmental purpose. They are trading organisations (their main income streams are revenues for goods and services provided, not grants or donations). Successful social enterprises generate surpluses or profits which are reinvested towards achieving their social mission. Their assets are often locked for community purpose.[30]

In MENA, similar challenges exist with some additional semantic ones. For example, the public generally accepts notions of charitable activities, as well as commercial ones, but conflating the two is often difficult to reconcile. Additionally, in Arabic, a term for social enterprise does not really exist.[31] Literal translations from the English are often confusing – more work still needs to be done in terms of Arabic terminology and lexicon.

But perhaps a more interesting question than "what is or what is not a social enterprise" is "how do they differ from traditional models". Social Enterprise UK notes quite specifically that social enterprises enable sustainable growth and increased social impact and are different from charities because they do not rely totally on grants and donations (although may use them) and, unlike charities, they "fund their social mission through trading activities – selling products and services to customers".

What is also key is having an "enterprise"-based approach to delivering social value and essentially a "commercial" mindset. This notably distinguishes social enterprises from more traditional non-governmental organizations (NGOs) who often underplay the concept of "social value". Social Enterprise UK has an interesting and important perspective on this point:

> Most products or services that you deliver need to be paid for by someone – whether that's the end user or an organisation buying the service on their behalf. Products or services not paid for by someone have to be cross-subsidised . . . This doesn't mean that your organisation can't provide any products or services "free" to some (or even all) of the people who use them but your business does not receive any income to just be there and exist, and this must always be kept in mind. Adopting a commercial mind-set is not just about selling things. It's about selling things at a profit – or at a loss that you understand and have budgeted for. One element of having a commercial mind-set is understanding how much it costs you to deliver a product or service. For example, if you run a community café, the cost of delivering a cup of tea does not just include the cost of the tea bag and the milk and sugar you put in.

As Newishy notes, social enterprise is essentially a "key disruptive innovation of our time . . . a hybrid breed placed at the intersection of the public, private and non-profit sectors" and responds directly to the failure of traditional models:

> Handing out cash may give people money to spend today, but it typically leaves them dependent on the giver and, in most cases, does not help them establish a source of sustainable revenue. The idea with social entrepreneurship is not to simply provide for the poor, but to actually move the poor from a lack of basic needs situation to a self-reliance situation.[32]

As authors, we engage in this definition debate reluctantly. As a successful Lebanese social entrepreneur Ziad Abichaker[33] puts it, "I don't care too much about definition – if you are creating social value and impact that's what counts." However, we acknowledge that in an academic publication ignoring theoretical definitions completely would be disingenuous. Definitions count a lot in understanding how this new hybrid model differs from its predecessor.

All too often that very difference is what defines social entrepreneurs – their lack of confidence in the aforementioned actors, the lack of results on the ground, the growing global discrepancies around socio-economic growth, income equality, and south–north divide that have led people to "take things into their own hands". This notion is something many implicitly reference, but rarely espouse vociferously. Regional social enterprise expert Gilbert Doumit, the managing partner at Beyond Reform and Development based out of Lebanon, touches on it when he says:

> If you're passionate for a cause and you want to change something in society; you're innovative; you want to use innovative means to solve a social problem . . . if I'm using business means, business discipline, business strategies to solve them and not being dependent on funding or on donors, it means . . . I'm a social entrepreneur.

### Regional social enterprises driving local solutions

The interesting thing about most social entrepreneurs is that they often do not define themselves as such. Rather they are often simply business people who believe that there are ways of applying business efficiency and principles to the challenges of resolving social issues, at scale and permanently. This characteristic seems to prevail, no matter what the country or the origin of the entrepreneur is. A cynic might even argue that those that overly propound the term "doth protest too much" and may be more focused on the novelty of the trend rather than the delivery of the mission. Indeed, numerous social entrepreneurs are business people who have successfully run various scalable and financially viable businesses in their former careers and are now keen to advocate for social change, rather than lifelong champions of the construct of social enterprise.

This point is reiterated by Feghali et al.[34] who undertook a survey of Lebanese cases and note that

Most participants did not create their enterprises with the intention of going into social entrepreneurship. Instead they wanted to fill gaps they personally identified in society. About 3% of the participants cited a personal experience that triggered their interest and drive to create the venture, ranging from war, death, interaction with marginalized people, or travel. Notably, each participant's enterprise and/or NGO does not overlap significantly with the other participants' indicating that the social enterprises are filling gaps uniquely.

Across the region, social enterprises are emerging as the "missing middle" between corporates, governments, and traditional social entities in responding to social challenges and pressing market demands on a variety of issues including diabetes, obesity, employability, and women's empowerment. The idea of applying business principles to create social value is gaining traction even in the oil economies of the GCC and particularly among young people.

One local Emirati entrepreneur, Faisal Al Hammadi, firmly believes in blending traditional capitalism with solutions that address the long-term needs of society. Al Hammadi has launched a food enterprise to address some of the most pressing health issues in the UAE – obesity and diabetes. Slices is an organic café, that uses locally grown organic produce, where every item on its menu is made freshly on the day. More than just a cafe, Slices donates what is left on its shelves at the end of the day to local community initiatives, setting an excellent example of reducing waste and dealing with leftover food.

Al Hammadi believes that an entrepreneurial approach to addressing social issues is often more effective than the traditional NGO model. "It gives you more control over operations and more flexibility. Generating an income base also means that unlike many NGOs, you can focus on the issue in hand rather than invest a lot of resources in fundraising," he said.

Khalid Al Khudair, is a Saudi social entrepreneur with a similar passion and a very strong corporate/business background. Al Khudair is an Ashoka Fellow, who co-founded and is now running Glowork. He is a businessman who understands the importance of equal access to the commercial sphere, economic empowerment, and human capital, especially as it relates to Saudi women. Glowork is a successful social enterprise that facilitates the entry of Saudi women into the local labour market. After watching his sister struggle to find employment upon her completion of graduate studies abroad and return to the Kingdom of Saudi Arabia, Al Khudair decided to start a business that acts as a channel to create jobs, develop skills, and bridge the gap between Saudi women and the private sector.

Glowork has grown to over 15,000 members in its network, 98 per cent of whom are Saudi. They have 180 employers in their database: 85 per cent are corporates and 15 per cent are NGOs. Thus far, roughly 5,000 Saudi women have secured jobs through Glowork and the organization has created three times that amount in terms of jobs through corporate lobbying to convert existing positions for Saudi women.[35]

While many might have taken a traditional NGO approach to resolving this particularly pressing social issue, Khalid's formal corporate background helped him to see the opportunity of applying a business-based approach to creating social value. Indeed, while his social metrics are impressive, the long-term sustainability of the enterprise has been secured on the back of its financial viability. In 2012, SAS Holding, a large software corporate, invested US$16 million for a share of 51 per cent equity in Glowork.[36]

Social entrepreneurship and women's empowerment have also united in Kuwait. Balsam and Lulwa Al-Ayoub, two Kuwaiti professional fencers, are using sports development and management to build female youth capacity across the region. Combining the social power of sports with business acumen, they founded Touche – a social enterprise that is a powerful means of helping women access the public sphere while also being a successful sports management agency. Balsam and Lulwa combine their business acumen with their sporting prowess and actively compete in international tournaments while also providing mentorship to youth across the region. They also use their business to advocate for systemic (in this case, regulatory) change by calling for the revision of sporting laws to equally qualify female athletes in international gaming events.[37]

Ziad Abichaker, the founder and CEO of Cedar Environment, argues that a business-based approach is optimal in terms of achieving financial viability and long-term sustainability. He argues that the traditional NGO approach too often means that organizations become slaves to their donors and the donor's agenda, whereas financial freedom offers a more sustainable model where social entities can focus on their social mission rather than chase their next grant.

David Munir Nabti, the chief entrepreneur and organizer of AltCity.ME, agrees. AltCity was designed "from the bottom up" to help facilitate, mobilize, encourage, and support high-impact entrepreneurship and innovation in Lebanon and beyond. Nabti notes that the mindset in the region is changing towards a market-based approach viewing the beneficiary as a client and not a dependent, which in turn allows for greater impact than traditional models.

Adopting a "commercial" mindset is not without hazard since, while it can lead to greater outcomes, it has to still ensure the creation of sustainable social value. Cedar Environment had turned down an offer of franchise despite a strong commercial opportunity, because the commitment to zero waste was not there.

Similarly, Slices noted that keeping social impact and ethics top of mind is critical when sourcing suppliers and ingredients. Charlotte Boyle, a board member of Al Fanar Foundation that invests in social enterprises, also highlights the importance of not getting side tracked by the desire to be financially efficient. Al Fanar, she said, provides financial resources but is still rigorous in tracking their social impact. A lot of Al Fanar's work also involves education and raising awareness of the concept of social enterprise in the community.

Interestingly, the social enterprise model also allows for effective institutionalized learning unlike its more traditional counterparts. Over and above strong financial nous, entrepreneurial skills, and a strong focus on social value, many social entrepreneurs agree that failure is a critical part of the journey to success. "Failure is not only natural," said Nabti,

> it is necessary. In many cases, incubators and investors will not extend their resources to start-ups unless they can demonstrate that the prototype has evolved and gone through various attempts. Failure is the best educator and incubators and investors know this. They expect to see it in the history of a proposal put in front of them.

Few NGOs or foundations would likely extol this approach.

While social enterprise may not solve all the region's ails, those entities that have emerged in the Arab World seem to be directly responding to the need to reduce dependence on government invest-ment and activity and do indeed focus on key regional challenges – job creation, youth empowerment, and developing human capital. In so doing, they clearly fill a gap in the market and address a "flaw" in the system, not only from an economic perspective but even from a social and political one.

## Building an enabling environment

Encouraging further social enterprise requires significant reform in the region. Both internationally and regionally, legislation remains one of the key influencing factors that support a thriving ecosystem for social entrepreneurship. Countries such as the United Kingdom and the United States have instituted specific laws to issue licensing, registration, and regulation of commercial entities aimed at resolving a social challenge while making and reinvesting profits.

Community interest companies (CICs) can be created under UK legislation that allows for the establishment of social purpose organi-zations under the Companies (Audit, Investigations, and Community Enterprise) Act 2004. The CIC legislation allows for an innovative type of limited company established specifically for operations target-ing community benefit rather than strictly the company's owners.[38] CICs can be run as a business whereby they are allowed to allocate specific assets and designate them for public benefit activities without acquiring charity status.[39]

A low-profit, limited liability company (LC3) can be established in the United States under a legislation instituted in 2008 as a response to the gap between non-profit and commercial entities. An LC3 is considered a for-profit venture, but simultaneously has a primary objective to provide a solution to a social challenge. Under this premise, LC3 entities have more flexibility in facilitating private funding to social programmes. Additionally, LC3 structures allow for philanthropic investment tranches from donors investing "patient capital" and expecting a higher rate of social return than a monetary one.[40]

Another more recently established US company model for facili-tating social enterprise business operations is the B-Corporation, also known as "B-Corps". B-Corps aim to more fluidly reconcile, within a corporate framework, entities with a business and social agenda.

The structure provides an index for each company that has a social mission embedded in the business model, which, in turn, affects the weight in the index. Companies that reach a score of 80/200 may convert to a B-Corps and subsequently receive the benefits of operating as one, for example, resources from B Labs.[41]

While in comparison to MENA markets, these models have been developed in relatively mature non-profit and private sectors, the CIC, LC3, and B-Corp structures and associated regulatory frameworks can still potentially serve as benchmarks for the region. However, the MENA region – and especially the GCC, where there is particularly high reliance on government to resolve social issues – will need to do more than simply address legal issues, if social enterprises are to thrive.

Legislation is just one piece of the puzzle in constructing an enabling environment for social enterprise that can lead to sustained and high social impact. There are several other equally important facets that need to be dealt with. These include policymaking and governance, institutional and operational support, and social and cultural awareness.[42]

Laws specifically instituting and/or regulating social enterprises are either non-existent or inchoate at best. This results in many social enterprises establishing themselves as either non-profits, commercial entities, or "flying under the radar" with no formal registration. In some areas, non-profit licensing is handled through the Islamic Affairs or Legal Departments, which is often restrictive in terms of the conditions imposed and further exacerbates the problem mentioned earlier, of not being able to reconcile the marriage of a social or "charitable" entity with one that is income generating or even profit making.

Where social enterprises register as formal commercial entities, they fail to benefit from their "social" status as they might elsewhere (e.g. from a fiscal/tax perspective) and face the same rules as their conventional counterparts. Moreover, due to the inconsistency in the licensing terms and structures that social enterprises can undertake, it becomes difficult to accurately regulate, track, or measure their impact.

In terms of operational and institutional support, again, existing legislation and regulation in the region stymie the potential impact of regional social enterprise and create multiple logistical challenges. These challenges surface in the form of set-up costs and funding, where conventional regulatory environments may offer relevant costs structures for commercial companies but are not fit for those entities aiming primarily at social impact. Typically, many social enterprises have longer term revenue-generating models, which may mean they have less available start-up capital and more complex access to capital than a traditional commercial enterprise. Many social enterprises find it difficult to sustain themselves financially even when they are clearly delivering social value – excessive "commercially benchmarked" establishment costs do not help.[43]

Once a social enterprise is able to establish itself, many face specific issues related to sourcing funding that their commercial counterparts do not. This can compound their ability to deliver social impact and further underlines the inappropriateness of traditional commercial registration as an option. Social enterprises often find it difficult to source investment notably from traditional investors who may challenge the ability of social enterprises to deliver a financial return. Equally – and somewhat ironically – they may struggle when seeking traditional charitable donations/grants if donors perceive them to be commercial and indeed if they are registered as such. Moreover, many current government setup fees are seen as prohibitive for start-ups, let alone for social enterprises who are seeking to create a "double"- or even "triple"-bottom line.[44] Additionally, some social enterprises rely on volunteers for staffing support initially, which is not permitted by some licensing terms under conventional commercial parameters.[45]

Mentorship is an area that could provide some real support to the sector but is also one that has yet to be fully matured or institutionalized in the region. While mentorship can play a critical role in the development of social enterprises, the lack of formal mentoring structures, databases, or support services means that social enterprises are often missing this pivotal development piece.[46]

Finally, the issue of social and cultural awareness continues to play a role in holding back the full potential of regional social enterprises. Arab society continues, in many cases, to view social impact and profit as mutually exclusive. Semantically, clear and precise terminology does not exist in Arabic in this space, with even the word "enterprise" being commonly translated in several different ways. While the idea is popular among certain circles (e.g. educated elite) and notably more mature business communities tend to operate in English (e.g. in Dubai/the UAE which has a small but vibrant "social enterprise" discourse and community and even a fairly well-established *Social Enterprise Week*),[47] its presence remains somewhat *ad hoc* and un-institutionalized.

## Social enterprise as a long-term solution

As the need is recognized for more egalitarian socio-economic standards, social entrepreneurship emerges as a sustainable solution. As mentioned earlier with Phelps and the essence of an inclusive capitalism model, social issues, particularly those in the MENA, beg for innovative responses – not just from governments, but from the private sector and individuals.

While the appetite and demand for social enterprise in the region is clearly on the rise, it has yet to be institutionalized inside formal structures, legislation, and regulation. It is also not yet well understood by the broader society. Notwithstanding global social enterprise actors, such as Ashoka, looking to build communities in the region,[48] local governments are still struggling to understand and process the concept. Regional social enterprises, such as those outlined in this report, are gaining voice and brand awareness. However, they have yet to acquire official status as social entities and/or relevant support from government or the investment community.

Some may argue that other parts of the world face similar structural challenges, and this may well be the case. However, few regions have such a pressing challenge of needing to create 80 million jobs in the next 15 years, engage a population of over 400 million of which half are under the age of 25, while also addressing ongoing issues within the public sector that relate to reduced spending, ongoing inefficiencies, and a loss of credibility among the broader public.

Social enterprise is clearly not a panacea for some of the socio-economic ails of the region. However, the efficiency of the model, its business-based approach which can allow for scale and financial sustainability more easily than its traditional counterparts and its ability to harness the energy and frustration of a whole wave of Gen-Y Arabs, means it is surely a subject that should be much higher up on the radar screen of regional leaders than it currently is.

We believe that a more concerted regional effort – built on learning from other markets and a commitment to create an enabling

environment "fit for purpose" – coupled with support, awareness raising, and investment in existing successful and scalable regional Arab
social enterprises, could go a long way to collapsing old developmental paradigms in the region and fast-tracking a new form of capitalism
much more in tune with the region's social and religious constructs
and its youthful ambitions.

Awareness needs to move from the organic community level to
the highest level of policymaking. And youth need to be reassured
that if they desire change and a more responsible way of delivering
value, they can be personally instrumental in building and delivering it through formal policy channels rather than revolution. As a
recent report by the Dubai School of Government on Social Media,
Employment and Entrepreneurship showed, "Arab youth are realizing that creating start-ups and enterprises can be just as empowering
as taking part in protests and demonstrations, not just for themselves
but for their communities as well, in the shape of social change and
economic development." They go on to suggest that "Some young
entrepreneurs believe that the political unrest of the past year may
actually be beneficial for their businesses, creating product demand,
encouraging investor to seek now opportunity beyond the large,
established businesses that may be floundering post 'Arab-spring',
and making governments sympathetic to the needs of start-ups."[49]

Creating more and stronger opportunities for youth engagement
through an enabling environment for social enterprises can also go a
long way to appeasing the current youth demand for more "voice" to
be heard by their leaders and to have a say in their future. An enabling
environment for social enterprise may not be a panacea for the ails
of a challenged region, but it most certainly could provide a very
real policy tool for the Arab World to leverage youth energy and
drive to create new, scalable ways of addressing old development
challenges in ways that are socially, economically, and financially
sustainable and viable. This would clearly distinguish them from the
models of the past and potentially create a whole new generation
of engaged and productive citizens, rather than a detracted, disillusioned, and disconnected one. It would also engender a new more
socially responsible way of deploying private capital.

In an ideal world, the social enterprise sector would evolve naturally out of a sophisticated non-profit sector; a socially engaged
private sector; and a progressive, enabling government one. MENA is

not there yet. However, if governments and businesses alike were to harness the energy and commitment of their innovative youth and create a clear strategy for the future that embeds social enterprise fundamentally in the fabric and structure of society, some of the region's underlying fundamental development challenges might look significantly less ominous.

## Notes

1. Gallup (2013). *State of the Global Workplace-Employee Engagement Insights for Business Leaders Worldwide.*
2. Dr Tzannatos, Z. (2013–2014). *The Youth and the Arab Spring,* Executive (www.executive-magazine.com).
3. Brookings (7 February 2014). *The Arab World Learning Barometer.* According to the report,

> over half of children in school are not acquiring foundational skills. Progress in school enrolment masks the crisis of learning in the Arab region. In many cases, even those who do attend and stay in school are not receiving a good-quality education and therefore not learning ... Based on 13 Arab countries with available data: Fifty-six percent of primary students and 48 percent of secondary students are not meeting basic learning levels; the learning crisis affects boys significantly more than girls. The share of boys in school that do not meet basic learning levels is higher than girls in almost every country in the region with available data; and, on average, rural children do not perform as well as their urban counterparts, and overlapping disparities based on income, gender and geographic location create stark divisions.

4. Dr Tzannatos, Z. (2013–2014). In *The Youth and the Arab Spring* notes that Arab students are below the global average, p. 50, Executive (www.executive-magazine.com).
5. O'Sullivan, A., Rey, M.-E. and Mendez, J. G. OECD (2012). *Opportunities and Challenges in the MENA Region.* "One of the reasons for high levels of unemployment for youth and the educated is a persistent gap between the skills acquired at university and the requirements of business. Enterprises often cite lack of suitable skills", p. 4.
6. World Bank (March 2010). *Trade Integration in the Middle East and North Africa,* available at http://go.worldbank.org/IZ7F77A120.
7. Al-Yahya, K. and Airey, J., Heart & Mind Strategies, *Leveraging Growth Finance for Sustainable Development,* p. 4. Supported by Shell Foundation and Citi Foundation.
8. Dr Tzannatos, Z. (2013–2014). In *The Youth and the Arab Spring* notes that Arab students are below the global average, p. 50, Executive (www.executive-magazine.com).

9. World Economic Forum (January 2014). *Global Agenda Council on Employment, Unemployment: Rising to the Global Challenge: An Agenda for Policymakers and Social Partners*, p. 5.

10. The GCC states comprise Saudi Arabia, the United Arab Emirates, Kuwait, Bahrain, Oman, and Qatar.

11. Jones, D. and Punshi, R. (2014). *Unlocking the Paradox of Plenty.* The authors note that despite GCC potential, "Gulf employees report some of the lowest levels of engagement in the world; youth unemployment... remains high; increasing female participation in the workforce remains a struggle; skills gaps in rapidly growing industries are significant; and Emiratisation is in full swing." As reported in the UAE daily *The National* on 11 February 2014.

12. 178 OXFAM Briefing Paper, 20 January 2014. *Working for the Few* – particularly shocking is the statistic reporting that the combined wealth of the world's richest 85 people is now equivalent to that owned by half of the world's population or 3.5 billion of the poorest people, p. 2.

13. The Center on Capitalism and Society. *Theory of Capitalism*, Columbia University, 2014, available at http://capitalism.columbia.edu/theory-capitalism.

14. Giddens, Anthony. *Critical Assessments*, ed. Christopher G.A. Bryant and David Jary. Routledge, New York, p. 52.

15. Ibid., p. 51.

16. Phelps, Edmund (1997). *A Strategy for Employment and Growth: The Failure of Statism Welfarism & Free Markets,* p. 2.

17. Ibid., p. 4.

18. Ibid., p. 5.

19. In 2012, the *Financial Times* launched an entire editorial series on the topic of "capitalism in crisis", and Richard Posner noted in his book *A Failure of Capitalism* published in 2009 that the 2007 global recession represented the greatest economic crisis since the Great Depression of the 1930s.

20. Cited in *Responsible Business*, Issue No. 3; July–September 2012, p. 7 *Quotables.*

21. Bryant, J. (2014). *How the Poor Can Save Capitalism*, Berrett-Koehler Publishers, USA.

22. When the OECD Development Assistance Committee met in Busan in 2011, the important role of philanthropy in development was formally recognized and captured in the communique.

23. See OECD Development Centre, 2014. *Venture Philanthropy in Development: Dynamics, Challenges and Lessons in the Search for Greater Impact.*

24. The United Kingdom alone now has 70,000 registered social enterprise according to www.socialenterprise.org.uk.

25. Cited in *Responsible Business*; Issue No. 6; April–June 2013, p. 7 *Social Enterprise Education on the Rise.*

26. Angel Gurria, Secretary-General of the OECD *Action for Youth* "Youth-oriented policies matter because they advance the cause of building a

stronger, fairer and cleaner post-crisis world. Today's young people don't need to be persuaded about the importance of fighting climate change, corruption or inequality." Published in the *OECD Observer*, No. 294 Q1 2013.

27. Dubai School of Government's October 2012 research *Social Media, Employment and Entrepreneurship – New Frontiers for the Economic Empowerment of Arab Youth* shows that 34 per cent of youth surveyed said they felt "empowered to influence social change through my own enterprise", p. 28.

28. See www.ashoka.org.

29. Ibid.

30. Available at http://www.socialenterprise.org.uk/about/about-social-enterprise/social-enterprise-dictionary.

31. Terminology for social enterprises or charities or foundations can often be used interchangeably with little distinction from newer constructs: for example, *al mashru'a al ijtima-'ai* simply means "social project" in English and yet is often used to mean social enterprise in Arabic.

32. Newishy, L. (February 2014). *Social Entrepreneur, What Drives You?* Published on www.linkedin.com.

33. Taken from the transcript of the panel held at Emirates Foundation's Philanthropy Summit on 11 November 2013 at which Mr Abichaker spoke.

34. Dr Feghali, T., Abuatieh, E. and Dandan, J., American University of Beirut (2013). *Social Entrepreneurship in Lebanon: Contexts and Considerations*. p. 3.

35. Baeshen, F. (March 2014). Telephone interview with Khalid Al Khudair.

36. Nina Curley (September 2013). "What's Next for Glowork after Its 16 Million USD Acquisition by SAS Holding?", www.wamda.com.

37. www.touchekuwait.com & www.ashoka.org.

38. www.legislation.gov.uk/.

39. Ibid.

40. Abdou, E., Fahmy, A., Greendwald, D., and Nelson, J. (2010). *Social Entrepreneurship in the Middle East: Toward Sustainable Development for the Next Generation* (Wolfensohn Center for Development at Brookings, Dubai School of Government, and Silatech).

41. www.bcorporation.net.

42. Abdou, E., Fahmy, A., Greendwald, D., and Nelson, J. (2010). *Social Entrepreneurship in the Middle East: Toward Sustainable Development for the Next Generation*, Wolfensohn Center for Development at Brookings, Dubai School of Government, and Silatech.

43. Emirates Foundation for Youth Development: Research & Advocacy Department (June 2013). *A Working Report on Social Entrepreneurship, NGOs, and Non-profits in the UAE*, Abu Dhabi, United Arab Emirates.

44. IFC-World Bank Report (29 May 2012). Press Release. Doing Business Report: "On average, businesses in the Arab world need to wait about 650 days to enforce a contract through the court, the third-longest average globally, while resolving insolvency is one of the most difficult among Arab economies."

45. Emirates Foundation for Youth Development: Research & Advocacy Department (June 2013). *A Working Report on Social Entrepreneurship, NGOs, and Non-profits in the UAE*, Abu Dhabi, United Arab Emirates.
46. Ibid.
47. Available at http://socentweek.me.
48. On 27 March, Ashoka hosted a meeting to discuss the Arab World Social Entrepreneurship Program (ASEP) seeking support from the business community and other sectors. ASEP will create a regional physical platform for the enhancement of social innovation in the Arab World. (Ashoka ASEP Program 2014 brochure.)
49. Dubai School of Government's October 2012 research *Social Media, Employment and Entrepreneurship – New Frontiers for the Economic Empowerment of Arab Youth* shows that 34 per cent of youth surveyed said they felt "empowered to influence social change through my own enterprise", p. 18.

# 6
# Scaling Social Enterprises and Scaling Impact in the Middle East

*David Munir Nabti*

The main purpose of this chapter is to examine how we can maximize the public benefit of entrepreneurial activity and increasingly engage the strengths of the private sector in boosting social impact in the Middle East through growth of scalable social enterprises. The chapter examines challenges to social enterprise scaling in the Middle East and offers recommendations for enhancing the scalability of social impact and social enterprises through using tools and adaptations of tools that have been developed for use in for-profit entrepreneurship and that address specific challenges to social enterprises in the region.

The foundations of this chapter are based on local, regional, and international research sources, plus extensive experience working in this sector in the Middle East over the last six years.

## Introduction – Framing the challenge

While a huge amount of money is invested in social and environmental programmes, development efforts, emergency relief, and the like, global problems remain, with some getting worse. Even if there was political will to do so, there are insufficient resources available globally to solve the world's problems in a sustainable way through traditional development or government approaches, and the mainstream private sector does not see that as its role in the world. We need to find alternative ways of addressing critical issues around the world.

At the same time, all around us are amazing innovations in science and technology, huge increases in access to information, new business models, and an ever-increasing global interconnectedness that are bringing us all closer together. Just as these changes are affecting how we work, live, interact, consume, and play, they can also play a greater role in improving the impact of social initiatives.

In the Middle East, the social and development challenges are combined with economic challenges on a grand scale. Growing populations and troubled economies have led to a high and increasing level of unemployment, in some places for some populations reaching above 50 per cent and in many places hovering between 10 and 20 per cent. The number is even higher if underemployment is included. According to the World Economic Forum, the region needs to create 75 million jobs by 2020 just to maintain current employment levels. As the WEF report states, "the consequences of not doing so could be more severe than a missed opportunity and slow growth; the region may lose its most promising youths to emigration, and social unrest is always a danger when large numbers of young people lack opportunities" (WEF, 2011). This is an incredibly ambitious goal, however, and does not take into account the additional job creation that is needed to address the persistently high unemployment and underemployment levels that exist today.

To further complicate the problem, if millions of new jobs are created that have the same level of negative side effects (air and water pollution, waste generation, water and energy consumption, etc.) as the jobs that already exist, then even if we are able to solve the unemployment crisis, we may exacerbate other problems at the same time.

These are not Middle East-specific challenges. As witnessed globally, "social problems have grown in magnitude and complexity, and non-profit organizations (NPOs) have proliferated to address these. However, traditional funding sources and institutional capacities have not kept pace. The search for new resources and more effective organizational approaches is bringing non-profits and corporations together" (Austin, 2000, p. 69).

This chapter focuses on two related concepts that have strong potential to contribute to positive development in this complex situation: "scalability" and "social enterprises". Social enterprises (also called "social ventures") are characterized by their adoption of a double- or triple-bottom line approach. While a normal company typically has one main measurable objective (financial returns), a social enterprise has two or three: (1) financial, plus (2) social and/or (3) environmental returns. A social enterprise could be legally registered as a for-profit or a non-profit entity or not registered at all (as an informal or unofficial entity), as long as they pursue objectives of both impact and financial return as core components of their work.

This article also focuses on "scalability" of social enterprises, meaning initiatives that are working to grow their impact to a substantial scale beyond their local community, addressing the challenge on the national, regional, or global level. A key part of the concept of "scalability" in both enterprises and social enterprises is the idea of developing a concept and strategy that can grow impact (and/or revenues) at a rate much faster than costs and staffing needed. A common guide is to develop an approach that has ten times growing returns and only two times growing costs, but those numbers can vary with each initiative and objectives of the enterprise founders (along with the success of the project). It is also important to note that small business start-ups are quite different from scalable start-ups. Growing a successful scalable start-up or social enterprise is difficult and risky, but has substantial potential upsides to the entrepreneurs and the community that a "small business" (or small organization) does not have.

Related to the issue of scalability, enterprises of a particular kind, "high-growth" or "fast-growing" enterprises, are particularly important. "The vital role of fast-growing SMEs ('gazelles') in employment creation has focused attention on the characteristics of high-growth firms, highlighting the importance of building their capacities and skills, while reducing constraints to their entry and operation" (Nasr and Pearce, 2012, p. 5).

While governments, international aid, and development assistance cannot be neglected or abandoned, we must work to leverage the strengths of the civic and business sectors (in the region and globally) much more effectively. This civic–business convergence in the form of scalable social enterprise is the focus of this chapter. It explores ways we can leverage, magnify, enhance, and celebrate the strengths of the private sector in creating jobs, fuelling innovation, creating livelihood opportunities, and generating income and wealth, in a sustainable manner and in a way that addresses critical social, environmental, and development challenges in the Middle East.

## Barriers to the growth of scalable social enterprises in the Middle East

Two primary components are needed for there to be a strong climate of social enterprise development and growth: (a) supportive "entrepreneurial framework conditions", or a country's (or community's) capacity to encourage and support start-ups, including all the relevant support systems, structures, laws, and culture; and (b) people with the right skills and motivations to go into business for themselves (Acs, 2006, p. 103).

In the Middle East, enterprises of all types face various challenges in the start-up and growth phases that make building stable and fast-growing organizations difficult. Core challenges identified by the Wamda Research Lab (2014) for scaling start-up companies in the Middle East include

1. market knowledge (access to research and data) and marketing talent;
2. access to strategic and smart finance, in terms of links and communications between investors and start-ups, willingness to invest in risky ventures, non-financial contributions by investors to start-up development, and the level of readiness of the start-ups;
3. finding and retaining top talent; and
4. business expansion into new countries in the region, access to new markets, identifying key partners, and addressing challenges related to registration, payment gateways, or other legal and business issues.

While that study was focusing on normal for-profit ventures, all those challenges exist for social enterprises as well, plus others. While people know well the concept of "non-profit associations", the concept of "social enterprise" is not widely understood, and various barriers exist for those working to develop social impact enterprises. In 2013, AUB and the Alliance for Social Entrepreneurship conducted a mapping study in Lebanon and identified key challenges to social entrepreneurship in the country (Figure 6.1).

These challenges are widespread around the Middle East. In addition, in some countries, "non-profit associations" are severely restricted or banned, limiting the opportunities and approaches for

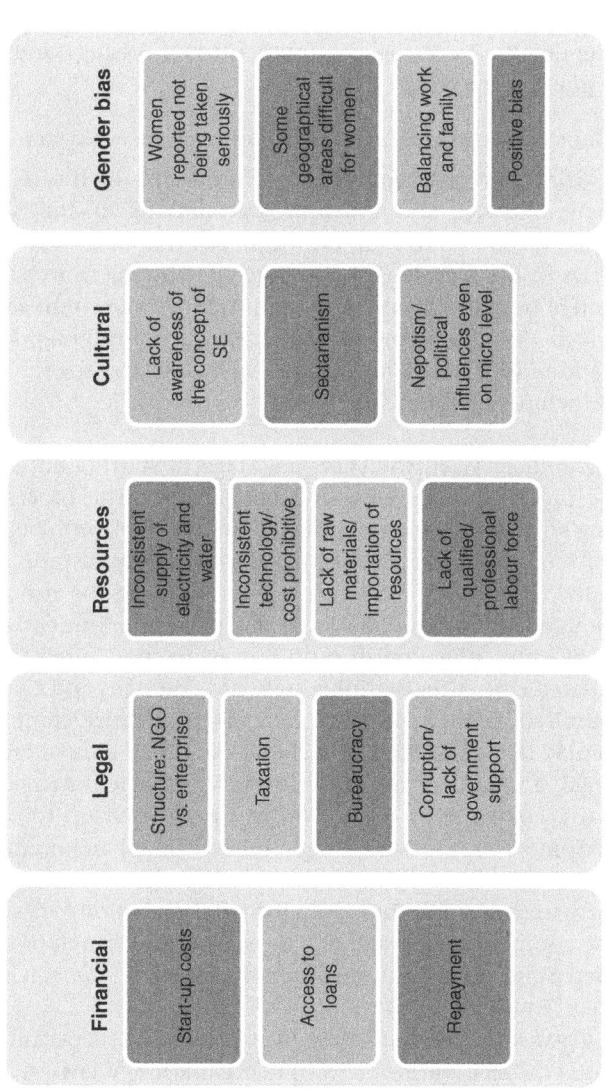

*Figure 6.1* Challenges to social entrepreneurship in Lebanon

*Source:* (Feghali et al., 2013, p. 9), produced jointly by the Alliance for Social Entrepreneurship and the AUB Olayan School of Business.

social enterprises that would otherwise register and operate as an NPO in another country. Various challenges remain, both from the side of the start-up/social enterprise ecosystem and from the side of the entrepreneur. Nevertheless, momentum is rising, and the situation is slowly improving.

### External: Gaps in the Middle East social enterprise ecosystem

While the social enterprise ecosystem is improving in the region, many obstacles and gaps still remain. Mixed rankings in the World Bank's "Doing Business" (Doing Business, 2014) index show that most countries in the Middle East are quite challenging from a business perspective (ranging from the United Arab Emirates ranked 23, to Libya ranked 187), but those rankings also do not fully represent the official and unofficial challenges that exist. Key challenges in the Middle East include the following:

- *Entity Registration*: From the very first stage of starting an enterprise, the process is expensive and challenging. The process of registering an NPO is difficult in most countries (Lebanon being a key exception), and in some countries in the Middle East it is near (or actually) impossible. Registering a company in the region is easier, though still substantially more expensive and time consuming than in some other countries in Europe or the United States. The estimated cost of registering a standard company in Lebanon (SARL – limited liability company, or SAL – joint stock company) is between $7,000 and $10,000, including required annual retainers for legal, accounting, and auditing services. The time needed to register a company in the region can also reach up to a few months. Some countries have high initial capital requirements (up to $20,000), which pose an additional barrier to registration. No country in the Middle East has a formal designation for "social enterprise company" equivalent to B (or Benefit) Corporations in the United States or community interest corporations (CICs) in the United Kingdom.
- *Other legal and procedural challenges*: IP protection, work permit and visa issues, contract enforcement, harsh bankruptcy laws, expensive customs duties and slow procedures for some imports, and physical office requirements also raise challenges and costs for new enterprises.

- *Access to finance*: Financing options are limited and very challenging, especially for early-stage and non-traditional companies. Banks are very risk averse, especially for enterprises that do not have traditional collateralizable assets. At the same time, since bankruptcy regulations are incredibly harsh, loans for new businesses are very risky for the entrepreneurs. Other kinds of early-stage capital, notably angel or seed investment, plus "smart capital" (where investors are engaged as advisors and supporters beyond their financial contribution) are still very limited in the region, but are slowly improving.
- *Infrastructure*: Internet and telecommunications are problematic in some countries in the Middle East, in terms of cost, speed and bandwidth, reliability, security, and privacy. Other countries face challenges in terms of provision of other basic infrastructure, including electricity and water. Some of these directly affect the costs needed for early-stage enterprise creation, while others can be remedied but may take time from an individual entrepreneur or small group that is distracting from their core work.
- *Education and human resource challenges*: Hiring and retaining people with proper talent and experience is difficult and often requires substantial on-the-job training. Brain drain also presents a substantial challenge in many countries in the Middle East, as many high-potential people leave their home countries for better education, work, and life opportunities in other parts of the region or the world.
- *Business processes and transactions*: While there are rapid changes happening globally in terms of how business is getting done and transactions processed, some of the key new tools and processes are not available to enterprises in the Middle East. PayPal, for example, has grown to become one of the largest and most trusted payment methods globally, but it is not available in several Middle East countries and is available in only a partial capacity in others.
- *Social constraints*: Friends, family, teachers, other respected community leaders, the media, and other social structures are critical enablers, encourages, supporters, or discouragers of innovation and entrepreneurship. Unfortunately, many of these influencers discourage entrepreneurship more than they encourage it, whether directly or indirectly. It is usually held in much higher esteem for someone to get a job in a big multinational company

versus start their own enterprise or work in a small enterprise. At the same time, more practical and applied careers (such as medicine, engineering, or law) are encouraged more than research-oriented fields (in those fields, or their more research or theoretical counterparts such as biology, physics, or philosophy).

- *Working behind the curve of global trends*: Entrepreneurs in the region are often working a few years behind global trends. Substantial effort is needed to help the region to be at the leading edge of innovation, not well behind it.
- *Insufficiently engaging expertise in the diaspora*: Too many people are leaving various countries in the region, or the region as a whole, to pursue their endeavours elsewhere, and there are insufficient efforts to encourage their participation and support of social enterprises in their home countries.
- *Gender constraints*: While overall trends for women participation are improving, there are still fields and activities where substantial gender bias affects opportunity.

While there is great opportunity for SME and social enterprise growth in the Middle East, there is critical need for ecosystem development, including a critical role for various actors, public and private, to foster a supportive investment climate and business regulations that encourage ease of exit, entry, and competition; [and] also a potential role for innovative finance, quality certification, mentoring and incubating, and effective competition policy (Bell, 2011). While many efforts are underway to address these issues, much more work is yet to be done to get to the point where the region should be in terms of fostering and supporting social enterprise development.

### Internal: Personal factors of the entrepreneur that affect scalable social enterprises

Apart from the ecosystem challenges, there are various personal issues on the part of entrepreneurs that limit the growth and development of scalable social impact ventures in the Middle East. These include the following:

- *Thinking too small*: It is common that entrepreneurs do not have the ambition to think big or are not aware of the option and opportunity to scale a social enterprise. It also happens that early decisions corner an effort and make it difficult to grow. Basic issues such as name, URL, language issues, and basic descriptions can reduce the scalability of an enterprise.

- *Thinking too big*: Many entrepreneurs aim for very big, complex, expensive, and very risky projects well beyond the scope of what would be strategic for a start-up enterprise at the earliest stages and disregarding new start-up approaches such as the lean start-up method, launching with a minimal viable product (MVP), or proper user and market validation.
- *Risk aversion*: Normal start-up risks in the Middle East are compounded by regional political, security, economic, and infrastructure issues. Entrepreneurs often have difficulty balancing and mitigating such instabilities and still pursuing innovative enterprises, which inherently involve an element of risk.
- *Creative/innovation limitations*: It is sometimes difficult for social enterprise leaders to think "outside" the box in terms of finding unconventional solutions to problems they want to address. At the same time, entrepreneurs and innovators should be more active in following regional and global trends, conducting research, understanding markets, and following innovations that are happening globally that could have relevance to their initiative. Curiosity, self-learning, and initiative are incredibly important traits, but are also very difficult to teach.
- *Esteem and prestige*: Many people consider positions in well-known multinational companies or stable jobs in a few sectors (doctors, engineers, lawyers, finance professionals, etc.) more prestigious than starting one's own small but potentially fast-growing enterprise. At the same time, there is a fear of failure along with a prejudice against those who tried an ambitious project but failed, rather than considering those efforts as powerful learning experiences that make someone more capable and valuable to work with.
- *Entrepreneurial motivation factors that inhibit pursuit of high-growth scalable social enterprises*: Research has shown that the motivation for an entrepreneur has a big impact on the aspirations of the entrepreneur. Many countries in the Middle East have a small middle class, meaning that most people seeking employment are from the quite large lower class (tending towards

"necessity entrepreneurship", which generally leads to less ambitious entrepreneurial ventures). People from the quite small wealthy class of the region generally have no need and low motivation to work in very risky and difficult entrepreneurial initiatives.

These issues are relevant to traditional for-profit entrepreneurs in the Middle East and are even more drastic for social entrepreneurs, since the systems for supporting social entrepreneurship and social enterprise are even less developed than for typical entrepreneurship and enterprise development.

## How to scale social enterprises and social impact in the Middle East

Rooted in the typical for-profit business sector discourse around capturing value, increasing profits, growing market share, and building sustainable and growing companies is the idea of "scaling" enterprises, basically the idea of growing small companies into bigger companies and at the same time increasing profits, durability, and competitiveness of the company. For some enterprises, this brings added financial benefits by way of positioning the enterprise for acquisition, larger investment, or IPO (initial public offering on a public stock exchange).

But organizational scaling has only partial relevance in the social enterprise space, where there is sometimes a stronger motivation to scale impact rather than scale profit. Depending on the specific activities of a social enterprise (the context, the primary issues addressed, the team capacities, the particular motivations of the leadership team, and other considerations), a group might choose any one of various options to scaling social impact that could focus on organizational growth, impact growth without organizational growth, or some mix between the two. These issues and decisions are also impacted by local context in the Middle East, where some approaches to scaling might be easier to achieve than others, given local and regional constraints and opportunities.

To understand better what "scaling" means in the social enterprise context, it is helpful to understand the breadth of scaling options that are in current discourse on the topic and how they relate to social enterprise scalability in the Middle East (Table 6.1).

While it is often true that "social entrepreneurs who are focused on social impact are indifferent to whether that impact is delivered directly through their organization or indirectly through the efforts of others" (Sherman, 2006, p. 22), it is important to note two key elements. First, as in the traditional for-profit business world, scaling impact or services should not come at the cost of quality provided to one's clients or beneficiaries. Even though "dissemination and loose affiliation strategies may reach more locations more quickly and at lower cost, these returns are only valuable if the innovation spreads in a form that delivers higher-quality services than already available" (Dees et al., 2004, p. 31). This is perhaps the key non-monetary element as to why maximizing impact may involve at least some component of scaling an organization, along with other key components and activities to ensure that quality of service is maintained as scaling is pursued.

Second, the wealth motive of the entrepreneur is a powerful motivator that can only be leveraged if there is at least some component of value-capture from scaling that is returned to the entrepreneur's organization. This is true in both traditional for-profit enterprises and social impact enterprises.

## Recommendations for increasing scalable social enterprises in the Middle East

There are various things that can be done to increase the number, strength, and impact of scalable social enterprises in the Middle East. Organizations and governments should take care to assess the critical barriers and opportunities to scalable social enterprise in each country, ideally starting with conducting a mapping and assessment study that includes all stakeholders in each context and then designing a work plan to improve these structures as feasible.

### External: Recommendations for support entities in the social enterprise ecosystem

The social enterprise support ecosystem should provide the necessary physical work facilities, legal and financial structures, qualified mentoring and advising, access to appropriate and diverse financing

*Table 6.1* Defining social innovations and strategies for scaling, and context in the Middle East

| Core social innovation | Related strategies for scaling | Strengths | Weaknesses | Middle East context |
|---|---|---|---|---|
| **Organization** (an overarching structure for mobilizing people and resources to serve a common purpose) | **Branching** (the creation of local sites of one large organization) or some form of franchise model | Greater control; ability to tap into the "wealth motive" through increasing value-capture by the organization | Resource intensive | Brick-and-mortar expansion is expensive, challenging (due to legal, bureaucratic, and logistical reasons), and time consuming. Nonprofit entities can have difficulty registering and operating in many countries, so this may be better suited to for-profit social enterprises in the Middle East

Efforts that want to expand through this approach must be well funded and with ample time to deal with near-inevitable delays and unanticipated challenges |
| **Programme** (an integrated set of actions that serve a specific purpose) | **Affiliation** (a formal relationship defined by an ongoing agreement between two or more parties to be part of an identifiable network) | Maintaining some level of control, moderate costs. Able to engage a wider network of motivated partners | Lacking some level of control, moderate costs | Initiatives that can expand by providing programmes and supports through existing organizations will be able to expand much faster and cheaper, but quality assurance may be difficult since professionalism, work ethics, and accountability can be challenging in the region

This approach includes expanding through technology or service adoption, or by working through a network of partners that already exist on the ground |

| Principles (general guidelines and values about how to serve a given purpose) | Dissemination (actively providing information, and sometimes technical assistance, to others looking to bring an innovation to their community) | Cheapest approach; ability to mobilize people based on shared values and principles; easiest to adapt or alter to fit specific circumstances | Least control and oversight on quality of service delivery; easiest to alter or manipulate so that it does not fulfil intentions of the original proponents | Monitoring and follow-up are critical to ensure quality of service

Principles can spread both very fast and very slow and are open to varied interpretation and implementation. Consistency and monitoring are difficult. Since there is wide diversity in the populations in the region, success at spreading principles can largely depend on adoption by leaders of various religions, political, or ethnic groups, or widespread dissemination through media channels

Civic and community engagement opportunities and participation are limited in the region, and strong leadership (from political, cultural, or business leaders) in this area is not widespread

Adoption by thought leaders is critical to spread principles and maintain adoption |
|---|---|---|---|---|

*Source:* Adapted from content in Dees et al. (2004), with additions by the author.

options, access to clients, talented individuals to hire or partner with, supports for research and development along with links to advanced educational systems, and a community of like-minded innovators and entrepreneurs to provide encouragement, feedback, inspiration, and project partners.

These key issues should be addressed to support social enterprise growth in the Middle East:

- *Increase availability of financing for social enterprises*: Ideally a diversity of financing structures should be available to social enterprises and social entrepreneurs, including loans, grants, investment (especially "smart investment", as discussed above), crowdfunding, and others. Each of these offers different benefits (and constraints) to the enterprises and funders, is suitable to social enterprises at different stages, and works with different strategies. The growth of various financing mechanisms for social enterprise globally should be matched in the Middle East.
- *Introduce legal reforms to make registration procedures and other legal processes simpler and cheaper*: When legal, registration, and other bureaucratic procedures are too complex or costly, social enterprises may not be able to afford those associated costs or they may choose to avoid registration (and operate unofficially) or register outside their primary country of operations. Streamlined legal procedures would enable more entities to access finance, legal protections, payment gateways, basic business procedures, proper hiring of staff, and other key business tools and processes.
- *Improve education to make it more relevant and more responsive to social enterprise needs*: Educational institutions should focus on developing skills that are necessary for scalable social enterprises and should use practical/applied project-based learning and interdepartmental activities to improve the real-world skills of students and improve work readiness. Entrepreneurial education should also not be restricted to business students. Instead, entrepreneurship should be treated as a core competency that students in all programmes should have basic awareness of. Soft skills (creativity, ambition, responsibility, team work, self-learning, etc.) are even more critical than hard skills, but are much less present in our education systems in the region.

- *Help social enterprises get early clients*: Governments and corporations in the Middle East should institute procurement rules that favour social enterprise start-ups from the region to help them during the earliest and most critical start-up phases.
- *Foster a community of practice*: Activities that build community around social enterprise generally or specific sectors are incredibly valuable to help people build links, get inspired, learn, find project partners, and much more. This could be through regular events, co-learning or presentation sessions, developing and hosting co-working spaces, or otherwise.
- *Support start-up accelerators and other programmes that encourage experimentation in possible high-impact scalable social enterprises*: Start-up accelerators, competitions, R&D grants, and other programmes can encourage enterprise development in unproven areas, which is critical to promote disruptive, catalytic, and high-impact innovation.

Start-up accelerators act as places of experimentation, rapid testing of business models, and intense start-up development designed to test the validity of a start-up idea, the approach of the start-up leadership team, and the capacities of the leadership team to deliver on the potential of the enterprise in formation. A start-up accelerator usually has these key characteristics:

- An application process that is open to all, yet highly competitive
- Provision of pre-seed investment, usually in exchange for equity
- A focus on small teams, not individual founders
- Time-limited support comprised of programmed events and intensive mentoring
- Cohorts or "classes" of start-ups rather than individual companies
  (Miller and Bound, 2011, p. 3)

It is estimated that there are now several hundred accelerators operating globally, including many that focus specifically on social enterprise, including some in the Middle East (Table 6.2).

Other social impact accelerators globally focus on the health, clean water, food security, affordable housing, or other sectors.

*Table 6.2*   Social enterprise accelerator examples globally and in the Middle East

| Sector | Examples |
| --- | --- |
| Education | www.kaplanedtechaccelerator.com<br>www.edtechincubator.com<br>www.imaginek12.com |
| Clean energy | www.greenstart.com<br>www.foresightcac.com<br>www.cleantechopen.org |
| Social enterprise (broad) | www.vilcap.com<br>www.agorapartnerships.org<br>www.thefsegroup.com |
| In the MENA region | Nabad (Lebanon; mixed cohorts of for-profit and non-profit groups; www.nabadarcenciel.org) |
| | Nahdet Mahrousa (Egypt; mixed cohorts of for-profit and non-profit groups; www.nahdetelmahrousa.org) |
| | AltCity (Lebanon; mixed cohorts of for-profit and non-profit groups; www.altcity.me) |
| | Sustaincubator (Egypt; focus on food, renewable energy, and water; www.sustaincubator.com) |

## Strategic choices: Choosing an organization- or non-organization-focused scaling strategy

One critical consideration is whether organization-focused scaling or non-organization-focused scaling is more appropriate for the issue being addressed, the chosen strategy, and the resources available.

### Organization-focused scaling

Like many growing traditional for-profit companies, many development organizations scale by setting up country operations in a number of countries to expand their operations. This approach can be most appropriate for some social enterprises as well, especially those that need a physical presence, for example, if a specialized space is needed (e.g. a health clinic) or if highly qualified or specialized personnel are needed who might be difficult to provide without a growing organizational structure in place. It also allows greater value-capture than other approaches, allowing the wealth motive to serve as a strong catalyst and motivator for the impact entrepreneurs.

A simple model that focuses primarily on organizational growth as a primary factor of scaling social impact is the SCALERS model. The acronym "SCALERS" stands for Staffing, Communicating, Alliance-building, Lobbying, Earnings generation, Replicating, and Stimulating market forces. First proposed by Bloom and Chatterji in 2009, the SCALERS model proposes that

> the "Scale of Social Impact" achieved by a social entrepreneurial organization – or the extent to which the organization has been able to scale "wide" (e.g., serve more people) and "deep" (e.g., improve outcomes more dramatically) – is influenced by how effective the organization has been at developing a combination of the seven capabilities outlined in the acronym.
>
> (Bloom and Chatterji, 2009, p. 5)

While the SCALERS model presents an interesting generic global model for scaling social enterprises, it also demonstrates some of the key unique challenges that are present in the Middle East, where many of the key drivers of successful scaling globally are much more difficult (or impossible) in some countries due to the local context. As mentioned above, staffing, lobbying, and earnings generation can be particularly challenging in the region.

One well-known example of the organizational scaling approach is Endeavor, a global non-profit working to support high-impact entrepreneurs around the world. Established in 1997, the organization now has 23 offices globally and has selected and supported over 500 companies to help them grow and create more jobs. Endeavor is now operating in several countries in the Middle East, including Egypt, Jordan, Lebanon, Morocco, Saudi Arabia, Turkey, and the United Arab Emirates.

Another interesting example in the Middle East is INJAZ Al-Arab, the regional programme for Junior Achievement Worldwide. JAW was founded as an NPO in 1919 and teaches young people about financial literacy, entrepreneurship, and other workforce training skills. The organization works in 121 countries and engages over ten million young people annually through a network of around 330,377 volunteers supported by 3,275 staff. INJAZ Al-Arab was launched in 1999 as an initiative of Save the Children Jordan and, in 2001, became affiliated with JAW as the regional office for MENA. Since then, the organization has grown to work in 15 countries in the MENA region and has engaged over 1.6 million students in their programmes since 2004. According to the INJAZ Al-Arab website, "a National Board of Directors leads each INJAZ country operation with the INJAZ Al-Arab Regional Board responsible for directing overall strategy and organizational governance".

At an earlier stage of organizational development, The Little Engineer is pursuing their growth and impact objective through a mixed organizational expansion and franchise model approach. According to their website, the company was started in Lebanon in 2009 to "have a positive social impact by encouraging education in general and improving scientific knowledge and skills in our society". They do a variety of science and technology courses for kids through activities directly in schools and through after-school activities in private centres. The company is now working in four countries in the MENA region and is seeking to further expand through both direct branching and a franchise model approach.

*Non-organization-focused scaling*

While there is growing interest in scaling social enterprises, there is also substantial interest in scaling social impact, regardless of the role of organizational scaling within that. The non-organization approaches could have strategic value in the Middle East, where barriers to enterprises (for-profit and non-profit) are oftentimes substantial. The "networked" non-profit or social enterprise works "by mobilizing resources outside their immediate control" in order to "achieve their missions far more efficiently, effectively, and sustainably than they could have by working alone". These organizations work "as nodes within a constellation of equal, interconnected partners, rather than as hubs at the centre of their non-profit universes" (Wei-Skillern and Marciano, 2008, pp. 40–42) and build on some of the key non-organizational scaling approaches noted in the charts above: focusing on programmes, principles, services, or behaviour change.

A key example of this "networked approach" is Habitat for Humanity Egypt (HFHE). HFHE was successful in producing many times more homes than the average of other Habitat for Humanity country programmes by working with a network of independent organizations that worked on different aspects of poverty relief. Not only did they build more homes, but they also engaged the constellation of partners to provide other supports, increase impact, and share best practices.

Wikimedia Foundation, another example, is the only non-profit to be listed in the top 20 websites globally (Wikipedia). Wikimedia Foundation employs around 150 people, has annual revenues of approximately $48 million, and works with hundreds of organizations and thousands of individuals worldwide. This hyper-networked organization enables thousands of people and organizations to build on its framework, contribute information, participate in decision-making, and use programmes and materials for a wide variety of purposes. Wikimedia has garnered modest participation across the Middle East, with efforts to increase contributions of Arabic content, contribute different perspectives to the collaborative documentation effort, and increase participation and contributions from women.

Another well-known effort is TED, a series of conferences, online activities, and online content owned and operated by the non-profit Sapling Foundation. There have been thousands of independently organized TEDx events in over 133 countries, and the online videos passed the one billion views mark in November 2012. There have been dozens of TEDx events across the Middle East, including Egypt, Lebanon, Yemen, United Arab Emirates, and Jordan.

Another example, Kiva.org facilitates microloans from people around the world. Though its only office is in San Francisco, California, it works with 247 partners in 76 countries and has facilitated over 700,000 loans, since its establishment in 2005. While Kiva has had limited success in the Middle East, they are expanding their programmes in the region in partnership with regional partners, including a recently launched initiative called "Change is in Your Hands" in partnership with Grameen-Jameel Microfinance Ltd (see the campaign at www.kiva.org/middleeast).

### Early-stage social enterprise idea development in the Middle East: Start with scaling in mind

Many social entrepreneurs in the Middle East are motivated by needs in their own communities, inspired by issues they see at the regional, city, community, or even neighbourhood level. Whether they have a particular passion or focus from the beginning, though, or they first get inspired to work on a social impact initiative and then go through the process of identifying what they want to work on, it is helpful to think about scalability from an early stage. Market research, market validation, and developing a scalable concept and strategy are important steps to make sure that there is strong product–market fit and that seemingly small decisions are not made early on, that limit the possibility of scaling an effort. This process is rarely easy, and "defining an innovation for scale is an iterative process" (Dees et al., 2004, p. 28).

The process for identifying scalable opportunities in the social impact space can be helped by looking at the situation on the ground in different communities and countries and seeing where there are common challenges that could be addressed by a shared solution. As mentioned above, it is usually more effective to start small – focusing on a local issue with local resources – and then build up from there after the organization, solution, team, and processes are refined and proven. In that process of idea/solution development and organizational development, however, it is also valuable to make sure that the solution being developed to address the local challenge also has relevance in a much larger context (Figure 6.2).

Since travelling and doing on-the-ground assessments in many different countries and communities is time consuming and expensive, a more efficient first step would be looking at what resources and

*Figure 6.2*   Identifying scalable ideas within concentric circles of opportunity

data sets are available to understand the key challenges that exist in different communities, countries, and regions.

| Local (neighbourhood, city, or country (if a small country)) | Country-based development reports, organizational assessments, anecdotal experience and interviews, own experience and observations in a community, and so on |
| --- | --- |
| Regional (e.g. MENA) or national (if a larger country) | Arab Human Development Report; regional reports from OECD, World Economic Forum, World Bank, discussion with people or organizations in different locales, and so on |
| Global (larger foreign expansion) | Millennium Development Goals, Skoll Global Threats, GEM – Global Entrepreneurship Monitor (global- and country-level data); global reports from OECD, WEF, WB, discussion with people and organizations in different locales, and so on |

Gregory Dees (et al.) identified in 2004 the five key points, called the 5 R's, to help entrepreneurs assess whether their social innovation is ready for scalability or help them make adjustments to maximize chances for success (Table 6.3).

While the challenges are greater to develop scalable social enterprises in the Middle East when compared to some other countries and innovation hubs, it is critical that social entrepreneurs and the social impact ecosystem look to adopt, refine, and effectively utilize best-in-class tools and methods to build scalable and competitive social enterprises. Rather than just use the tools and strategies developed elsewhere, groups in the Middle East should aim to work smarter, more efficiently, and more strategically than elsewhere, in order to counterbalance the greater challenges that exist in the region.

A few such tools include the "lean startup method" and the "social impact business model canvas". While these tools (or variations of them) have widespread use in other innovation hubs globally, they have less prominence in the social impact sector, and even less so in the Middle East. In a recent (April 2014) start-up event in Beirut, for example, not one of the 25 participants (largely university students and recent graduates) was aware of the "lean startup method", a standard tool in the start-up toolbox in the United States and Europe.

*Table 6.3*   The 5 R's for scalable innovations, and notes regarding scaling in the Middle East

| | |
|---|---|
| Readiness | Is the innovation ready to be spread? |
| | Mideast: Are quality, cost, design, and competitiveness factors well established and ready for growth? |
| Receptivity | Will the innovation be well received in target communities? |
| | Mideast: Can it spread within the originating country, or can it extend to other countries in the region? Are there language, religious, or cultural reasons that would inhibit the spread of an innovation? |
| Resources | What resources, financial or otherwise, are required to get the job done right? |
| | Mideast: Are there resources to expand this in different countries, with sufficient resources and time to deal with possible delays and challenges? |
| Risk | What is the chance the innovation will be implemented incorrectly, or will fail to have impact? |
| | Mideast: Are some countries and contexts more risky than others? |
| Returns | What is the bottom line? Impact should not just be about serving more people – it should be about serving them well |
| | Mideast: What is the level of need in different countries in the Middle East, and how does the intended impact relate to the challenges and need in different contexts? |

*Source*: Adapted from content in Dees et al. (2004), with additions by the author.

While the business model canvas is an incredibly helpful tool for early-stage enterprises to think about key elements of their early-stage venture, it lacks any specific elements that relate to social enterprise. Through our work at AltCity coaching start-ups and social impact start-ups, we went through our own process to assess what was missing and how it could be improved for this specific purpose. We adapted the BMC by adding two boxes to include social/environment costs and benefits to the chart, so those elements can be included as a core part of the enterprise formation thought process (Figure 6.3).

AltCity has successfully used these tools to help aspiring social entrepreneurs refine their concepts and develop a more strategic

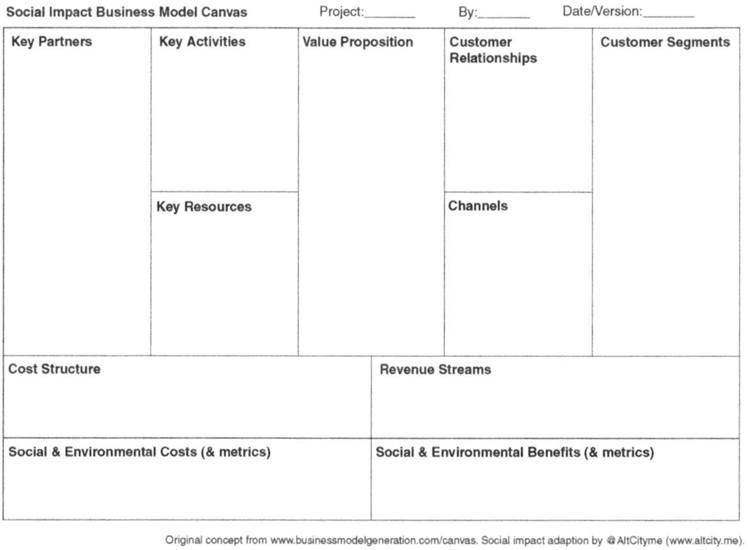

| Social Impact Business Model Canvas | | Project:_____ | By:_____ | Date/Version:_____ |
|---|---|---|---|---|
| **Key Partners** | **Key Activities** | **Value Proposition** | **Customer Relationships** | **Customer Segments** |
| | **Key Resources** | | **Channels** | |
| **Cost Structure** | | **Revenue Streams** | | |
| **Social & Environmental Costs (& metrics)** | | **Social & Environmental Benefits (& metrics)** | | |

Original concept from www.businessmodelgeneration.com/canvas. Social impact adaption by @AltCityme (www.altcity.me).

*Figure 6.3*   The social impact business model canvas
*Source*: Adapted by AltCity, from Osterwalder (2008).

approach to their social enterprise initiative. Overall, these tools (among others) can increase the efficiency, impact, and competitiveness of social impact enterprises in the Middle East.

## Conclusion

Leaders of social impact initiatives are often hesitant to scale, fearing that the scaling process itself will have a negative impact on their organization or their intended beneficiaries. While it may be possible to identify examples where scalability in the social impact space would not be helpful, that is more likely attributable to a limited understanding of how scaling can be applied and the levels of flexibility that exist. There is no one model for scaling that can be used by all social impact initiatives, just as there is no one model for scaling purely for-profit businesses. There are numerous approaches to scalability that can be adapted to different contexts, different approaches, different issues, and different challenges.

Of course, there are valid reasons why a social impact initiative would not scale. These could relate to limitations of the opportunity or limitations of the resources available. There are always risks, as well. Regardless of the strategy chosen, "more than 70% of new businesses fail within eight years of their inception". Both large-scale social impact and "substantial profits, although not impossible to achieve, are hard to come by" (Dees, 1998, p. 5). Still, the potential benefits of scaling on the wider ecosystem, at the national, regional, and global levels, are substantial. While immense expenditures on international aid will continue for some time to come and it is critical that they do continue (and grow), many global issues will only be resolved when a multitude of high-impact, scalable initiatives can successfully address them in a sustainable manner.

On the larger scale of a community or an economy, "social entrepreneurs serve as a learning laboratory for society: They develop, test, and refine innovative solutions to social problems....Only by fostering a wide range of experiments can we hope to find which proposed solutions are viable, cost-effective, and scalable" (Dees, 2005, p. 4). This link between "social impact change" and "commercial innovation" goes even further, potentially providing tangible economic benefits to those that provide them, while also dramatically shifting how we live and function as a society.

These reasons and more provide sufficient justification to foundations, donors, governments, and entrepreneurs interested in positive and sustainable development in the Middle East to invest time, finances, and other resources in supporting scalable social enterprises in the region.

## Acknowledgements

Special thanks to the AltCity team and co-founders, and especially Dr Dima Saber, for their appreciation of research and knowledge production as part of our work at AltCity and for supporting me in my efforts to bridge academic work and our applied start-up support efforts. Special thanks also to Dr Patricia Nabti for being a key reviewer and editor for this paper.

## Bibliography

Acs, Z. (Winter 2006). How Is Entrepreneurship Good for Economic Growth? *Innovations*. Boston, MA.

Austin, J. E. (2000). "Strategic Collaboration between Nonprofits and Business", *Nonprofit* and *Voluntary Sector Quarterly*, 29, 69–97.

Bell, S. (2011). *iMENA: An Innovation Agenda for Jobs* (No. 89, 66102). World Bank, Washington, DC.

Bloom, P. N. and Chatterji, A. K. (2009). "Scaling Social Entrepreneurial Impact", *California Management Review*. Berkeley, CA.

Dees, J. G. (January–February 1998). "Enterprising Nonprofits", *Harvard Business Review*, 55–67. Boston, MA.

Dees, J. G. (2005). "Social Ventures As Learning Laboratories", *Tennessee's Business*, 20, 3–5. Murfreesboro, TN.

Dees, J. G., Anderson, B. B. and Wei-Skillern, J. (Spring 2004). "Scaling Social Impact – Strategies for Spreading Social Innovations", *Stanford Social Innovation Review*. Stanford, CA.

Doing Business [WWW Document] (2014). World Bank Doing Bus. Rank, available at http://www.doingbusiness.org/rankings.

Feghali, D. T., Abuatieh, E. and Dandan, J. (2013). *Social Entrepreneurship in Lebanon: Contexts and Considerations*. Beirut, Lebanon: Darwazah Center for Innovation Management & Entrepreneurship, American University of Beirut. Beirut, Lebanon.

Miller, P. and Bound, K. (2011). *The Startup Factories: The Rise of Accelerator Programmes to Support New Technology Ventures*. NESTA. London, UK.

Nasr, S. and Pearce, D. (2012). *SMEs for Job Creation in the Arab World – SME Access to Financial Services* (No. 71551). The World Bank. Washington, DC.

Sherman, D. A. (2006). "Social Entrepreneurship: Pattern-Changing Entrepreneurs and the Scaling of Social Impact", Case Western Reserve University, Weatherhead School of Management, 29. Cleveland, OH.

WEF (2011). *Accelerating Entrepreneurship in the Arab World*. World Economic Forum (WEF) with Booz & Company, Geneva, Switzerland.

Wei-Skillern, J. and Marciano, S. (2008). "The Networked Nonprofit", *Stanford Social Innovation Review*, 7. Stanford, CA.

# 7
# Bridging Impact and Investment in MENA

*Jamil Wyne*

## Introduction

The practice of impact investment is becoming increasingly prominent. The Monitor Institute posits that in the past few years, hundreds of new impact investment funds with billions of dollars in potential investments have appeared across the globe.[1] According to a 2012 survey of over 100 impact investment funds by the Global Impact Investment Network (GIIN), participating funds committed US$8 billion in capital to impact investments and planned to commit another US$1 billion in the following year.[2]

A growing pool of institutions is championing this practice of investors bridging financial, social, and even environmental returns. Institutions such as the GIIN, along with the Rockefeller Foundation, Acumen Fund, and the World Economic Forum, just to name a few, have each contributed to laying the foundation for impact investment globally. Even global investment banks such as J.P. Morgan, Credit Suisse, Goldman Sachs, and Deutsche Bank have created special programmes dedicated to impact investment.

Though these players have different agendas, investment tools, and criteria, they share a common belief that investing for profit is not mutually exclusive from investing for social and environmental impact. Many practitioners and supporters would argue it represents the future of investment where financial capital is intrinsically linked to social impact and vice versa.

## Defining impact investment

Globally, the term is still developing. Though its focus on social and environmental impact connotes a philanthropic deployment of capital, impact investment is not charity. It is also important to distinguish impact investment from socially responsible investing. The latter connotes a focus on investing in companies that do not have any damaging repercussions on society or the environment, acting with the philosophy that you can do good by not causing harm.[3]

A 2013 report from the World Economic Forum points to several key criteria that characterize this practice. Though the definition will take on new forms over time, for intents and purposes of this chapter, the criteria provided in Table 7.1 offer an overview of three core components: approach, intention, and measurement.

Perhaps the most important component of impact investment is that it blends the venture capital and social enterprise fields to achieve scale. It is a hybrid method of spreading capital to innovative scalable social enterprises with the expectation that financial, social, and/or environmental gains will be made. Though these social enterprises may have good teams that develop scalable products and services, they often lack the financial backing to help them grow their operations or develop new products and services; scale is

*Table 7.1* Key components of impact investment[4]

| | Components | Details |
|---|---|---|
| 1 | Approach | Impact investment should be understood as a strategy for deploying capital rather than an asset class itself. It also cannot be understood as charity or philanthropy, as investors seek a return |
| 2 | Intent | Investors are driven to leverage their capital to achieve some form of social and/or environmental impact and not solely financial return. While investments that seek purely a financial gain can indeed have an impact, if the intention is not there, the investment is not as closely affiliated with impact investment |
| 3 | Measurement | Careful and active measurement of financial, social, and environmental returns is embedded in the practice of impact investment. These measurements are jointly used to determine the full impact of each investment |

diminished with the chances of impact being limited as well. Likewise, these enterprises often need more than cash to realize their full impact. Networks, know-how, and mentorship – staple services of the venture capital approach – can be much needed as non-financial support for social entrepreneurs. Financing is, of course, critical, but investors can also support through helping portfolio companies develop growth strategies, build new products, and, in general, serve as a sounding board for new ideas and solutions to challenges.

Impact investors also bring an emphasis on milestones and measurement, which also bodes well for social enterprises. Setting key performance indicators in both financial and non-financial areas can push the enterprise to excel while also developing accountability. Tying financial goals to social and environmental ones can place greater responsibility on both the investor and investee to perform to higher standards, especially if there is a mutually held interest in achieving both sets of goals.

Of course, the venture capital model is not without flaws nor do all funds function with the same methods and capacity. Likewise, big impact is not a certainty if a social enterprise is part of an impact investment fund's portfolio. However, the combination of financial capital alongside mentorship, access to networks, and measurement that investors can bring can indeed enhance growth and impact prospects for a social enterprise. This hybrid investment approach allows for capital to be more easily deployed to market-driven solutions for development challenges.

## MENA's entrepreneurship ecosystem

Experts interviewed for this chapter agreed that, in order for impact investment to take root in any country or society, there much first be an entrepreneurial culture and the basic foundations of an entrepreneurship ecosystem – the network of investors, incubators, non-governmental organizations, and other initiatives created to support entrepreneurs.

In the past 4–5 years, the MENA region has witnessed enormous change in its entrepreneurship ecosystem. Barely existent several years ago, there are now over 150 institutions working with entrepreneurs in the region, not including micro-finance initiatives (Figure 7.1).[5]

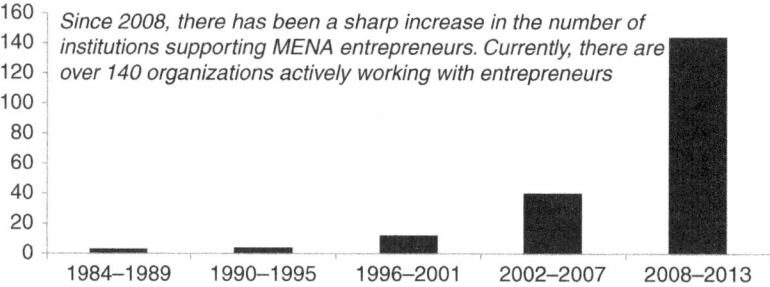

*Figure 7.1* Rise in entrepreneurship support organizations in MENA (1984–present)[6]

Countries such as Jordan, Lebanon, Egypt, and the United Arab Emirates have been home to some of the most actively developing ecosystems, with institutions such as the Oasis 500 (Jordan), Flat 6 Labs (Egypt), and Bader (Lebanon), among many others, providing holistic support to start-ups while fast-growing enterprises such as Souq and Namshi have their headquarters in the UAE. Governments have also become involved in this ecosystem, particularly in the UAE, where institutions such as the Khalifa Fund and Dubai SME have established robust programmes dedicated to supporting private enterprise growth domestically. These countries are also home to some of the most active venture capital funds in the region: Dash Ventures, MENA Venture Investments, Middle East Venture Partners, Wamda Capital, Ideavelopers, and Sawari Ventures to name a few. Over the past several years, each of these funds has deployed smart capital to young start-ups, primarily in the information and communication technologies industries and, in the process, developed a portfolio of promising enterprises.

Additionally, the rise in financing for entrepreneurs signifies two key shifts in the mindsets of the MENA private sector. One, more investors are embracing risk and open to thinking long term; and two, there is an explicit interest in searching for young companies that have potential for big impact. In investors' eyes, these companies could be vanguards, bringing new technologies and business models to MENA to lay the foundation for new industries.

Indeed, this movement has much ground to still cover, but it demonstrates that there is a growing population of investors and other stakeholders that have their sights set on big impact through entrepreneurship. Steadily, business innovation is being embraced as a tool to introduce new solutions to industries, accelerating MENA's private sector development.

This phenomenon is, of course, not unique to MENA. Discourse on emerging markets over the past several years has consistently touched on the importance of entrepreneurship and the innovation of grass-roots start-up communities in enhancing economic growth. Countries in Latin America, sub-Saharan Africa, and Southeast Asia have all garnered recognition for their ability to grow entrepreneurship ecosystems. In fact, research from Endeavor Insight has pointed to how such ecosystems can develop in spite of limiting business environments that often characterize these developing economies.[7]

> Vibrant cultures that already have entrepreneurship well-established, such as India, Kenya, Brazil, each have fairly long established traditions in which people are comfortable and recognized for taking risks, failing and trying again. Linking this cultural attribute to local social challenges creates a growing pipeline of potential deals for impact investors.
>
> Simon Winter, Senior vice president for Development,
> Technoserve

These geographic areas, where poverty and limited access to basic resources and infrastructure has threatened economic and social development, have also proven to be fertile ground for innovative companies that do not simply sustain and grow the enterprise, but have a positive social and/or environmental impact. Not only do entrepreneurs provide the much-needed innovation and leveraging of scant resources, they appear to be doing so with increasing focus on the public good.

Global examples in the utility and growth of impact investment such as Omidyar Network, Soros Economic Development Fund, Triodos Bank, and Root Capital have all deployed capital to combat socio-economic challenges with market-based solutions in these countries. The involvement of such institutions, though driven in part by a search for social impact, is also the result of perceived attractive investment opportunities. However, while impact investment has become increasingly common in these economies, it has a minimal presence in MENA, despite its own growing entrepreneurship ecosystem.

## Lack of MENA presence in global impact investment

In 2010, the GIIN identified 1,105 impact investment deals that took place across the globe in that year. Within this pool of investments, only six were made in MENA, accounting for less than 1 per cent of reported deals.[8] In fact, MENA was the least represented region on this list, aside from Australia and New Zealand and the South Pacific, which had no impact investment activity. Furthermore, the average investment size of these deals was noticeably lower in MENA than it was in other regions. On average, the deals reported in MENA were each just over US$800,000 compared to an average of US$3,360,097 per investment in Canada and the United States, US$1,214,953 in South and Southeast Asia, US$1,555,555 in sub-Saharan Africa, and US$2,480,769 in western Europe (Figure 7.2).[9]

The following year, GIIN doubled the size of its survey, and MENA had marginally higher representation. Of the 2,106 identified impact investments, the region was home to 2 per cent of the deals and 1 per cent of the total dollar amount invested.[10] In 2012, GIIN administered its largest impact investment survey to date, with MENA still having the lowest representation of any region that participated in the survey. Of the 99 impact investment institutions who responded to the survey, only 10 per cent had a focus on investment

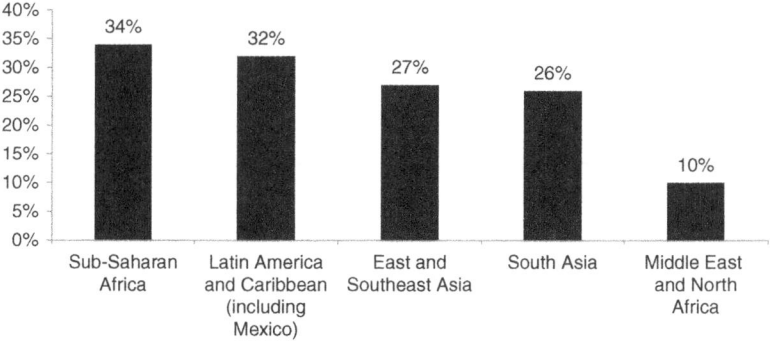

*Figure 7.2*   Geographic focus of impact investors[11]

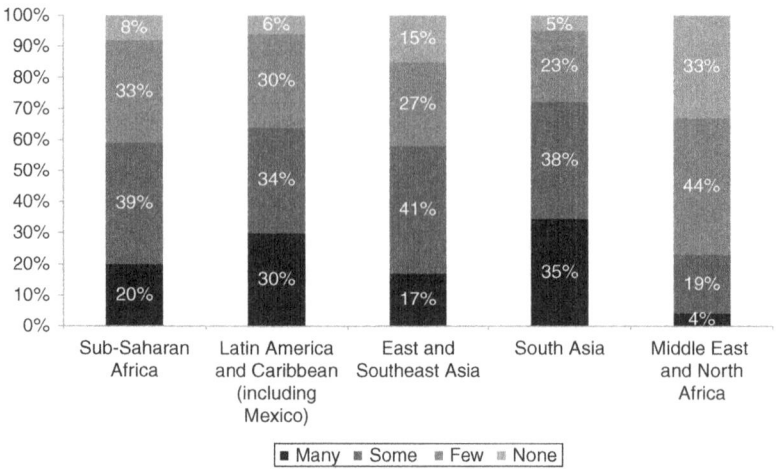

*Figure 7.3*  Number of investment opportunities considered in 2012 that passed initial impact and financial screen[12]

in MENA. The region was also labelled as the most challenging area to identify viable investments.[13] Compared to regions such as Latin America, sub-Saharan Africa, and South Asia, each of which was identified as having viable impact investment opportunities by at least 50 per cent of GIIN survey respondents in 2012, MENA lags far behind (Figure 7.3).

Of course, the GIIN study is not inclusive of all impact investment activity globally. It only includes funds that manage at least US$10,000,000 in impact investment capital and, even among funds of this size, the survey results are not representative. However, a closer look at the MENA region's impact investment landscape reveals minimal activity.

Only two funds in the region are actually identified as impact investment-focused: Willow Impact in the United Arab Emirates and MC Egypt, created by Mercy Corps and based in Cairo. There are several other venture capital and investment vehicles that focus on funding enterprises that have financial, social, and/or environmental returns, including Catalyst Private Equity in Jordan, which focuses on clean-tech, and E2E holding company in Jordan that focuses on the energy sector.

However, this is not due to a lack of demand for market-driven solutions for overcoming the region's development challenges. The MENA region is home to some of the most water-scarce countries in the world, as the United Nations claimed that, as of 2007, many MENA countries already existed at a level of stressed, if not scarce, access to freshwater.[14] Of equal concern, by some estimates, by 2035, energy consumption in the region will increase by 70 per cent.[15] These environmental constraints are just as, if not even more, pressing as the employment challenge and they too demand solutions.

The healthcare space is in need of reform, which can best be understood through the prevalence of diabetes. Saudi Arabia, Kuwait, and Qatar have some of the highest prevalence of diabetes globally with roughly one quarter of the adult population in each country afflicted by the disease. The region's adult population itself has the highest rates of diabetes in the world, as roughly one in ten adults is diabetic. This number is expected to rise over the next 20 years by 96.2 per cent, creating large demand for quick solutions.[16]

Innovation in these fields could bring more efficient and affordable access to much-needed services to sustain and enhance human development regionally. Impact investment can play a significant role in this process as well. Yet, as it has not established a presence in the MENA entrepreneurship ecosystem, it is not a part of the conversation on how to efficiently counter these challenges.

## Explaining the gap

The challenges to growing an impact investment community in the region can be understood through analysing a series of factors. The limited number of investors with an interest in fusing financial and social returns and the number of viable social enterprise investment deals are two challenges currently holding back the growth of the sector. These two obstacles contribute to creating a lack of success stories and viable benchmarks that can help to garner more support for impact investment in MENA.

- *Little public interest in fusing social and for-profit methods*: During interviews with experts, many pointed to a lack of public interest in blending social and financial agendas. While some explained it as a general lack of understanding of how the two can complement one another, others pointed to a stigma towards the social sector in MENA. According to interview findings, the private sector tends to view non-profit organizations as supply-driven and inefficient, lacking the management capacity and strategy needed to have a tangible impact. As such, investors are not interested in engaging in social impact.

Local populations see the issues but don't understand social enterprise – they understand charity and business, but not a fusion.

(Rama Chakaki, Baraka Ventures)

Additionally, other experts pointed to how the private sector sees a need for supporting social causes – as evidenced by a growing trend of corporate social responsibility in the region – yet see such efforts as purely charitable, thus not capable of yielding any financial return. This pervading opinion has the direct consequence of overlooking the symbiotic relationship between financial and social objectives.[17]

---

**Case Study 1  Levan Impact Ventures**

After having spent years studying in the United States and working in leading private investment institutions in MENA, Jordanians Hamed Masri and Mohammed Nasif turned their attention to creating a fund that invested in for-profit enterprises with the potential for both significant financial and social returns. Their hypothesis was that though there was a high demand for social goods and services, social impact represented a subset in the economy that was often neglected by the private and public sectors. Yet, this neglect also provided a larger opportunity in terms of both financial return and impact. However, there was minimal interest from potential investment partners, bringing an end to fundraising efforts. Masri explains their inability to raise capital by a few factors. First, the pool of investment strategies and financial tools in MENA is still a young practice. While venture capital and more nuanced approaches to funding companies had evolved in other markets, MENA was and still is experimenting with basic forms of risk capital, resulting in few investors that had even heard of impact investment. Second, the more active venture capital funds and angel investors in the region who were instrumental in popularizing risk capital in MENA had not yet explored the impact investment space. During their fundraising efforts, the LIV team consistently encountered limited partners who equated social impact with pure philanthropy. Their lack of interest diminished the chances of encouraging investors to follow suit. Third, Masri pointed to the long waiting period for realizing returns that come with impact investment as a deterrent for recruiting investors. The LIV team often met with potential limited partners seeking quick turnarounds on investment, much shorter waiting periods than impact investments allowed. The LIV story embodies several of the core challenges facing impact investment in MENA. A lack of thought leadership, interest in blending financial and social goals, as well as an expectation of faster returns on investment held back LIV's efforts, and these same factors impinge on the development of impact investment in MENA.

- *Venture capital itself is still developing in MENA*: Over the past several years, multiple new venture capital funds have been created in MENA. In Jordan, MENA Venture Investments, Silicon Badia, and Dash Ventures have inhabited this space, while Egypt's Ideavelopers and Sawari Ventures have become leaders in this field and Lebanon's Middle East Venture Partners has steadily grown both its portfolio and its fund over the past three years. Saudi Aramco also recently entered the venture capital field in MENA by creating Wa'ed Ventures, which joins STC Ventures for two prominent funds for start-ups in Saudi Arabia. Palestine has also launched a venture capital fund, Sadara Ventures, which is funded by Cisco, Google, Skoll Foundation, Case Foundation, the European Investment Bank, and the Soros Economic Development Fund.

Developing an angel investment and VC space could be a natural and important step before impact investment.

(Saurabh Lall, Aspen Network for Development Entrepreneurs)

However, this venture capital activity is still young, and few funds have realized a substantial return on investment or a successful exit. Indeed, such progress will come with time, but it is arguable that regional investors will need to prioritize mastering traditional venture capital before exploring how social impact and financial return can be symbiotic.

- *Few investment-ready for-profit social enterprises*: The gap can also be explained by MENA's impact investors' inability to identify any social enterprises that have matured to a stage at which they will be ready for investment. Nadine Kettaneh, from Willow Impact Investors, an impact investment fund with a focus on both MENA and East Africa, points to this issue as a recurring challenge for implementing their investment agenda in the region. Though there are indeed social enterprises with revenue-generating mechanisms in MENA, few have matured to a point in which an investor can effectively enter the picture and disburse capital to the company.

  Impact investment funds in the US and UK often come with backing from foundations and development funds in order to get them started and support operational costs. What impact investors don't have in the Middle East are backers like government funds or big foundations that have a pool of money committed to impact investment.

  (Nadine Kettaneh, Willow Impact)

  GIIN research suggests that, globally, impact investors tend to focus on later-stage ventures rather than seed and early stage. In GIIN's most recent study on global impact investment trends, funds focusing on growth stage represented over 70 per cent of surveyed entities, while those focusing on early stages represented less than 20 per cent.[18]

- *Lack of success stories*: Ultimately, recruiting more investors and capital to support impact investment will hinge on finding success stories, where a fund has invested in a social enterprise that has met with measurable financial and social returns. These case studies will create more confidence around the sector by giving

---

**Case Study 2   Willow Impact Investors**

Willow Impact is an impact investment and advisory firm with offices in Dubai, UAE, and Nairobi, Kenya. Its investment agenda focuses on East Africa and MENA, with a focus on social enterprises in the environmental, agricultural, educational, and health sectors, focusing on firms that yield high financial and social returns. To date, the fund's only investments have been in East Africa, despite an active search for viable investment deals in MENA. Nadine Kettaneh, co-founder and managing partner of Willow Impact, points to a few reasons for why the fund has yet to invest in any social enterprises in the region. In terms of the investment environment itself, though some of the potential investments in MENA that Willow has vetted have been promising, the fund team has not been able to identify a company that is mature enough to meet its investment criteria. While they have identified social enterprises that could eventually yield high financial term as well as significant impact, the track record and performance milestones needed to inform investment decisions are lacking. This points to a potentially good social investment landscape in the coming years, yet currently there is little that impact investors such as Willow can do to add value to these companies. Beyond the deal flow, Kettaneh also points to foundational factors in the region's education system that hold back the development of quality social enterprises and impact investing, in general. A stronger emphasis on science and the arts is needed, according to Kettaneh, which could ultimately help to educate people on investing for good.

---

the public evidence of tangible impact. Many point to Yahoo!'s purchase of Jordanian company Maktoob.com in 2009 as a primary reason for the rise in funds, incubators, and general events supporting the region's start-ups in recent years. Shortly after news of the acquisition was made public, the founders and investors became instant celebrities. In fact, within the Jordanian start-up community, many often discuss how the creation of the country's premier business accelerator, the Oasis 500, was a direct result of the Maktoob acquisition, as King Abdullah II sought to replicate its success. The impact investment space would benefit from a similar breakthrough. It may not necessarily be an acquisition, but could come in the form of a significant partnership, endorsement from the public sector, or large investment from a foreign fund. In large part, these challenges are rooted in cultural, financial, and market readiness elements. A combination of few viable impact investment deals in MENA, limited exposure to concepts, successful practices of impact investment and a young market, all currently limit the speed at which this field can have a stronger foothold in the region. However, none of these challenges is insurmountable and arguably, as the market evolves, opportunities for impact investment will naturally appear. Additionally, there are already several positive signs that this trend can come to fruition, which are due in part to current resources and developments in the region's entrepreneurship ecosystem.

## Positive developments

There are indeed noticeable gaps, and none can be closed with any quick-fix solutions. However, addressing these gaps can be achieved by looking at currently existing resources and activity in MENA's entrepreneurship and philanthropic communities. Despite a list of substantial challenges, there are some positive signs that deserve our attention and can be used as a starting point for advancing this field in the region.

- *Nascent pipeline developing*: First, there is a general consensus among institutions and thought leaders in the region's entrepreneurship ecosystems that there are a growing number of good business ideas that fuse for-profit business models with social and environmental impact. Ehaab Abdou, an Ashoka Fellow and Founder of Egyptian social enterprise incubator Nahdet Al Mahrousa, says that there is a noticeable number of social enterprises at national and regional business plan competitions.

Out of every 100 entrepreneurs we see between 5 and 10 that are tackling a big social issue that have the potential for large impact.

Con O'Donnell, MC Egypt

Though the companies competing in such events are often in the very early stages, it is encouraging for supporters of impact invest- ment to see evidence that more entrepreneurs are exploring this sphere precisely because they could mature into viable investments. Also, as shown in Table 7.2, there are clear examples of companies

*Table 7.2* Examples of MENA companies blending social and profitable objectives

| Company | Focus area | Model | Country |
| --- | --- | --- | --- |
| Saphon Energy | Wind energy | Patented wind turbines that use "zero-blade" technology, an innovation that differs from traditional bladed turbines, which generate energy more efficiently and with less pollution | Tunisia |
| Pi-Slice | Microfinance | Social platform that links individuals and companies with microfinance institutions in MENA to enhance micro-lending practices in the region | UAE |
| Al-Tibbi | Health care | Online Arabic healthcare portal that seeks to enhance communication between patients and physicians and provide more accurate and accessible online medical information across the Arab region | Jordan |
| Souktel | Unemployment | Builds customized mobile services to foster employment opportunities and enhance development across a variety of sectors including education, emergency response, and agriculture | Palestine |

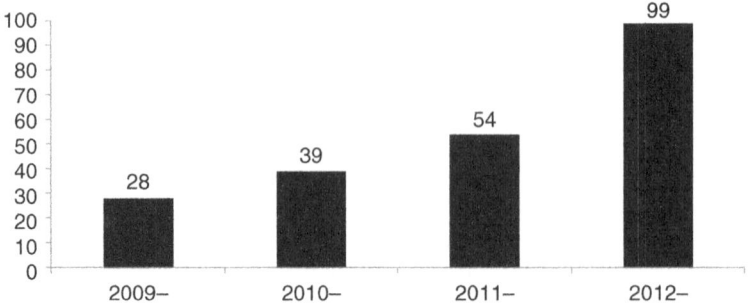

*Figure 7.4*   Number of investments by year[19]

that have already begun to blend social and financial objectives across the region.

- *Early-stage infrastructure is coming into place*: Second, the region's blossoming start-up and venture capital community can lay a foundation for more nuanced investment approaches. There is tangible evidence that investments in start-ups have increased notably in recent years. In a 2014 study from the Wamda Research Lab, of the entrepreneurs surveyed, over three times as many received investment in 2012 compared to 2009 numbers.[20] There is still much learning, experimenting, and potential to be realized in MENA's entrepreneurship ecosystem. However, as knowledge around this space accumulates, there will be a foundation on which impact investors can begin to develop their operations.

Insights into different investment tools, portfolio management, and general market knowledge will all grow with time (Figure 7.4). In parallel, the number of investors and funds will also grow. As this community expands and more institutions and high net-worth individuals become involved, there will be an increasing number of opportunities for impact investment entities to organically develop.

- *The field is being populated slowly*: Third, there is already a small contingent of impact investment practitioners and social entrepreneurship support organizations growing in MENA.

As mentioned earlier in this chapter, Willow Impact and MC Egypt are two examples of formal impact investment funds. Additionally, there may be other funds that are currently being created and others that may have stalled or never come to fruition. The latter group can be particularly helpful to understanding potential mistakes and challenges other funds can learn from. In parallel, non-governmental organizations, such as Ashoka, Nahdet Al Mahrousa, and Synergos, among others, are supporting social entrepreneurs across the region. Of course, many of these entrepreneurs do not have sustainable business models, but they are still instrumental in popularizing the general concept of social entrepreneurship in MENA. Collectively, these players have the capacity to test models and share knowledge and can help to educate new institutions seeking to enter this field.

- *Strong philanthropic practices*: Fourth, and last, the Arab region has a rich tradition of philanthropy. In the post-Arab Spring era, there has been a rise in regional philanthropy, which some say has become substantially more strategic.[21] Of course, there are stark differences between philanthropic giving and impact investment, so an increase in the former does not equal an increase in the latter. Additionally, philanthropy in the region must continue to evolve as practitioners move from sporadic charitable donations to more targeted, structured giving with long-term goals.[22] However, positive developments in the region's philanthropic space bodes well for institutionalizing impact investment in the long term. Put differently, there is already a culture of giving to social causes, thus the next step becomes ensuring that this trend in philanthropy becomes effectively fused with a measurable investment strategy.

## Conclusion

Of course, the impact investment space has much room to grow globally. It is a practice whose institutionalization is still in its infancy, which leaves much room for testing and honing of the model. Likewise, it has many sceptics. Concerns over adequate deal flow, estimated date of receiving a return on an investment, and trading off between social and financial return are several areas that have slowed the field's entrance into the mainstream. Research from Endeavor Insight suggests that social enterprises should prioritize financial goals over social ones in order to maximize both, yet more studies are needed to settle this debate.[23]

However, the near absence of this field in MENA needs to be addressed. Part of the process for developing impact investment in the region will also include a broader understanding of what can be accomplished through supporting entrepreneurs. Though many stakeholders have already zeroed in on the critical role new start-ups can play in fostering employment, the growing impact investment across the globe is also demonstrating how social enterprises can help in delivering solutions to other development challenges.[24] The same must become true in MENA, and the below recommendations and the proposed high-level framework can help to begin this exercise in sparking the impact investment agenda in the region.

## Recommendations

- *Mobilize the diaspora*: The MENA diaspora has a large role to play in fostering interest in impact investment regionally and, in general, expanding the perceived role of entrepreneurs in society. Though active in emerging markets, many of the largest impact investment institutions have headquarters in the United States and the European Union. The phenomenon of diaspora bringing back knowledge and resources to their home countries is common, with practices of the Indian diaspora serving as perhaps the best case study of how professionals can move abroad, gain knowledge and wealth, then carry it with them back to their home country. Similarly, in interviews, several experts pointed to countries such as India and Kenya, both of which have a lot of impact investment activity, as areas where many diaspora or expatriates have relocated to start companies and investment funds.

So many people in the Diaspora with backgrounds in investment banking, venture capital and private equity as well as new technology are bringing back ideas to the region that they have been inspired by and trying to apply them to develop the social sector.

(Myrna Atalla, Alfanar, Arab Venture Philanthropy
Organization)

Many professors, consultants, investors, and entrepreneurs from MENA have worked or studied in western countries. In doing so, they have been exposed to new technologies, business models, partnerships, and investment strategies. Bringing new approaches to development challenges, with impact investment being among them, could be one direct output of tapping into the knowledge of MENA's diaspora.

- *Increase research and knowledge sharing*: Studying current social enterprises and demonstrating their financial, social, and environmental outputs can help build a knowledge base around impact investing in MENA. More knowledge exchange, through media, networking events, or advocacy between social enterprises, investors, and even corporations can help to clarify needs and interests from each side. These efforts must also involve careful analysis and understanding of how the social and for-profit agendas can merge. If done strategically, doing so will also have an advocacy function as such research can be used to inform policymakers and other decision-makers to allocate resources to support this field.
- *Adopt a gradual approach*: Any individual or institution looking to enter the impact investment space in MENA, as an investor, entrepreneur, or other stakeholder, should start small and build gradually. Introducing too large a fund or attempting to invest in too much infrastructure early on could do more harm than good. Though there is a pipeline of viable investments developing, it is still young and many would argue that these companies are not investment ready. Workshops, information sessions, media articles, and case studies are low-cost tools that can be used to create more knowledge around impact investing and build capacity of social enterprises, which can help to bolster the early-stage pipeline. Though more expensive, events and small competitions are also viable solutions for spurring awareness and interest in this field. Though creating funds is a crucial endeavour, without a pipeline of viable investment-ready enterprises, investors will have no business.
- *Focus on capacity building*: Anecdotally, many of the new up and coming social enterprises in MENA need mentorship, capacity building, and early-stage financing in order to develop them

to a condition wherein an impact investor could enter. Programmes such as Coach and Consult for a Cause in Dubai provides extensive workshops for social entrepreneurs to help build their capacities in developing communication strategies, business models, and board structuring among other areas. Similar models can help social enterprises work through the early-stage growing pains of getting their business up and running, in turn, helping them evolve to a state where investors would be able to become involved.

- *Do not look for a panacea*: Impact investment is by no means a panacea that will solve all socio-economic development challenges in MENA. It is indeed underused and under-represented in the region, yet if over-promoted, its natural role will not be realized. Supporting impact investment, like supporting entrepreneurship itself, must be part of a larger economic development agenda that includes public, private, and civil sector players and the unique services each brings to the table, both financial and non-financial. Incorporating impact investment into a grand development vision will not only allow it to fulfil its natural role, but also allow it to find symbiotic relationships with other components of the agenda.

Scholars and practitioners working to building entrepreneurial communities often point to a range of financing, support services, cultural, educational, and policy matters that are required to build thriving entrepreneurial ecosystems. Though impact investment is still a developing field globally, similar components and measures needed to build a healthy environment for entrepreneurship can be used for shaping good conditions for impact investment.

Based on the findings from interviews and literature review conducted for this chapter, the following high-level framework for enhancing the impact investment sector in MENA is suggested as a starting point for understanding where and how different players and resources can contribute to this space. Many players and resources are needed to grow, sustain, and scale impact investment in the region. As such, this framework is not intended to be inclusive, but it provides initial insight into what efforts will play key roles in this movement (Table 7.3).

*Table 7.3*  An initial framework for advancing impact investment in MENA

| Focus area | Key players | Details | Intended outcomes |
|---|---|---|---|
| Thought leadership | Research institutions, media, and investors | Research and media can help to promote the concept of impact investment, and investors can become more active in discussing the importance of this field. These efforts can help to better integrate impact investment principles into the mainstream | Increased exposure for impact investment and subsequently more investors and general supporters entering this field |
| Funding | Investors, foundations, and aid organizations | Current angel and venture capital investors in the region could be likely sources of impact investment in the near term. They can collaborate with and learn from the small population of impact investors in the region. In parallel, foundations and aid organizations can provide grant funding at the early stages of new funds to help them sustain | More risk capital is made available to profitable, scalable social enterprises while more funding is made available to sustain impact investment vehicles in the short term |
| Capacity building | Incubators and training organizations | To develop a pipeline of potential investments for impact investors in MENA, incubators and training institutions can help build the capacity of social enterprises in the region. By enhancing the skills of founders and their teams, these institutions can help them to become more investment-ready | Social entrepreneurs receive training in important competencies that will help them to better operate their companies and make their enterprises more attractive to investors |
| Policy | Research institutions, media, investors, incubators, foundations, and aid organizations | Policy reform and the creation of a regulatory system that is friendly to social enterprises and impact investment funds are a long-term process. Knowledge and resources from all relevant players will be needed to advocate for and shape policies that create a more supportive environment for this field | Creation of policies tailored to the needs of social enterprises and investors that protect funders and allow social entrepreneurs to operate in their countries |

## Appendix 1 Methodology

This chapter was compiled through conducting 21 interviews with impact investors, venture capital investors, social entrepreneurs, and institutions supporting social entrepreneurs in MENA. Additional data was gathered through desk research and insights collected from the Wamda Research Lab studies on regional trends in entrepreneurship development. Interview candidates were chosen based on a literature review of the institutions working in the impact investment field as well as references from impact investors and experts in this field. The following questions comprised the core topics explored during the interviews:

• What are the viable examples of impact investment in MENA?
• Why is impact investment not yet widely practiced in MENA?
• How have impact investment funds, communities, and general practices taken root in other regions?
• Are there certain indicators for when a country or region is favourable for impact investors?
• How can investors and other entrepreneurship stakeholders in MENA replicate these conditions?
• Does a population of venture capital funds need to precede the creation of impact investment funds?
• Should and how can MENA investors (i.e. angel and venture capital) evolve their strategies to include more impact investment?
• What currently available resources and knowledge in MENA can be leveraged to help to grow the region's impact investment sector?

Most of the questions were discussed during each interview, with some receiving more attention than others depending on the background and expertise of the interview participant. For instance, questions specifically focused on MENA are not as relevant to experts with experience in other regions, so other questions were used in those interviews.

## Notes

1. Koh, H., Karamchandani, A. and Katz, R. (2012). *From Blueprint to Scale: The Case for Philanthropy in Impact Investing*. Monitor Institute in collaboration with Acumen Fund and the Bill and Melinda Gates Foundation.

2. Saltuk, Y., Bouri, A., Mudaliar, A. and Pease, M. (2013). *Perspectives on Progress: The Impact Investor Survey*. J.P. Morgan and the Global Impact Investment Network.
3. Freireich, J. and Fulton, K. (2009). *Investing for Social and Environmental Impact: A Design for Catalyzing an Emerging Industry*. Monitor Institute.
4. Drexler, M. and Noble, A. (2013). *From the Margins to the Mainstream: Assessment of the Impact Investment Sector and Opportunities to Engage Mainstream Investors*. World Economic Forum in collaboration with Deloitte Touche Tohmatsu.
5. Numbers based on calculations from Wamda Research Lab MENA Entrepreneurship Mapping.
6. Wyne, J. (2014). *The Next Step: Breaking the Barriers to Scale for MENA's Entrepreneurs*. Wamda Research Lab.
7. Ambrose, E. (2012). *Impact of Endeavor Chile, and the Endeavor Multiplier Effect, Network Map of Buenos Aires Tech Sector (2013)*, Endeavor Insight.
8. O'Donohoe, N. and Brandenburg, M. (2010). *Impact Investment: An Emerging Asset Class*. J.P. Morgan, the Global Impact Investment Network and the Rockefeller Foundation.
9. O'Donohoe, N. and Brandenburg, M. (2010).
10. Saltuk, Y., Bouri, A. and Leung, G. (2011). *Insight into the Impact Investment Market: An In-Depth Analysis of Investor Perspectives and over 2,200 Transactions*. J.P. Morgan and the Global Impact Investment Network.
11. O'Donohoe, N. and Brandenburg, M. (2010).
12. Saltuk (2013).
13. Saltuk,Y., Bouri, A., Mudaliar, A. and Pease, M. (2013). *Perspectives on Progress: The Impact Investor Survey*. J.P. Morgan and the Global Impact Investment Network.
14. Bucknall, Julia (2007). *Making the Most of Scarcity Accountability for Better Water Management in the Middle East and North Africa*, MENA Development Report, World Bank.
15. Ramjin Jalilvand, D. (2012). "Renewable Energy for the Middle East and North Africa, Policies for a Successful Transition", *Friedrich Ebert Stiftung*.
16. International Diabetes Federation (2013).
17. Shehadi, R. et al. (2013). *The Rise of Corporate Social Responsibility: A Tool for Sustainable Development in the Middle East*. Booz & Company.
18. International Diabetes Federation, 2013.
19. Wyne, J. (2014). *The Next Step: Breaking the Barriers to Scale for MENA's Entrepreneurs*. Wamda Research Lab.
20. Wyne, J. (2014). *Enhancing Access: Assessing the Funding Landscape for MENA's Startups*. Wamda Research Lab.
21. Zidi, M. (2013). *Giving in Transition and Transitions in Giving: Philanthropy in Egypt, Libya and Tunisia 2011–2013*, John D. Gerhart Center for Philanthropy and Civic Engagement, American University in Cairo.
22. El-Gamal, M. (2014). *How to Unlock Arab Philanthropy*, McKinsey on Society – How We Give.
23. Rottenberg, L. and Morris, R. (2013). "If You Want to Scale Impact, Put Financial Results First", *Harvard Business Review*.

24. Ayyagari, M., Demirguc-Kunt, A. and Maksimovic, V. (2011). "Small vs. Young Firms across the World: Contribution to Employment, Job Creation, and Growth," Policy Research Working Paper Series 5631, The World Bank. See also: T. Kane (2010), "Firm Formation and Economic Growth, The Importance of Startups, in Job Creation and Job Destruction", Kauffman Foundation.

## Works cited

Ambrose, E. (2012). *Impact of Endeavor Chile, and the Endeavor Multiplier Effect, Network Map of Buenos Aires Tech Sector (2013)*, Endeavor Insight.

Ayyagari, M. Demirguc-Kunt, A. and Maksimovic, V. (2011). "Small vs. Young Firms across the World: Contribution to Employment, Job Creation, and Growth," Policy Research Working Paper Series 5631, The World Bank. See also: T. Kane (2010). *Firm Formation and Economic Growth: The Importance of Startups, in Job Creation and Job Destruction*, Kauffman Foundation.

Brandenburg, M. (2010). *Impact Investment: An Emerging Asset Class*. J.P. Morgan, the Global Impact Investment Network and the Rockefeller Foundation.

Bucknall, Julia (2007). *Making the Most of Scarcity Accountability for Better Water Management in the Middle East and North Africa*, MENA Development Report, World Bank.

Drexler, M. and Noble, A. (2013). *From the Margins to the Mainstream: Assessment of the Impact Investment Sector and Opportunities to Engage Mainstream Investors*. World Economic Forum in collaboration with Deloitte Touche Tohmatsu.

El-Gamal, M. (2014). *How to Unlock Arab Philanthropy*, McKinsey on Society – How We Give.

Freireich, J. and Fulton, K. (2009). *Investing for Social and Environmental Impact, a Design for Catalyzing an Emerging Industry*, Monitor Institute.

Han Cho, Nam and Whiting, David (2013). *International Diabetes Federation, Diabetes Atlas*, 6th Edition, International Diabetes Federation.

O'Donohoe, N. and Brandenburg, M. (2010). J.P. Morgan, the Global Impact Investment Network and the Rockefeller Foundation.

Ramjin Jalilvand, D. (2012). *Renewable Energy for the Middle East and North Africa, Policies for a Successful Transition*. Friedrich Ebert Stiftung.

Rottenberg, L. and Morris, R. (2013). "If You Want to Scale Impact, Put Financial Results First", *Harvard Business Review*.

Saltuk, Y., Bouri, A. and Leung, G. (2011). *Insight into the Impact Investment Market: An In-Depth Analysis of Investor Perspectives and over 2,200 Transactions*. J.P. Morgan and the Global Impact Investment Network.

Saltuk, Y., Bouri, A., Mudaliar, A. and Pease, M. (2013). *Perspectives on Progress: The Impact Investor Survey*. J.P. Morgan and the Global Impact Investment Network.

Shehadi, R. et al. (2013). *The Rise of Corporate Social Responsibility: A Tool for Sustainable Development in the Middle East*. Booz & Company.

Wyne, J. (2014a). *The Next Step: Breaking the Barriers to Scale for MENA's Entrepreneurs*. Wamda Research Lab.

Wyne, J. (2014b). *Enhancing Access: Assessing the Funding Landscape for MENA's Startups*. Wamda Research Lab.

Zidi, M. (2013). *Giving in Transition and Transitions in Giving: Philanthropy in Egypt, Libya and Tunisia 2011–2013*. John D. Gerhart Center for Philanthropy and Civic Engagement, American University in Cairo.

# Interviews

| Person | Institution | Country |
| --- | --- | --- |
| Amr Adly | Stanford University | United States |
| Ankur Shah | Acumen Fund | United Arab Emirates |
| Ben Matranga | Soros Economic Development Fund | United States |
| Cornelius O'Donnell | Mercy Corps | Egypt |
| George Khalaf | Synergos | United States |
| Hamed Masri | Sequence Labs | Jordan |
| Heather Henyon | Balthazar Capital | United Arab Emirates |
| Jim Villanueva | Eleos Foundation | United States |
| Kareem Elbayar | United Nations Development Program | Iraq |
| Muhammed Mekki | Astrolabs | United Arab Emirates |
| Myrna Atalla | Al Fanar Foundation | United Kingdom |
| Nadine Kettaneh | Willow Impact | United Arab Emirates |
| Nafez Al Dakak | Queen Rania Foundation | Jordan |
| Raghda El Ebrashi | Alashanek Ya Balady | Egypt |
| Rama Chakaki | Baraka Ventures | United Arab Emirates |
| Reem Khouri | Independent Consultant | Jordan |
| Sarina Beges | Stanford University | United States |
| Saurabh Lail | Aspen Network for Development Entrepreneurs | United States |
| Simon Winter | Technoserve | United States |
| Steven Haley | Mercy Corps | Egypt |
| Zina Sanyoura | Bamboo Finance | Switzerland |

# 8
# From Necessity to Opportunity: The Case for Impact Investing in the Arab World

*Ali El Idrissi*

### Introduction: The promise of impact investing

Impact investing refers to the practice of investing with a dual objective: generating positive social and/or environmental impact while also achieving a financial return.[1] Impact investments are often characterized by (i) the pursuit of an identified social and/or environmental impact, often with the view of benefiting an underserved or excluded segment of the population, (ii) the measure of the impact post-investment to be able to track progress, (iii) a longer term approach to the investment cycle (impact investing is also sometimes described as "patient capital"), and (iv) an innovative approach to structuring investments (impact investing is often considered part of a broader "innovative finance" field). Although there is still much debate around terms and definitions, the concept has gained considerable traction in recent years and moved to the centre stage of the discussion on how to tackle some of our most pressing challenges with limited, sometimes decreasing, resources.[2]

The power of impact investing resides in its potential to unlock significant amount of private capital and its promise to bring together and reconcile various perspectives and stakeholders, often deemed incompatible if not antagonistic, by moving beyond old-fashioned dichotomies opposing charity and business or non-profit and for-profit endeavours. In this new approach, investors, philanthropists, and governments are pioneering innovative partnerships and structures to support ventures (often referred to as social enterprises)[3] that use market-based tools to address social and/or environmental issues.[4] This support includes the provision of risk capital to social enterprises that have typically found it very challenging to attract funding to grow, but even most importantly it recognizes the need to build robust ecosystems that, beyond financial support, will enable those ventures to reach their full potential. In this respect, the growth of impact investing, which has been hailed as "the new venture capital",[5] should be viewed as intrinsically connected to the growth of social enterprises (we will refer to "social business" when designing both social entrepreneurship and impact investing). Appendix I provides some examples of and background information on leading impact investors.

For all its promise and appeal, impact investing is still a nascent industry with an elastic definition and a limited amount of market data. A number of recent studies estimated it at about US$40 billion of capital invested, a very small number compared to the US$62 trillion financial assets managed globally or the US$3.5 trillion managed by private equity firms.[6] Still, impact investing is growing, and a recent survey released by J.P. Morgan and the GGIIN of 125 leading impact investors found that this group was expected to commit 19 per cent more capital to impact investments in 2014 than in 2013. However, the report also highlighted significant disparities across regions. Indeed, while the majority of impact investments are directed to emerging markets, some regions such as the Middle East and North Africa (MENA)[7] are still under-represented and attract significantly less attention and capital than, for example, sub-Saharan Africa, Latin America, or South Asia.[8]

Growing an impact investing market in MENA can offer an opportunity to access vast untapped potential in the Arab World while contributing to tackling some of the most pressing needs in the region through innovative, market-based approaches. The MENA region displays the highest youth unemployment rate in the world, currently recorded at over 25 per cent, with North Africa reporting approximately 24 per cent.[9] At the same time, the rate of new business registrations in the region is one of the lowest in the world at 0.63 new firms per 1,000 people per year versus 1.31 for Latin

America and the Caribbean, 0.79 for South Asia, and 0.58 for sub-Saharan Africa (2004–2009 average).[10] The objective of this chapter is to explore the rise of impact investing globally and the reasons behind the under-representation of MENA, as well as identify some of the main challenges and opportunities to its growth in the region. The main thesis is that the current relatively low level of impact investments in MENA is not surprising as investment opportunities are still limited and the main conduits through which it developed in other regions are themselves underdeveloped in MENA. However, the current cultural shift and unprecedented momentum behind social business in the region can pave the way for vast opportunities to accelerate economic growth and social progress, if a robust and holistic ecosystem is built over the next decade. In doing so, market players and policymakers in MENA have a unique opportunity to leverage the region's assets, such as its various sources of capital, and need to work hard to reduce existing barriers to the growth of the market, including longstanding regulatory hurdles.

## The underlying trends supporting the emergence of impact investing globally

Although impact investing has gained significant momentum in recent years, it is important to note that its emergence is linked to underlying trends that have been and will likely be at play for many years. Demographic and economic trends have created opportunities to invest in emerging markets with rising middle classes. Technological advances have enabled to reach millions of customers in frontier markets with innovative and impactful business models, for example, increasing financial inclusion through mobile banking in sub-Saharan Africa. Investment trends have reflected the growing adoption of sustainability and development targets by investors, and social trends refer to the increasing discontent with the current economic growth model and the awareness around the role the private sector can and should play in tackling social and/or environmental issues. These trends are intertwined and help explain the increasing momentum behind impact investing. We describe and illustrate some of them in Table 8.1:

*Table 8.1*  Underlying trends supporting the emergence of impact investing

| Nature | Illustration |
|---|---|
| Demographic trends:<br>*Growth mainly in*<br>*developing countries* | • World's population expected to reach 9.1 billion people by 2050 and the growth being almost entirely attributable to less developed countries[11] |
| Economic trends:<br>*Re-balance and*<br>*emergence of middle*<br>*class in developing*<br>*countries* | • Emerging markets now accounting for about half of global GDP[12]<br>• Africa home to seven of the ten fastest growing economies today[13]<br>• Emergence of large middle classes in certain geographies<br>  • Asia Pacific expected to be home to two-thirds of the global middle class by 2030 (versus less than a third today)[14]<br>  • In Brazil, about 40 million people (the size of Argentina) joined the middle class between 2003 and 2011[15] |
| Technology trends:<br>*Technological advances*<br>*open new markets* | • Internet penetration growth rate of about 3,600 per cent in Africa between 2000 and 2012 (current penetration rate of 15.6 per cent of the population, largely below the world average of 34.3 per cent)[16]<br>• Proliferation of mobile phone subscribers in the developing world from 1 subscriber per 100 inhabitants in 1997 to 45 subscribers per 100 inhabitants in 2007.[17] Mobile phone subscriptions in sub-Saharan Africa have risen from 16mm in 2000 to 376mm in 2008[18] |
| Investment trends:<br>*Growth of sustainable*<br>*investing and*<br>*commercial*<br>*microfinance* | • Sustainable investing[19] growing at an annual rate of 11 per cent in the United States between 1995 and 2012[20] and estimated to represent, as of 2012, about US$14 trillion globally, accounting for 49 and 11 per cent of assets managed in Europe and the United States, respectively[21]<br>• Evolution of microfinance in the past decades from a donor-based model to a scalable commercial model attracting foreign investment<br>  • Between 2005 and 2007, foreign investments in microfinance increased fivefold and amounted to US$13 billion in 2010[22] |

*Table 8.1*  (Continued)

| Nature | Illustration |
|---|---|
| Social trends: *Necessity for private resources to complement governments and philanthropic resources and desire to target a more sustainable and inclusive model of economic growth* | • Development aid has decreased by 6 per cent in the past three years and is likely to remain under pressure with developed nations facing long-term budget challenges, highlighting the need for increased private sector contribution[23] <br> • Growing desire for a new economic growth model to tackle lasting challenges such as global inequalities (the bottom half of the global population owns less than 1 per cent of total wealth, the richest 10 per cent holds 86 per cent of total wealth, and the top 1 per cent alone accounts for 46 per cent of global assets)[24] <br> • Continuous debate about the limits of GDP as an indicator, with recent initiatives such as the Social Progress Index by Deloitte[25] |

At the global level, a thesis of opportunity (reflected by the long-term trends described above) has supplemented the thesis of necessity (the strains on current resources in the face of persisting social challenges). This dual thesis has combined with a shift in investor mindset, exacerbated by the recent financial crisis, to build significant momentum for impact investing.

The case for impact investing in the Arab World is supported by a similar dual thesis. The MENA region accounts for 6 per cent of the global population with 300 million people, of which about 23 per cent live on less than US$2 a day.[26] More than half of the MENA population is under 24, and the youth population is expected to reach 100 million people by 2035.[27] The average median age in the region is 25 years, which is well below the average of other emerging regions such as Asia (29 years) and Latin America and the Caribbean (28), and well below the average of developed countries.[28] A large portion of this young population is highly connected and the region displayed an Internet penetration growth rate of about 2,640 per cent between 2000 and 2012 (and a current penetration rate estimated at 40.2 per cent of the population, in line with the 43 per cent for Latin America and the Caribbean but largely above the 15.6 per cent for Africa and the 27.5 per cent for Asia).[29] This "demographic gift"[30] combines with a number of gaps and market failures that impact investing naturally targets and aims to fill. In addition to youth unemployment, we can highlight the very low participation of women in the labour force (the region's female labour force participation rate of 26 per cent is well below the 39 per cent rate in low and middle income countries),[31] the large funding gap for small- and medium-sized enterprises (SMEs, with estimates that more than half of them do not have access to credit or are in need of additional financing),[32] and underperforming education systems with school dropout rates that remain high in segments of populations in some countries (2007 estimates of nearly ten million illiterate youth in the region, with girls representing over two-thirds of that group).[33] The promise of impact investing in the region is to view such challenges as opportunities that can be addressed using market-based approaches.

## Spotlight on the current impact investing market

Given the young age of the impact investing industry and its remaining definitional challenges, there have been relatively few attempts to size the market in terms of the amount of capital committed. Table 8.2 below provides a summary of some of these attempts over the past few years.

The 2014 J.P. Morgan/GIIN survey of 125 leading impact investors provided, for the first time, detailed insight into asset allocation trends across regions, sectors, and financial instruments. The report, which features leading investors in the market like the Omidyar Network, the Bill & Melinda Gates Foundation, CDC, and LeapFrog Investments, found that respondents collectively managed US$46 billion of impact investments. These respondents expected to commit US$12.7 billion in 2014, up from US$10.6 billion committed in 2013, a 19 per cent increase. While 80 per cent of respondents were based in either the United States and Canada or Europe, 70 per cent of the capital was invested in emerging markets. As shown in Figure 8.1, the three main investment destinations for this sample were Northern America (22 per cent), Latin America (19 per cent), and sub-Saharan Africa (15 per cent), and the MENA region attracted only 2 per cent of the capital. The survey found that development finance institutions (DFIs)[34] managed 42 per cent of total assets, followed by fund

*Table 8.2*   Select market sizing reports on impact investing over the past few years

| Author | Year | Description |
|---|---|---|
| Monitor Institute | 2009 | Estimated that the impact investment market could potentially reach US$500 billion by 2020[35] |
| J.P. Morgan, The Rockefeller Foundation, and the GIIN | 2010 | Estimated a potential investment opportunity of between US$400 billion and US$1 trillion in the next decade[36] |
| Global Sustainable Investment Alliance | 2012 | Sized the global sustainable investment market at US$14 trillion, with impact investing less than 1 per cent at US$89 billion[37] |
| World Economic Forum (WEF) | 2013 | Published a first report of a series on impact investing where it sized the market at between US$25 billion and US$40 billion of capital committed globally[38] |
| J.P. Morgan and the GIIN | 2014 | Released a survey of 125 leading impact investors that collectively managed US$46 billion of impact investments[39] |

managers with 34 per cent of total assets, among a relatively well-diversified investor group also including foundations, banks, pension funds and insurance companies, as well as family offices. The survey also showed that microfinance and financial services accounted for about 40 per cent of respondents' impact investments and that a majority of the capital (68 per cent) was invested in private markets (44 per cent in private debt and 24 per cent in private equity).

## Why is MENA under-represented in impact investing?

The picture of the impact investing market drawn above highlights the leading role of international investors, particularly DFIs and fund managers, and how they invest predominantly in microfinance and financial services through private (debt and equity) instruments. While this survey does not claim to be fully representative of the

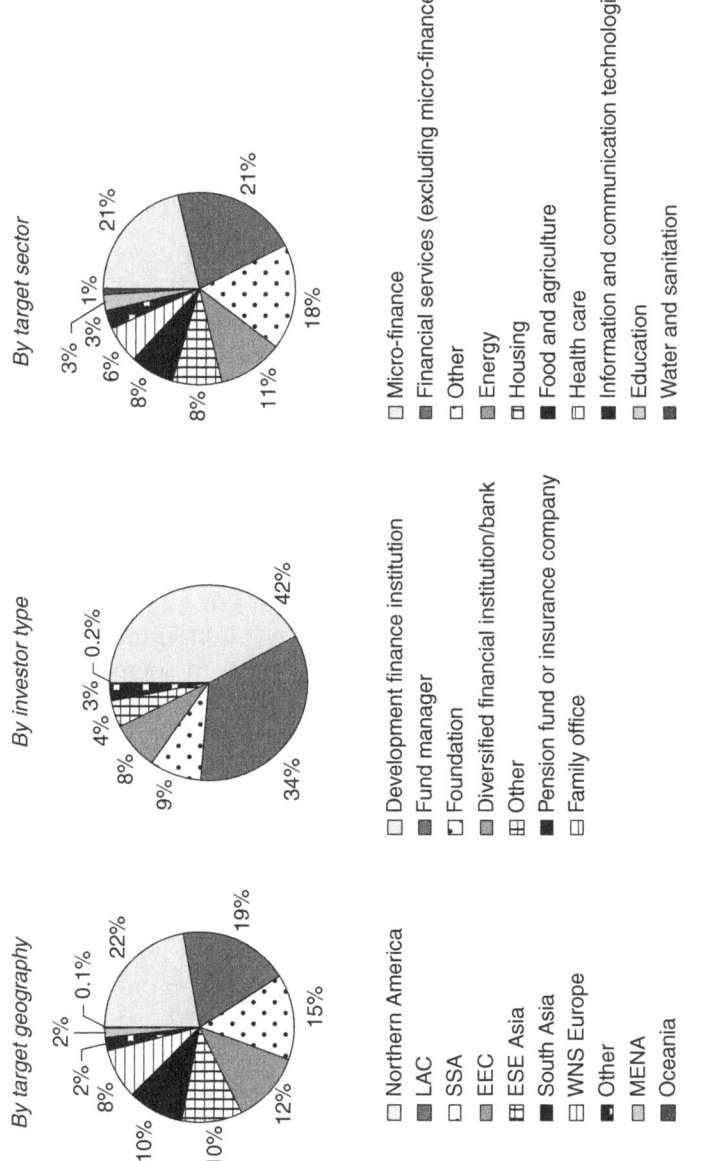

*Figure 8.1* Breakdown of impact investment assets under management[40]

*Note:* n = 124; AUM-weighted average; total AUM = US$46 billion.

*Source:* J.P. Morgan, GIIN, *Spotlight on the Market* (May 2014).

broader impact investing market, these indications provide a good starting point to explore the reasons behind the low percentage of impact investing capital currently allocated to MENA. Indeed, as described in more detail in Table 8.3, the region is characterized by a lower capital allocation from DFIs relative to other regions, a nascent venture capital industry and related small number of fund managers, and significant obstacles to investing in microfinance, which has been an essential stepping stone for many, if not most, impact investors.

In other words, because impact investing is often using existing conduits (such as sustainable investing, microfinance, and venture capital) that have been themselves underdeveloped in MENA, it is hardly surprising that the region attracts today only a small percentage of global impact investments. Importantly, this lower attention from investors also results from a lower availability of impact investment opportunities in the region when compared to other emerging regions. A recent report from the WEF analysed the number of companies that provided impact data to the GIIN and highlighted that while companies in this sample span multiple geographies, only 3 per cent came from MENA compared to 26 per cent from Latin America and the Caribbean; 25 per cent from South and East Asia and Pacific; and 22 per cent from sub-Saharan Africa.[41] The J.P. Morgan/GIIN survey also highlighted the difficulty for investors to source impact investment deals in MENA, as shown in Figure 8.2. Indeed, 47 per cent of the respondents actively considering MENA indicated that "None" of the opportunity they assessed passed their initial impact and financial screens, and 26 per cent said that "few" did, with only 26 per cent reporting that "many" or "some" did ($n = 38$). While, again, the survey does not claim to be fully representative of the whole market, it is telling to compare these results with responses for other emerging regions like Latin America and sub-Saharan Africa where, respectively, 64 and 53 per cent of respondents indicated that "many" or "some" of the opportunities they assessed in these regions passed their initial impact and financial screens ($n = 62$ and $n = 73$).

## Growing momentum for social business in MENA

For most people who grew up in MENA, it is easy to understand why entrepreneurship is so underdeveloped in most countries of the

*Table 8.3* Select explanation factors for the low level of impact investments in MENA

| Explanation factor | Illustration |
| --- | --- |
| Lower capital allocation from DFIs | • The International Finance Corporation (IFC), the private sector investment arm of the World Bank Group, had only 12 per cent of its portfolio allocated to MENA, as of June 2013, versus 33 per cent to Europe, Central Asia, and South Asia; 22 per cent to Latin America and Caribbean; and 16 per cent to sub-Saharan Africa[42]<br>• European DFIs, in aggregate and as of 2012, had 30 per cent of their portfolio invested in Africa, 27 per cent in Asia, 20 per cent in Central and South America, and only 8 per cent in the Mediterranean, North Africa, and Middle East[43] |
| Nascent nature of the venture capital industry and very low number of impact funds | • According to Walid Hanna, Managing Partner at Middle East Venture Partners, one of the first venture capital firms in MENA, "the number of venture capital firms [in the MENA region] is increasing but is still extremely low [...] the number of funds managed by venture capital firms is still very low"[44]<br>• On ImpactBase, an online database maintained by the GIIN and referencing almost 300 active impact investing funds, we currently find only three that include MENA as part of their regional focus[45] |
| Obstacles to investing in microfinance and resulting low level of foreign investment | • The MENA microfinance sector is still small and the vast majority of microfinance institutions (MFIs) in the region are still non-profit entities.[46] According to the World Bank, "Microcredit accounts for just 0.2 percent of the region's Gross Domestic Product. Lending by microfinance providers reaches only 1.8 percent of the adult population, half the rate of South Asia or Latin America and the Caribbean"[47]<br>• Foreign investment in the microfinance sector in MENA is constrained and the region represents only about 1 per cent of the capital invested by microfinance investment vehicles (MIVs) in 2012, versus 36 per cent for Latin America and Caribbean; 33 per cent for Europe and Central Asia; 20 per cent for East Asia, Pacific, and South Asia; and 7 per cent for sub-Saharan Africa.[48] According to MicroRate, "countries in the Middle East and North Africa continue to play no significant role in MIV microfinance portfolios (0.7%), a reflection of longstanding obstacles to investing in the region's microfinance sector and more recent instability following the Arab spring"[49] |

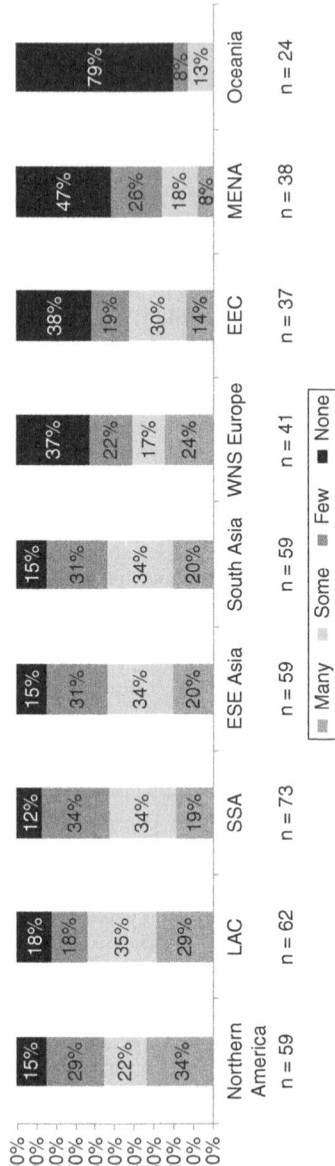

*Figure 8.2* Respondents' indications of the deals that passed initial impact and financial screens in markets they considered[50] Number of respondents for each region is shown below each bar; some respondents chose "did not consider investments in this region" and their responses are not considered here.

*Source*: J.P. Morgan, GIIN, Spotlight on the Market (May 2014).

region. Of course, as many will state, one form of entrepreneurship is abundant, the one that consist of quick fixes and sustaining businesses. But in societies so plagued with elitism and where upward social mobility rarely occurs and is never collectively celebrated, the non-privileged youth have too often been burdened by a deep sense of fatalism, hardly conducing to a desire to build the right skills and act on their aspirations. One Arabic word captures the essence of this, *hogra*, which can refer to the contempt for the small and vulnerable people, even when they are trying to grow. Not only have *hogra* and fatalism wasted vast amounts of potential, but they have often combined with a cultural celebration of secure jobs in the public sector or in large corporations, viewed as prestigious, and the lack of understanding and tolerance for constructive entrepreneurial failure. In short: the cultural opposite of an entrepreneurship and venture capital mindset.

For anyone who travels across and looks closely at the region now, it is also easy to sense the cultural shift and the unprecedented momentum behind entrepreneurship, including but not limited to social entrepreneurship. On the cultural front, there are signs of progress and real reasons for optimism. First, the region starts to benefit from a more strategic use of the power of storytelling. Success stories – such as Maktoob, the Arab/English online portal sold to Yahoo![51] or Souktel, the Palestinian job-matching company praised by the Gates Foundation and partly funded by George Soros and Jeff Skoll[52] – are increasingly spread and discussed, even if they remain limited in number. At least as important if not more, stories of failures and lessons learned are also increasingly shared. Platforms like Wamda, with its media coverage of entrepreneurship stories across the region, are playing a critical role in supporting this cultural shift.[53] Second, the region has seen a flurry of new initiatives promoting and supporting entrepreneurship in the past few years, with both new and existing programmes expanding their operations in the region. Some are focused on raising awareness and providing forums for entrepreneurs to meet mentors and investors, for example, through business plan competitions such as the Hult Prize, the MIT Enterprise Forum Arab Startup Competition, or the MIT Global Startup Workshop that, this year and for the first time, took place in a MENA country (the event was co-organized with OCP in Marrakech in March 2104).[54] Others have started or expanded their capacity-building operations, opening regional branches and expanding their programmes in the region such as Oasis500, a technology-focused incubator based in Jordan,[55] Flat6Labs, a Cairo-based accelerator expanding in Saudi Arabia and Abu Dhabi,[56] and international networks like Endeavor and Ashoka. In addition to these efforts, the increased involvement of figureheads such as Fadi Ghandour, chairman of Wamda and founder of the logistics company Aramex – established in 1982 in Jordan and the first Arab-based company to trade on NASDAQ in 1997 – is boosting and accelerating this necessary shift to a cultural acceptance and celebration of entrepreneurship. In the case of social entrepreneurship, there will need to be a progressive and consistent education of market players in MENA around the nature of social ventures and the benefits of blending commercial objectives with the pursuit of measurable impact targets. The opportunity (and challenge) for the region in this regard is twofold: it coincides with the broader movement around entrepreneurship and it addresses some of the most pressing social issues in the region. In this respect, it is interesting to note that in many start-up competitions in the region, ventures that have an explicit social mission make up for a significant portion of the businesses presented. This was the case, for example, at the 7th MIT Enterprise Forum Arab Startup Competition that took place in Cairo in May 2014, where prize categories also included "Business with the Best Social Impact" and the "Best Woman Entrepreneur".[57]

Beyond cultural barriers, some of the factors hindering the emergence of a thriving social business market in MENA are related to the low provision of capital (the supply side) and others to the low availability of investable opportunities (the demand side), as described above. To achieve significant and lasting progress in the region, there needs to be a more holistic approach to ecosystem building.

## The case of the UK social business market

One interesting case that could help inform this agenda is the emergence of a social business ecosystem in the United Kingdom over the past 15 years, which is arguably one of the most innovative and advanced today. In 2000, a Social Investment Taskforce (SITF) was formed at the request of the UK government and was chaired by Sir Ronald Cohen, the founder of Apax Partners – one of Britain's first venture capital firms – who has been acting as a figurehead for the social investment movement since then.[58] As Sir Ronald Cohen describes,

> the impetus was a concern on the part of the UK government that while standards of living were rising in society as a whole, the gap between rich and poor was increasing. I was asked to approach the whole issue from the perspective of a private equity investor and [...] to create a system to support business-like approaches to the scale and sustainability of social organizations that are trying to deal with massive social issues.[59]

Since 2000, the SITF and related initiatives in the United Kingdom adopted a holistic and innovative approach to ecosystem building, focusing on increasing both the supply of and the demand for social investment, as well as improving the overall environment for social investment, including through regulatory improvements.

Looking at the supply side, many studies show an annual social investment market size in the United Kingdom of between GBP150mm and GBP200mm, with a potential to reach GBP750mm by 2015.[60] The most groundbreaking initiative on the supply side was the creation of a social investment bank, Big Society Capital (BSC), which was launched by the UK Prime Minister David Cameron in April 2012 with a total funding potential of GBP600mm. Interestingly, GBP400mm come from UK dormant bank accounts, and a further GBP200mm come from Britain's four largest banks.[61] BSC provides funding exclusively to intermediaries, mostly fund managers investing in social businesses or channelling capital to philanthropic organizations, as opposed to investing in companies directly.[62] BSC generates a multiplier effect by stimulating the emergence of an intermediary market which has seen the entry of many new impact investing funds over the past few years.[63]

On the demand side, various estimates indicate that social enterprises contribute between 1.5 and 5 per cent of the UK GDP and employ 800,000 to a million people in the United Kingdom.[64] A number of initiatives have been launched to provide investment readiness and business capability support to these social ventures beyond the provision of finance itself. For example, the Cabinet Office within the UK government has launched a GDP10mm Social Incubator Fund to support incubators for social ventures, as well as a GBP10mm Investment and Contract Readiness Fund (ICRF), which is "the world's first fund dedicated to helping charities and social enterprises acquire the skills they need to raise investment and compete for public service contracts".[65] Since May 2012, 94 social ventures have received GBP8.9mm in grants to fund support services such as legal advice and financial management support.

In terms of improving the general environment for social investment, beyond the role the UK government is playing as a catalyst and a convener, a number of initiatives related to legal and regulatory barriers are being tackled. The most recent example is a 30 per cent tax relief for social investments, announced in March 2014 with the objective of encouraging retail investors to invest in this sector. It is expected to create up to GBP500mm in additional investment over the next five years.[66]

## Leveraging MENA assets to build an ecosystem beyond entrepreneurs

We can derive a number of considerations from the UK experience that could be discussed in the MENA context. First, it focuses on a holistic approach that goes beyond entrepreneurs to build the various layers of the ecosystem. Second, it highlights the importance of sequencing the various building blocks to ensure that supply, demand, and an enabling environment are developed in tandem (which is critical to avoid a prohibitive mismatch between supply and demand). Finally, it opens an interesting discussion on bold and innovative approaches to building the ecosystem – for example, using dormant bank accounts to fund a social investment bank – and leveraging country-specific assets – for example, the tax relief announced in the United Kingdom.[67]

There are signs that market players in MENA are already starting to adopt a more holistic approach to ecosystem building and to recognize that, despite the growing momentum for entrepreneurship and social business, there are still very limited amounts of high-quality investment opportunities and active financial partners, especially when compared to other emerging regions. While demand-side initiatives are increasing, there should be a focus on broadening and deepening the range of services provided to ventures as well as the scope of ventures supported. In an insightful research report released earlier this year, Wamda surveyed over 900 entrepreneurs and experts in MENA and identified four key barriers MENA entrepreneurs struggle with in growing their ventures: finding talent and building teams, access to finance, access to new markets, and marketing.[68] To tackle these barriers, an effective ecosystem should include but not be limited to events, business plan competitions, and community building (e.g. through provision of common working space). Capacity-building organizations should be equipped to provide high-quality business support (including design, financial management, intellectual property, marketing, and access to investors to name a few areas) and be properly staffed with experienced business people to deliver so. These initiatives should also gradually broaden their scope to support more ventures outside of the technology sector and ensure they do not focus only on the very small portion of ventures that are already investable and generating revenues, while early-stage ventures are those that need most help and support. In addition, there should be an increased focus on scaling ventures, especially those that need to reach enough volume to achieve a commercial scale attractive to impact investors. Increasing involvement in the region from organizations like Endeavor and Ashoka and initiatives like OCP Entrepreneurship Network in Morocco, where a large corporate like OCP can leverage its resources and play a champion role, are promising. On the supply side, while the emergence of a vibrant risk capital industry may still be a medium-term prospect, there are indications that the market is at a turning point, especially in the technology sector. Indeed, it is reported that three times as many technology investments took place in the 2010–2012 period than in the 2006–2009 period in MENA.[69] A recent important headline was the announcement of a partnership between Fadi Ghandour, through Wamda Capital, and the IFC to set up a US$75mm MENA venture capital fund which will provide funding between US$1mm and US$3mm to technology companies.[70] In a similar fashion, Cisco announced recently an investment alongside the European Investment Bank (EIB) and King Abdullah Fund for Development as an investor in the Badia Impact Fund targeted at early-stage technology start-ups in Jordan.[71] These initiatives on the demand and supply sides are encouraging and there should be a strong focus on building all the layers of the ecosystem, including stimulating a richer and more diversified supply side. The objective is to address the funding and business support needs of companies during their first few years and to fill the multiple gaps between accelerators and incubators, on the one hand, and established fund managers targeting proven and growing business models, on the other hand. A more challenging area is around the need to improve the environment for impact investments. The regulatory challenges to investing in microfinance have been discussed above, with still a large majority of microfinance institutions being non-profit organizations limited in the products they can offer. Legal and ownership challenges are also commonly emphasized in the case of ventures that want to expand in the region and face significant difficulties in finding partners and setting up affiliates.[72]

To accelerate the social business agenda, policymakers and market players in MENA should seize the opportunity to leverage assets specific to the region. More specifically, MENA is home to various sources of capital that could play strategic roles in the social business ecosystem. Philanthropic capital could play an important role in filling the early-stage gap and providing funding for investment-readiness programmes, exclusively targeted to early-stage ventures to help them get to a stage where they can receive more commercial funding. On the other hand, sovereign capital composed of sovereign wealth funds (SWFs) and development funds (DFs) could be leveraged to accelerate the emergence of an intermediary market. Table 8.4 describes in more detail the potential use of these capital sources for impact investments in MENA.

While these various sources of capital – foundations, large corporates, Islamic Finance, development funds and SWFs – have different primary objectives than supporting entrepreneurship in the region, they could be leveraged to stimulate specific parts of the ecosystem and could view their involvement as a strategic opportunity to act as pioneers and champions in building the market. If done with the right sequencing, ensuring that capacity is built gradually and across both the demand and supply sides, and with governments acting in parallel to reduce some of the most pressing regulatory barriers, such an agenda could pave the way for vast opportunities over the next decade.

## Conclusion: From necessity to opportunity

In other emerging regions, impact investing has often used existing conduits to grow, to a large extent out of foreign investments

*Table 8.4*  Leveraging philanthropic and sovereign capital for impact investments in MENA

| Nature of capital and objective | Opportunities and illustration |
|---|---|
| Philanthropic capital to fill the early-stage gap and catalyse the impact investing market: *Foundations, large corporates, and government-related entities* | • Opportunity for large philanthropic organizations and corporates to act as pioneers in providing catalytic capital, either directly to social ventures or by partnering with investment funds to de-risk their investments (e.g. through the use of guarantees)[73]<br>• A probably longer term perspective relates to the potential role of Islamic Finance and charity in impact investing. Indeed, it is reported that billions of dollars are raised annually through zakat, and many Islamic finance experts say a large part of it is mismanaged, disbursed with very little transparency and tracking of impact. A recent estimate put global Muslim charity at around US$200 billion, with more than half related to zakat, constituting a huge potential pool of capital that could be channelled towards business-oriented forms of development, including microfinance and SME funding[74]<br>• One precedent of using zakat for development outcomes was in 2007 in Egypt, where the Grand Mufti considered that a fundraising campaign to open 57357 Hospital, a new children's cancer hospital, would constitute legitimate zakat. The hospital, financed completely through donations, is now the second largest in the world dedicated to paediatric cancer care[75] |
| Sovereign capital to accelerate the emergence of an intermediary market: *SWFs and DFs* | • Opportunity to create a regional social investment bank which would play a similar role to the one BSC is playing in the United Kingdom<br>• With regard to SWFs, since 2007, the assets they control globally have risen from around US$2.2 trillion to more than US$5 trillion, with about 30 per cent in the hands of SWFs in MENA.[76] SWFs could be considered as natural candidates for impact investments as their mandate is to ensure prosperity for future generations and they have a longer investment horizon and more flexibility than other large institutional investors |

196

*Table 8.4* (Continued)

| Nature of capital and objective | Opportunities and illustration |
| --- | --- |
| | • Today, SWFs have low involvement in the market and as noted in a recent WEF study, "despite one-off examples, SWFs infrequently allocate capital to impact investment funds and products"[77] |
| | • However, SWFs are very active in certain areas close to impact investing like renewable energy as well as private equity. For example, Abu Dhabi-based Mubadala heavily invests in the renewable energy sector and is building Masdar City, the first low-carbon, low-waste sustainable city.[78] An interesting trend to note, given the importance of private (debt and equity) instruments in impact investing, is the reported increase in private equity allocations of MENA SWFs in the past few years, from 5 per cent in 2011 to 13 per cent in 2013, in order to diversify their portfolios[79] |
| | • With regard to development funds, it is worth noting that, as reported by the World Bank, "Arab donors, predominantly the Kingdom of Saudi Arabia (KSA), Kuwait and the United Arab Emirates (UAE), have been among the most generous in the world, with Official Development Assistance (ODA) averaging 1.5 percent of their combined gross national income (GNI) during the period 1973–2008, more than twice the United Nations target of 0.7 percent and five times the average of the OECD-DAC countries"[80] |
| | • Some of these funds, such as the Abu Dhabi Fund for Development (ADFD), have already pioneered innovative approaches to development and established investment portfolios that commit capital to both companies and funds internationally[81] |

in microfinance, private equity (and debt) investments, and venture capital. These conduits are, in many cases, less or underdeveloped in MENA, with the most obvious case being microfinance where foreign investment still plays a negligible role. However, there are increasing signs that a cultural shift supporting entrepreneurship, including social entrepreneurship, is taking place in the region. Beyond this cultural shift, a more holistic approach to ecosystem building is emerging through initiatives focused on increasing the supply of capital to entrepreneurs and supporting early-stage ventures to grow. An area that appears more challenging and that deserves special attention is the need to improve the regulatory framework for recipients of capital, whether they are microfinance institutions or early-stage ventures trying to expand regionally. In building a robust ecosystem for entrepreneurship and social entrepreneurship, market players and policymakers in MENA should leverage some recent experiences from abroad, notably the case of the United Kingdom. For instance, a groundbreaking initiative like the creation of a social investment bank for the MENA region could accelerate this agenda. A number of institutions in the region, from foundations to large corporates, development funds, and SWFs, have a significant opportunity to champion this market and play a pioneering role in its emergence.

The social business market will grow as a subset of the broader entrepreneurship ecosystem and movement and benefit from a more dynamic venture capital industry. Given the nascent stage of both fields and the pressing need to create jobs in the region, it is difficult, and not necessarily desirable, to draw a hard line between entrepreneurship and social entrepreneurship. The bigger opportunity is to embed a culture of social impact in all entrepreneurs, hence making entrepreneurship a more effective tool to respond to social challenges.

Like other emerging markets, MENA displays a number of challenges and barriers to the growth of social business. But equally important, the region is blessed with unique assets that, if properly leveraged, can create vast opportunities. While many commentators focus, and rightly so, on the shockingly high unemployment rates among youth and women and the low rate of new business creation what they are articulating is a thesis of necessity. They are telling us, rightly so, that there is a necessity to confront these issues and come up with appropriate solutions. But for a social business market to grow, for impact investors to allocate capital to the region, this thesis of necessity needs to be supplemented with a thesis of opportunity. This thesis of opportunity should better articulate the Arab story, with its emerging consumer class, its innovation potential, and its youth's growing aspirations and connectivity to the world.

## Appendix I – Select leading impact investors

All the below firms are members of the GIIN Investors' Council. The GIIN Investors' Council is a leadership group of active large-scale impact investors. Comprised of asset owners and asset managers with diverse interests across sectors and geographies, the Investors' Council provides a forum for experienced impact investors to strengthen the practice of impact investing and accelerate learning about new areas in the field (Table 8.5).

*Table 8.5*   Select leading impact investors

**Acumen**
Acumen invests patient capital in business models that deliver critical, affordable goods and services to the world's poor, improving the lives of millions. Since 2001, Acumen has invested more than US$85mm in enterprises that provide access to water, health, energy, housing, agricultural services, and education to low-income customers in South Asia and sub-Saharan Africa. Acumen was incorporated on 1 April 2001, with seed capital from the Rockefeller Foundation, Cisco Systems Foundation, and individual philanthropists. Headquartered in New York City, Acumen also has offices in Kenya, Pakistan, India, and Ghana

**Big Society Capital**
Big Society Capital Ltd (BSC) is an independent financial institution established in 2012 to develop and shape a sustainable social investment market in the United Kingdom. The overarching aim of BSC is to help frontline social sector organizations increase their social impact by improving their access to long-term, effective finance. BSC is financed with GBP400mm from the English share of dormant bank accounts (i.e. those that have been inactive for 15 years or more), which will be transferred to BSC as equity investment capital over four years. In addition, four banks – Barclays, HSBC, Lloyds Banking Group, and RBS – are each investing GBP50mm in BSC

## The Bill & Melinda Gates Foundation

The Bill & Melinda Gates Foundation works to help all people lead healthy, productive lives. In developing countries, it focuses on improving people's health and giving them the chance to lift themselves out of hunger and extreme poverty. In the United States, it seeks to ensure that all people – especially those with the fewest resources – have access to the opportunities they need to succeed in school and life. Based in Seattle, WA, the foundation is led by CEO Jeff Raikes and Co-chair William H. Gates Sr., under the direction of Bill and Melinda Gates and Warren Buffett

## Bridges Ventures

Started in 2002, Bridges Ventures, a UK-based investment company whose commercial expertise is used to deliver both financial returns and social and environmental benefits, has grown over the past eight years from an initial GBP40mm fund to about GBP150mm under management and with ambitions to hit GBP1 billion over the next few years, according to its founder and chairman, Sir Ronald Cohen. Sir Ronald launched Bridges Ventures after chairing the United Kingdom's Social Investment Task Force from 2000

## CDC

CDC is the United Kingdom's development finance institution, owned by the British Government's Department for International Development (DFID). CDC is a provider of scarce long-term capital to private sector entrepreneurs in developing countries and as such is one element of the U.K.'s endeavour to reduce poverty and help people prosper in the poorest countries in the world. CDC recently redefined its investment policy to embed development impact into its investment strategies. It supports building businesses and creating jobs and focuses on Africa and South Asia, especially the poorer regions

## FMO

Founded in 1970, FMO is the Dutch development bank. FMO supports sustainable private sector growth in developing markets by investing in ambitious entrepreneurs. FMO specializes in sectors where its contribution can have the highest long-term impact: financial institutions, energy, and agribusiness, food, and water. With an investment portfolio of EUR 6.3 billion, FMO is one of the largest European bilateral private sector development banks

## IGNIA

IGNIA is an impact investing venture capital firm based in Monterrey, Mexico, that supports the start-up and expansion of high-growth social enterprises serving the base of the socio-economic pyramid in Latin America. IGNIA empowers entrepreneurship and generates social impact with investments in health services, basic utilities, and education, while targeting market-rate financial returns for its investors. IGNIA has raised US$77mm of equity funding in addition to US$25mm raised for a credit facility from the Inter-American Development Bank

*Table 8.5*   (Continued)

---

**IFC**

The International Finance Corporation (IFC), a member of the World Bank Group, is the largest global development institution focused exclusively on the private sector. Established in 1956, IFC is owned by 184 member countries with offices in nearly 100 countries. IFC's vision is that people should have the opportunity to escape poverty and improve their lives. IFC addresses development challenges in emerging markets through direct investments and advisory services to firms. As of 30 June 2012, IFC had a committed portfolio of US$45.3 billion, and in fiscal year 2012 it invested 15.5 billion in 576 projects

**JPMorgan Chase & Co.**

JPMorgan Chase & Co. is a global financial services firm with assets of US$2 trillion. Operating in more than 60 countries, the firm is a leader in investment banking, consumer financial services, small business and commercial banking, financial transaction processing, asset management, and private equity

J.P. Morgan's Social Finance business was launched in 2007 to serve the growing market for impact investments in direct response to client interest and the increasing recognition that innovative business models can complement limited public sector and philanthropic resources by delivering market-based solutions to achieve sustainable and scalable social and environmental impact. The group publishes research to provide thought leadership to the market, commits J.P. Morgan capital to impact investments, and provides investment services to its clients

**LeapFrog Investments**

LeapFrog Investments is a profit-with-purpose fund manager with assets under management of US$135mm. It invests in high-growth companies in Africa and Asia that serve emerging consumers with financial tools, including insurance, savings, and mobile financial services. LeapFrog's fund targets top-tier returns alongside sustainable social impact, with its portfolio companies serving the vast untapped market of low-income people seeking affordable financial safety nets and springboards

**Lok Capital**

Lok Capital is a venture capital fund investing in enterprises serving the lower income and base of the pyramid (BoP) segments in India. Lok Capital has two funds with a combined corpus of almost US$90mm under management as of June 2012

With a focus on financial inclusion, education, health, and livelihoods, Lok Capital aims to promote inclusive growth by supporting the development of high-potential social enterprises that deliver basic services to the BoP in a scalable, affordable, and commercially viable manner

**Omidyar Network**
Omidyar Network is a philanthropic investment firm dedicated to harnessing the power of markets to create opportunity for people to improve their lives. Established in 2004 by eBay founder Pierre Omidyar and his wife Pam, the organization invests in and helps scale innovative organizations to catalyse economic and social change. To date, Omidyar Network has committed more than US$622 mm to for-profit companies and non-profit organizations that foster economic advancement and encourage individual participation across multiple initiatives, including entrepreneurship, financial inclusion, property rights, government transparency, consumer Internet, and mobile

**responsAbility**
responsAbility Investments AG is one of the world's leading independent asset managers specializing in the development-related sectors of emerging economies such as finance, agriculture, health, education, and energy. responsAbility provides debt and equity financing to non-listed companies with business models that target the lower income segment of the population and can thus drive economic growth and social progress

Founded in 2003, responsAbility currently has assets under management of over US$1.4 billion, invested in over 400 companies in around 80 countries. responsAbility is headquartered in Zurich and has offices in Paris, Lima, Mumbai, and Nairobi

**The Rockefeller Foundation**
The Rockefeller Foundation, a global philanthropic organization based in New York City, supports work that expands opportunity and strengthens resilience to social, economic, health, and environmental challenges. The Rockefeller Foundation realizes that there is not enough public and charitable capital to solve the world's social and environmental problems. In response, the foundation created a US$42 mm Harnessing the Power of Impact Investing initiative, as a complement to charity and government in an effort to bring social and environmental solutions to scale

**UBS**
UBS is a global financial services firm headquartered in Zurich and Basel, Switzerland. The UBS Group has four business divisions, including Wealth Management & Swiss Bank, which serves high net worth and ultra-high net worth individuals globally, as well as private and corporate clients in Switzerland. As of 2009, social investing, philanthropy, and strategic charitable services have been unified within the Wealth Management unit under a new dedicated Philanthropy & Values-Based Investing team

---

*Source*: GIIN and company website.

# Notes

The author is a member of J.P. Morgan Social Finance, a unit of the bank which was launched in 2007 to service the growing market for impact investments. The views and opinions expressed here are those of the author and do not necessarily represent the views or opinions of J.P. Morgan.

1. Impact investing is sometimes referred to as "social impact investing", "social venture capital", "double-bottom line investing", or "blended value investing", among other appellations.
2. Impact investments are defined by the Global Impact Investing Network (GIIN) as "investments made into companies, organizations, and funds with the intention to generate social and environmental impact alongside a financial return. They can be made in both emerging and developed markets, and target a range of returns from below market to market rate, depending upon the circumstances". The GIIN is an organization acting as a trade association for the impact investing sector and dedicated to building the infrastructure and increasing the effectiveness of impact investing. A more detailed discussion on definition can be available at http://www.thegiin.org/cgi-bin/iowa/resources/about/index.html.

    It is often useful to describe what impact investing is not to better framing the concept. Impact investing differs from charity, as it expects financial return. It overlaps with venture philanthropy in an active pursuit of impact but excludes those forms of venture philanthropy where return of principal is not expected or targeted. It often differs from sustainable investing (also called "socially responsible investing") by actively targeting the creation of positive impact (sustainable investing is generally associated with minimizing or avoiding negative impact).
3. We will use here the terms "organizations", "enterprises", and "ventures" interchangeably, unless specified. We will use "social organization", "social enterprise", and "social venture" to designate both social and/or environmental focus.
4. Although it is important to note that the scope of impact investing is not limited to supporting social enterprises.
5. Sir Cohen, R. and Sahlman, William A. (January 2013). "Social Impact Investing Will Be the New Venture Capital", *Harvard Business Review*.
6. Boston Consulting Group (BCG) (July 2013). *Global Asset Management 2013: Capitalizing on the Recovery* and Preqin (February 2014). *2014 Preqin Global Private Equity Report.*
7. In this chapter, we will use interchangeably MENA, Arab World, and Middle East to refer to the Middle East and North Africa region.
8. J.P. Morgan and the Global Impact Investing Network (GIIN) (May 2014). *Spotlight on the Market.*
9. IFC and the Islamic Development Bank (April 2011). *Education for Employment: Realizing Arab Youth Potential.*
10. World Bank/Kauffman Foundation data, accessed through the Early Stage Innovation Financing (ESIF) Facility draft document, available at http://

inforesources.assystuc.com/infodevfiles/resource/InfodevDocuments_
1203.pdf.

11. IMF. *Global Demographic Trends 2006*, available at http://www.imf.org/
external/pubs/ft/fandd/2006/09/picture.htm.
12. The Economist (July 2013). "When Giants Slow Down".
13. The Economist (December 2011). "Africa Rising".
14. Ernst & Young (April 2013). "Hitting the Sweet Spot".
15. FGV/CPS (March 2012). "Back to the Country of Future: European Crisis,
Forecasts and the New Middle Class in Brazil" and World Bank (November
2012). "In Brazil, an Emergent Middle Class Takes Off".
16. World Internet Usage and Population Statistics (2012) available at http://
www.internetworldstats.com/stats.htm.
17. World Bank Database.
18. *Journal of Economic Perspectives, Mobile Phones and Economic Development
in Africa*, 24, Summer 2010.
19. The World Economic Forum notes that

> socially responsible investing typically refers to the screening of
> investments that may have some sort of negative impact to society or
> to the environment (negative screen). On the other hand, sustainable
> investing refers to the active incorporation of ESG criteria into the
> investment decision (positive screen); sustainable investing priori-
> tizes financial returns above social or environmental returns. While
> certainly impactful, these activities are not "impact investing" by def-
> inition given that they do not intentionally and explicitly set out
> to deliver the dual objective of social/environmental outcomes and
> financial returns.

20. US SIF Foundation's 2012 Report on Sustainable and Responsible Investing Trends.
21. 2012 Global Sustainable Investment Review.
22. The evolution of the microfinance industry has been extensively docu-
mented. See Deutsche Bank, *Microfinance in Evolution*, September 2012.
23. OECD (March 2013). Aid to poor countries slips further as governments tighten budgets, available at http://www.oecd.org/dac/stats/
aidtopoorcountriesslipsfurtherasgovernmentstightenbudgets.htm.
24. 2013 Credit Suisse Wealth Report, available at https://www.credit-suisse.
com/ch/en/news-and-expertise/research/credit-suisse-research-institute/
news-and-videos.article.html/article/pwp/news-and-expertise/2013/10/
en/global-wealth-reaches-new-all-time-high.html.
25. Available at http://www.socialprogressimperative.org/data/spi.
26. World Bank MENA Overview, available at http://web.worldbank.org/
WBSITE/EXTERNAL/COUNTRIES/MENAEXT/0,,menuPK:247619~page
PK:146748~piPK:146812~theSitePK:256299,00.html.
27. Education for Employment (September 2012). *Arab Youth and Businesses
Partner for Growth*.

28. World Economic Forum (October 2011). *Arab World Competitiveness Report 2011–2012.*
29. World Internet Usage and Population Statistics (2012) available at http://www.internetworldstats.com/stats.htm.
30. World Bank (2004). *Unlocking the Employment Potential in the Middle East and North Africa: Toward a New Social Contract.*
31. World Bank (April 2010). *Middle East and North Africa: Women in the Workforce.*
32. See McKinsey & Company (May 2013). *SME Banking Opportunity in MENA.*
33. Population Reference Bureau (April 2007). *Youth in the Middle East and North Africa: Demographic Opportunity or Challenge?*
34. Overseas Development Institute (January 2011). *Comparing Development Finance Institutions.* DFIs are government-backed entities in developed countries that invest in viable private businesses in poorer developing countries to contribute to economic growth that benefits the poor. The ten largest DFIs are the International Finance Corporation (IFC), the European Bank for Development and Reconstruction (EBRD), the European Investment Bank (EIB), the African Development Bank (AfDB), Investment and Promotion Company for Economic Cooperation, France (Proparco), German Investment Corporation (DEG), Netherlands Development Finance Company (FMO), Inter-American Development Bank (IADB), CDC Group plc UK (CDC), and Asian Development Bank (ADB).
35. Monitor Institute (January 2009). *Investing for Social and Environmental Impact.*
36. J.P. Morgan, the Rockefeller Foundation and the Global Impact Investing Network (GIIN) (November 2010). *Impact Investments, an Emerging Asset Class.*
37. Global Sustainable Investment Alliance (January 2013). *2012 Global Sustainable Investment Review.*
    We should note here that this US$89 billion number includes US$61 billion of investments made by community development finance institutions (CDFIs) in the United States. CDFIs were established in the United States following the Riegle Community Development and Regulatory Improvement Act of 1994. Some analysts exclude CDFIs from the impact investing market given their reliance on significant subsidy through government grants and tax credits.
38. World Economic Forum (September 2013). *From the Margins to the Mainstream Assessment of the Impact Investment Sector and Opportunities to Engage Mainstream Investors.*
39. J.P. Morgan and the Global Impact Investing Network (GIIN) (May 2014). *Spotlight on the Market: the Impact Investor Survey.*
40. Region codes used for this graph are as follows: Northern America (United States and Canada), WNS Europe (Western, Northern, and Southern Europe), Oceania (Oceania), SSA (sub-Saharan Africa), LAC (Latin America and Caribbean including Mexico), South Asia (South Asia), ESE Asia (East and Southeast Asia), MENA (Middle East and North Africa), EEC (Eastern

Europe, Russia, and Central Asia). Total impact investment assets under management represents 124 respondents, due to one respondent not providing this data in the survey.

41. World Economic Forum (September 2013). *From the Margins to the Mainstream Assessment of the Impact Investment Sector and Opportunities to Engage Mainstream Investors.*

42. IFC, Annual Report 2013.

43. EDFI Annual Report 2012.

44. See Walid Hanna presentation as part of the CFA Institute Middle East Investment Conference in Dubai, March 2013, available at http://blogs.cfainstitute.org/investor/2014/01/27/emerging-trends-in-private-equity-and-venture-capital-in-mena-video/.

45. While this is probably not an entirely fair reflection of these funds' focus on MENA, given a number of them would put MENA under their "global" focus, or "Africa" focus, it does illustrate the under-representation of the region among fund managers. ImpactBase is available at http://www.impactbase.org/.

46. Microfinance Information Exchange (March 2011). *2010 Arab Microfinance Analysis & Benchmarking Report.*

47. McConaghy, P. (August 2013). A Boost for Microfinance in the Arab World, World Bank blog.

48. MicroRate (November 2013). *The State of Microfinance Investment 2013.* Microfinance investment vehicles (MIVs) are independent investment entities with more than 50 per cent of their non-cash assets invested in microfinance and which are open to more than one investor.

49. MicroRate (November 2013). *The State of Microfinance Investment 2013.*

50. Region codes used for this graph are as follows: Northern America (United States and Canada), WNS Europe (Western, Northern, and Southern Europe), Oceania (Oceania), SSA (sub-Saharan Africa), LAC (Latin America and Caribbean including Mexico), South Asia (South Asia), ESE Asia (East and Southeast Asia), MENA (Middle East and North Africa), EEC (Eastern Europe, Russia, and Central Asia).

51. See Wamda (October 2013). *The Story of Yahoo's Acquisition of Maktoob,* available at http://www.wamda.com/2013/10/case-study-yahoo-acquisition-maktoob.

52. See Higgins, C. (December 2013). 6 Ways Cell Phones Are Changing the World, available at http://www.impatientoptimists.org/Posts/2013/12/6-Ways-Cell-Phones-Are-Changing-the-World-Beyond-the-Ways-Youre-Probably-Thinking and Forbes (December 2012). *Billionaire-backed Palestinian VC Fund Sadara Invests in Mobile Job-Matching Firm Souktel,* available at http://www.forbes.com/sites/kerryadolan/2012/12/18/billionaire-backed-palestinian-vc-fund-sadara-invests-in-mobile-job-matching-firm-souktel/.

53. See www.wamda.com.

54. Office Chérifien des Phosphates (OCP) is the national Moroccan phosphates company and the world's largest exporter of phosphates. See www.ocpgroup.ma.

55. See www.oasis500.com.
56. See www.flat6labs.com. Flat6Labs was created and funded by Sawari Ventures, a Cairo-based private equity firm.
57. See http://www.mitarabcompetition.com/the3tracks.php.
58. See www.socialinvestmenttaskforce.org and Social Investment Taskforce (April 2010). *Social Investment: Ten Years On.*
59. See available at http://evpa.eu.com/wp-content/uploads/2011/06/Interview-with-Sir-Ronald-Cohen.pdf.
60. See Big Society Capita (October 2013). *Social Investment Compendium* and Boston Consulting Group (September 2012). *The First Billion: A Forecast of Social Investment Demand.*
61. See available at http://www.bigsocietycapital.com/ and http://www.theguardian.com/society/2012/apr/04/david-cameron-big-society-fund. On dormant bank accounts, see http://www.theguardian.com/money/shortcuts/2012/apr/04/dormant-accounts-big-society-capital. In the United Kingdom, an account is declared dormant after a bank or building society has failed in attempts to contact the holder; legislation came into force in 2009 allowing the government to use money that has been untouched for at least 15 years (but this money can still be reclaimed by the owner). It is also interesting to note that while BSC was launched by the government, it is now independent from the government.
62. Big Society Capital, Social Investment: From Ambition to Action, Annual Review 2013. During 2012 and 2013, its first two years of operation, BSC committed GBP149mm investment across 20 social finance intermediaries, and this comes as matching funds (meaning these funds need to raise funding from other investors to receive BSC funding, which helps to align incentives).
63. Many impact investing funds have now been launched in the United Kingdom, in some instances with the support of BSC. Some of the most established include Bridges Ventures, Nesta Impact Investments, The Social Investment Business, LGT Impact Ventures UK, Esmée Fairbairn Foundation Finance Fund, and Big Issue Invest.
64. See HM Government (February 2011). *Growing the Social Investment Market* and Social Enterprise UK (June 2013), available at http://www.socialenterprise.org.uk/news/the-social-apprentice-campaign-launched.
65. See HM Government (June 2013). *Growing the Social Investment Market, 2013 Progress Update* and see SIB Group Press Release (April 2014). *World-leading Fund Helps Charities and Social Enterprises Win Multi-Million Pound Deals.*
66. Budget 2014, HM Treasury, and Big Society Capital Press Release (March 2013). *Big Society Capital Welcomes the Chancellor's Commitment to Introduce Tax Incentives for Social Investment.* For a broader update on government initiatives to support social investments, see J.P. Morgan and the GIIN (May 2014). *Spotlight on the Market*, p. 19.
67. The UK tax relief is very specific to the United Kingdom as it builds off of existing investment schemes for UK retail investors.

68. Wamda Research Lab (March 2014). *The Next Step: Breaking Barriers to Scale for MENA Entrepreneurs.*
69. *Wall Street Journal* blog (March 2014). *As Arab Startups Get More Serious, So Too Does VC Investment* and Sindibad Business (December 2012). *MENA Internet and Technology Investment Report for 2012.* In addition, according to MENA Private Equity Association Third Venture Capital in the Middle East & North Africa Report, 2013, 47 per cent of the deals completed in the past three years were in the technology sector.
70. *Wall Street Journal* blog (March 2014). *IFC, Aramex Founder to launch VC Fund for MENA Tech Startups.*
71. Cisco Press Release (March 2014). *Cisco Announces First Venture Capital Funding Allocation in Jordan to Badia Impact Fund.*
72. Wamda Research Lab (March 2014). *The Next Step: Breaking Barriers to Scale for MENA Entrepreneurs.*
73. For a discussion on the use of catalytic capital in impact investing, see GIIN (October 2013), *Catalytic First Loss Capital.*
74. *Bloomberg Business Week* (April 2014). *Charity Begins at Home* and IRIN (June 2012). *A Faith-based Aid Revolution in the Muslim World?* The obligatory zakat is 2.5 per cent of an individual wealth.
75. IRIN (June 2012). *A Faith-based Aid Revolution in the Muslim World?* See www.57357.com.
76. KPMG (May 2013). *Emerging Trends in the Sovereign Wealth Fund Landscape* and McKinsey (2012). *A Growing Role for Sovereign Wealth Funds.*
77. World Economic Forum (September 2013). *From the Margins to the Mainstream, Assessment of the Impact Investment Sector and Opportunities to Engage Mainstream Investors.*
78. www.masdar.ae. Abu Dhabi is also home to the International Renewable Energy Agency (IRENA).
79. Invesco Middle East Asset Management Study 2013 and *Financial Times. Middle East Sovereign Wealth Funds Bypass Private Equity,* May 2013.
80. World Bank (September 2010). *Forty Years of Development Assistance from Arab Countries.*
81. Abu Dhabi Fund for Development, Annual Report 2012.

# 9
# Arab Diasporas: A Catalyst for the Growth of Social Ventures in the Middle East?

*Irene Kapusta*

## Introduction

Social enterprises are full of economic and social promise for the Middle East. Social entrepreneurship raises hopes in difficult times for the Arab World. The Middle East and North Africa (MENA) region suffers from the highest unemployment rate worldwide (ILO, 2014). Egypt is undergoing a severe economic crisis (World Bank, 2014). While 2.5 million refugees have fled Syria to neighbouring countries and North Africa, 6.5 million have been internally displaced in March 2014 (OCHA, 2014). Iraq, under reconstruction, has been plunged into chaos by ISIS.

The potential impact of social ventures in the region is commensurate with the scale they can reach. Yet scaling (as opposed to starting or institutionalizing) is "the most challenging development phase for entrepreneurs in the MENA region" (Wamda Research Lab, 2014).

Locally, mentorship and funding opportunities for social ventures in the Middle East are limited. Could Arab diasporas be instrumental in unlocking the growth potential of social enterprises in the region?

In the past few years, attention to diasporas surged globally. Diaspora members are, if not courted, at least targeted by governments, non-profits, and businesses. The latter seek to leverage diasporas' financial resources (investments or donations), and to a limited extent their time, knowledge, and network (through repatriation or remote support). Diasporas are no more (or rather not only) seen as a missed opportunity (brain drain) and dismissed as a political threat. Their idealization of the country of origin or ancestry, sense of responsibility, knowledge of the businesses environment, connections, skills, and wealth are true assets.

Notwithstanding, large-scale diaspora mobilization is complex – in any country. Diaspora individuals reside abroad and their time and resources are limited. Gaining diaspora trust is a challenge. In addition, diaspora members differ in many ways, not least through emigration context, diaspora generation, country of residence, level of integration, homeland links, age group, income, and education. Diaspora heterogeneity results in different motivations, involvement options, and possible communication channels.

Globally, diaspora participation in development is a historical, spontaneous phenomenon (Agunias and Newland, 2012). Already in the late 19th and early 20th centuries, the Lebanese diaspora contributed to the modernization of Lebanon, among others via remittances (Khater, 2001). Arab diaspora individuals and organizations still actively support their countries of origin. Worldwide, active diaspora courting began in the 20th century and took off this century. Yet few attempts to rally Arab diasporas succeeded on a large scale.

Are diasporas a missed opportunity in the Middle Eastern social entrepreneurship space? What kind of engagement model should be established between Arab diasporas and social ventures in the region in the near future?

## Definitions and scope

Diaspora definitions abound. Most are far from the classical Babylonian concept – implying forced migration. In this chapter, "diaspora" will be understood in a broad sense: "Emigrants and their descendants who live outside of the country of their birth or ancestry, either on a temporary or permanent basis, yet still maintain affective and material ties to their country of origin" (IOM, 2012, p. 15). This choice (especially the inclusion of multiple diaspora generations) is rooted in pragmatism and utilitarianism rather than in theoretical debates. Contribution to the social entrepreneurship movement in the Middle East is likely to rally those who never set a foot there, are deprived of their citizenship, and others. Undoubtedly, the IOM diaspora definition excludes many expatriates and descendants who are disconnected from their country of origin or descent. Yet the significance of the Arab diaspora population is evidenced by remittances representing 6 per cent of GDP in the countries studied – namely, Egypt, Lebanon, Jordan, Syria, Palestine, Iraq, and Yemen (World Bank, UN Data, see Table 9.2).

In this chapter, a "social enterprise" will be defined as an organization – whether registered as a business or as a non-profit – that pursues a social mission and is financially self-sustaining. Social enterprises that are in their infancy (which form the vast majority of social enterprises in the Middle East) will be depicted as social ventures or social start-ups.

Although the focus of this book is on social entrepreneurship, this chapter largely refers to the development and business spheres. Globally and in the Arab World, the social economy is embryonic. Diaspora mobilization has been experimented with for homeland development and more recently for start-ups and SME growth in countries of origin or descent. Social enterprises are at the crossroads between non-profits and regular commercial businesses. Lessons can be learnt from (tentative and actual) diaspora engagement by governments, international organizations, non-profits, and start-ups.

This chapter focuses on the Middle East. Yet it will leave aside non-Arab countries of the region, namely, Turkey, Iran, and Israel – as they do not share Arab culture. The chapter also excludes GCC countries. In the latter, nominal GDP per capita exceeds US$20,000, while other Arab Middle Eastern countries (Egypt, Lebanon, Jordan, Syria, Palestine, Iraq, and Yemen) show nominal GDP per capita below US$10,000 (World Bank, 2012). In the GCC, the high level of development and government budget limit the relevance of diaspora mobilization in the social enterprise sphere – all the more as diaspora communities from Gulf countries are minor in size. Throughout the chapter, "Middle East" and "Arab" will refer to the seven countries listed above: Egypt, Lebanon, Jordan, Syria, Palestine, Iraq, and Yemen.

Limitations of this chapter mostly concern the data gap on Arab diasporas and on diaspora engagement in the Middle East, as well as the multinational geographical scope of the book (i.e. the heterogeneity of Arab diasporas and countries).

## "Arab diaspora" landscape

Each diaspora is singular. Based on Cohen's well-known diaspora model, Arab diasporas fall into different categories (Cohen, 2008). For example, the Palestinian diaspora is what Cohen describes as a "victim" diaspora fighting for an existential cause and a state while the Lebanese diaspora is considered as a "trade" diaspora, fruit of a long tradition of emigration, vast and dispersed. Combined with diaspora singularity, the variety of country contexts excludes a one-fit-for-all diaspora strategy.

Arab diasporas are far from forming a single diaspora. Notwithstanding, they are united by a pan-Arab sense, evidenced by the existence of pan-Arab diaspora groups and networks, not least in business (e.g. Arab Bankers Association of North America), academia (like the Columbia University Middle Eastern [student] Discussion Group in the United States), and arts and culture (e.g. Club Sirio Libanes in Argentina). The language (despite dialects) and culture that bind Arab diaspora individuals nationally also tie them to other Arab diasporas, hence, for example, a feeling of belonging to an "Arab-American community" in the United States (Rignall, 2006). Diaspora engagement models relevant in one country seldom make sense in others. However, some approaches are relevant across Arab diasporas. This chapter seeks to identify them.

As noted by Cohen (2008), literature on diasporas has much developed since the mid-1990s. Diaspora research has mushroomed in the form of new entities (e.g. Migration Policy Institute – MPI, International diaspora Engagement Alliance – IdEA) and within existing organizations (such as the World Bank, Calvert Foundation, and Ashoka). Yet literature remains thin on Arab diasporas and Arab diaspora engagement.

If the diaspora data deficit is a worldwide issue (Agunias and Newland, 2012), it is particularly acute in the Middle East. Contradictions abound. Lebanese diaspora estimations fluctuate between 3 and 17 million (including descendants). The variety of definitions of the term "diaspora" certainly does not help. Estimations by countries of residence (including organizations like OECD) are limited in geographic scope, do not necessarily take into account dual citizens, and usually encompass first-generation diaspora only (excluding descendants). They largely underestimate diaspora sizes.

Statistics by countries of origin – if any – are inconsistent. For example, estimations of the number of Jordanian workers in the Gulf by the Jordanian Ministry of Labour and the Jordanian Department of Statistics show a 300 per cent discrepancy (2008). In Lebanon, the last national census dates back to 1932.

Arab diasporas are scattered. While migration to Middle Eastern countries (including the Gulf) is usually considered as "temporary", Arab migrants to Latin America started settling in the 19th century and form a long-standing community. North America, Europe, and Australia were and still are major destination countries.

Arab diasporas have formed various formal and informal groups – including academic, professional, cultural, and religious networks and organizations.

Even though this chapter refers to examples across seven Middle Eastern countries, particular attention will be dedicated to Lebanon, given the availability of literature on its diaspora. Such literature owes much to the demographic importance of the Lebanese diaspora community (relatively to the country population) and to the substantial number of Lebanese diaspora initiatives (Table 9.1).

## Diaspora involvement in development and business in the Middle East

Social entrepreneurship in the Middle East is a novel phenomenon mostly unexplored by Arab diasporas. However, the latter have been involved in the development and business spheres in their countries of origin, although research on the topic is scarce.

### Spontaneous diaspora contribution for development

In the Middle East, diaspora contribution in development remains largely out of control of governments and philanthropic entities. It mostly takes the form of remittances to relatives. Overall, remittances in the seven countries studied amount to US$37 billion (World Bank, 2012; see Table 9.2), without taking into account unofficial diaspora transfers and in-kind support. Gulf countries are a major source of remittance to Arab countries. Diaspora remittances are so sizeable that Middle Eastern governments depend and count on them economically (Sirkeci, Cohen and Ratha, 2012). Jordan and Lebanon

*Table 9.1* Promising diaspora, challenging engagement: the Lebanese example

---

The Lebanese diaspora is an extreme case on the international stage in terms of both complexity and potential support

Lebanon has been an emigration country for centuries. Its diaspora is "near to global" (Tabar, 2009, p. 33), dispersed across the Americas, Europe, Africa, the Gulf, and Oceania. Lebanese diaspora profiles vary tremendously – especially through diaspora generation, level of integration, and socio-economic status. Given religious divisions and the sectarian distribution of powers in Lebanon, any diaspora involvement threatens to overwhelm the political balance, hence the past state negligence towards the Lebanese diasporas. "Many Lebanese have lost their citizenship [...] or their property while abroad" (Brand, 2007, p. 10). The Lebanese diaspora created multiple groups and societies abroad – many of them with religious and political affiliations. The main Lebanese diaspora organization (WLCU), set up in 1960 by the government, lost its legitimacy and power in the 1975–1990 war (Hourani, 2007) and was paralysed by internalized political and religious quarrels. Lebanese diaspora engagement is particularly challenging

Yet the Lebanese diaspora boasts a huge potential for the country, for various reasons, especially its demographic size, one to four times as large as the country population (Brand, 2007). Lebanon's diaspora counts many business leaders worldwide, such as Carlos Slim in Mexico – the second richest person worldwide (Forbes, 2014) and Carlos Ghosn, the Lebanese Brazilian CEO of Renault and Nissan. Diaspora remittances represented 18% of Lebanon's GDP in 2013 and as much as 24% in 2007 (World Bank), translating into the highest level of remittances per capita worldwide in 2003 (Özden, 2006). The Lebanese diaspora proved to be instrumental in shaping Lebanon's middle class in the last two centuries. It contributed to financing schools, universities, and hospitals (Hourani, 2007). In 1991, the Lebanese government created diaspora bonds to reduce government debt, raising around US$35 million (Hourani, 2007). The Lebanese diaspora showed persistent support and loyalty in times of crisis. For example, remittances increased during the July 2006 Israeli war (Tabar, 2011). The diaspora's "memory and vision of the homeland [and] commitment to restoring Lebanon to its old glory has driven them to maintain and nurture a continuing relationship with the homeland" (Hourani, 2007, p. 3)

---

feared the consequences of the 2008 global economic downturn on the remittance influx (Table 9.2).

Organizations have been set up by Arab diaspora members in their residence countries to channel diaspora resources and skills towards

*Table 9.2*   Formal remittances to the Middle East, 2012 (unless otherwise stated)

| | Remittances in US$ billion | Remittances as a percentage of GDP |
|---|---|---|
| Egypt | 19.2 | 7.3 |
| Lebanon | 6.7 | 15.6 |
| Jordan | 3.5 | 11.3 |
| Yemen | 3.4 | 10.5 |
| Palestine | 2.1 | 18.3 |
| Syria (2010) | 1.6 | 2.7 |
| Iraq | 0.3 | 0.1 |

*Sources*: World Bank http://data.worldbank.org, UN Data http://data.un.org.

philanthropic goals. Some of these entities are standalone organizations; others have been formed as philanthropic arms of networking, religious, professional, or cultural organizations.

Diaspora support proved to be considerable in crises, not least in Lebanon during the 2006 Israeli conflict (Hourani, 2007), in Palestine via recurring donations (Hilal, 2007), and in Egypt for Tahrir via SMS, email and Twitter (Eldin et al., 2013). The Syrian diaspora has been instrumental in organizing and financing relief supply in the current Syrian crisis (HPG and ODI, 2012; Syrian American Medical Society, 2013).

Over history, Arab diasporas have actively contributed to the development of the Middle East. How successful have been states, non-profits, and start-ups in gathering their support?

### Diaspora courting by governments

Tools deployed by Middle Eastern governments to harness diaspora resources have largely focused on financial contributions. Governments offered remittance incentives (e.g. tax breaks in Egypt), remittance securitization (as in Lebanon and Egypt), special savings accounts – with low interest rates, fiscal advantages, and foreign denomination (e.g. in Lebanon), diaspora bonds with discounted or nil interest rates (e.g. in Egypt and Lebanon), and investment promotion (e.g. in Jordan through conferences targeting wealthy diaspora individuals). Few government schemes have sought diaspora contributions for development uses.

Arab diasporas have limited trust in governments in the Middle East. They systematically associate public entities in the region with corruption and inefficiency. A study conducted among Egyptian diaspora members in Kuwait, the United States, and the United Kingdom showed that Egyptian consulates and embassies have a bad reputation even in the eyes of diaspora members who never set a foot in these offices (Zohry and Debnath, 2010). Diaspora suspicion towards Middle Eastern public bodies is not only the reflection of what is perceived as a long-standing corrupt system. It is also fuelled by local politics (including authoritarianism and sectarianism) and conflicts.

On their side, many governments in the Middle East (e.g. Syria, Egypt) have limited budget and capacity to coordinate diaspora engagement initiatives. Diaspora ministries or sub-ministry institutions (set up in Egypt, Syria, Lebanon, Iraq, and Yemen) are fragile. In Yemen, the official diaspora entity closed and reopened under new names multiple times (Agunias and Newland, 2012).

Furthermore, states in the region tend to fear the politicization of diaspora aid. As a result, they have been reluctant to grant political rights to diasporas. Diaspora outreach is determined by ad hoc government needs (especially elections and fund-raising). Governments in the region consider diasporas as a commodity confined to the economic sphere. The relative state negligence of Arab diasporas, on political rights (e.g. citizenship, voting) and social benefits, limits incentives for participation.

In recent years, some governments in the Middle East attempted to connect with their diaspora more thoroughly, especially through diaspora consultation and conferences (as in Lebanon in 2014). Other countries are betting on diaspora repatriation as a tool for development. In 2013, Iraq announced it would dedicate US$86 million to a diaspora return scheme (O'Hannelly, 2013). States even initiated cross-country cooperation via MedGeneration, a new discussion forum on diaspora mobilization for development launched in 2013 by governments and diaspora representatives of Jordan, Lebanon, and Palestine (ANIMA, 2014).

Arab diasporas may be keener to trust Middle Eastern governments and municipalities when the latter partner with international organizations or IO (e.g. Transfer of Knowledge Through Expatriate Nationals or TOKTEN) and foreign states (e.g. Germany's Returning

Experts Programme). TOKTEN, a brain-gain temporary return scheme initiated by the United Nations in 1977 and implemented in various countries (including Palestine, Egypt, and Lebanon) is considered as a success. TOKTEN rallied over 500 diaspora experts (volunteers) in Palestine between 1994 and 2008 (United Nations Volunteers, 2008), for short-term consultancy projects with public, non-profit, and private entities. However, IO diaspora programmes in the Arab region have shown limitations in scaling because of rigidity (in the case of physical return programmes like TOKTEN) and of insufficient coordination and participation (in the case of virtual networks for remote knowledge exchange like UNDP's PALESTA in Palestine). New initiatives are promising but require time before success can be assessed – as with Live Lebanon, an internet platform set up in 2010 by UNDP to connect the Lebanese diaspora with local community projects and leveraging diaspora Goodwill Ambassadors.

As governments, non-profits in the Middle East have encountered challenges in attempts to mobilize Arab diasporas because of insufficient trust.

### Diaspora solicitation by non-profits

Arab diasporas perform charity contributions to local entities in the Middle East – especially towards education and youth, health care, religious communities, and village organizations. Religion is a key motivation underlying philanthropy among Arab diasporas.

Interestingly, Arab diaspora donations tend to be directed towards faith-based organizations, local initiatives (in villages or communities of origin), and projects undertaken by relatives, rather than towards Middle Eastern non-profits. Globally, there is "a general lack of [diaspora] trust in the nonprofit sector [ . . . ] in countries of diaspora origin" (IOM and MPI, 2012, p. 201). Charities in the Middle East particularly arouse suspicion among Arab diasporas. Some Palestinian diaspora members fear they might end up on a terrorist list if they donate to one of the many Palestinian non-profits.[1] Out of fear for corruption and incompetency, Arab diasporas tend to mistrust non-profits in their country of origin or descent, unless they have personal connections to them. Leadership also significantly influences Arab diasporas in gauging trustworthiness of Middle Eastern initiatives or non-profits. The importance of personal ties and non-profit leadership in the philanthropic choices of Arab diasporas is outlined in a study on Arab-American giving (Rignall, 2006). Arab diasporas seem to have greater confidence in international NGOs operating in the Middle East (such as the Red Cross and the United Nations), than in local Middle Eastern non-profits.

Lastly, there is a fear associated with lending in the Middle East among Arab diasporas. The latter have a tendency to mistrust microloan mechanisms on platforms like Kiva and Pi Slice. Notwithstanding, the younger generation (under 35) seems to be more confident than other Arab diaspora members in microcredit for the Middle East. Paradoxically enough, Arab diasporas seem to prefer donation systems (such as Zoomaal, a crowdfunding website for MENA) to lending platforms in the region.

The diaspora outreach history, albeit recent, of Middle Eastern governments and non-profits, contrasts with the novelty of diaspora mobilization efforts from local entrepreneurship stakeholders. The Arab start-up ecosystem has seen promising diaspora initiatives in the past few years.

### Diaspora rallying in start-up and SME growth

There is no shortage of business leaders among Arab diasporas. Their financial resources (as investors), experience (as advisors or returnees), and connections are valuable to Middle Eastern ventures and small businesses.

Few start-ups and SMEs have access to diaspora support in the Middle East, not only because Arab diaspora mobilization is difficult, but also because the Middle Eastern entrepreneurship ecosystem is still what was depicted as an "out-of-balance ecosystem" (Saddi and Soueid, 2011, p. 12). Start-up incubators, accelerators, and venture capital funds have been mushrooming in the Middle East in recent years. The entrepreneurship ecosystem is particularly developed in Jordan, led by Oasis 500 (a major start-up accelerator, incubator, and seed investment company in the Arab region). Nevertheless, diaspora readiness to contribute to start-up and SME growth in the Middle East is constrained by risks, such as deficient legal frameworks and highly hypothetical exit opportunities. A report written by a Lebanese diaspora network of financial professionals (LIFE) in a view to foster the growth of the high-tech industry in Lebanon outlines well the start-up ecosystem gaps (or risks) limiting diaspora involvement in Lebanon (Bejjani, 2012).

Arab diaspora members are rarely invited to be agents of change (as opposed to contributors – typically investors or mentors) in the business sphere. Arab diaspora groups thus took action and set up organizations to build the Arab entrepreneurship ecosystem in their country of descent (as LFE, see Table 9.3) and to provide local start-ups with resources from their country of residence (e.g. TechWadi, see Table 9.4).

*Table 9.3*   LFE's local model: diaspora organizations helping build the technology start-up ecosystem in Lebanon

---

Lebanon For Entrepreneurs (LFE) was set up in 2013 "to accelerate the development of the Lebanese IT start-up ecosystem through the active involvement of diaspora organizations". It was launched by three US-based Lebanese diaspora entities (LIFE, LebNet, and SEAL). It is headed by a diaspora returnee based in Beirut, instilling trust locally in LFE and in the Lebanese diaspora alike, and easing discussions between LFE and local stakeholders (start-ups, government, businesses, and universities). The diaspora organizations behind LFE ensure the diaspora perspective is built into the start-up ecosystem and generate confidence in LFE projects among diaspora members

---

*Source*: LFE (2014), http://www.lfepartnership.com/.

*Table 9.4*   TechWadi's remote model: accelerating the growth of Arab start-ups in the Silicon Valley

---

TechWadi is a pan-Arab-American diaspora non-profit founded in the United States in 2006 to build bridges for entrepreneurship between the Silicon Valley and the emerging Middle Eastern start-up ecosystem. TechWadi leverages the network and knowledge base of the Arab diaspora community in the Silicon Valley to offer training, mentorship, and acceleration programmes to high-impact Middle Eastern ventures. TechWadi organizes conferences, networking sessions, workshops, business plan competitions, and investor pitches, among other events. Support to entrepreneurs is provided not only by members and volunteers (including diaspora members and others) remotely, but also in person (entrepreneurs are flown to the United States). TechWadi partners with other organizations in the United States (including the Skoll Foundation, Google for Entrepreneurs, and the Plug and Play Silicon Valley accelerator) and entities in the Arab World (like the American University of Cairo and the MIT Enterprise Forum of the Pan Arab Region), to maximize impact on start-ups from the Middle East

---

*Source*: TechWadi (2014), http://techwadi.org/.

Arab diaspora organizations catalysing the growth of Middle Eastern start-ups tend to be focused on technology and/or financial help and based in the United States. Support initiatives include venture capital funds (e.g. Silicon Badia in New York), incubators and accelerator programmes (such as PITME in Silicon Valley), events (like the MENA Innovation DemoDay in Silicon Valley), and networks facilitating connections between diaspora professionals and local entrepreneurs (e.g. the Lebanese Business Network). Directly, diaspora start-up initiatives provide support to Arab entrepreneurs (through access to mentorship and funding); indirectly, they improve awareness about ventures abroad.

Most of these Arab diaspora start-up projects involve collaborations with large corporations (as sponsors), universities, non-profits, and/or other diaspora organizations. Such partnerships enhance the impact, scale, and image of diaspora initiatives.

Governments in the Middle East are starting to engage their diasporas in start-up growth at home. Interestingly, some residence countries showed interest in helping them in such endeavours. The Jordanian government is partnering with the US Department of State through Partners for a New Beginning on a project meant to engage US-based diaspora members in business in Jordan (Aspen Institute, 2013). France offers incubation services to selected Lebanese and North African students and graduates from the French higher education system who would like to set up innovative companies in the South Mediterranean region (IRD/PACEIM).

The first steps of Arab diasporas in the start-up sphere in the Middle East can serve as inspiration for the social enterprise field.

## Diaspora engagement in social entrepreneurship in the Middle East

Social enterprises combine the social mission of non-profits and the scaling potential of commercial entities. They do not rely on continuous donation injections and are not expected to generate high financial returns. There is an opportunity to position social ventures as a new frontier, halfway between development and business.

In addition, the Arab philanthropic culture among the wealthy shows a certain appetite for social entrepreneurship. The top charitable cause among millionaires in the Middle East overall (beyond the seven countries studied) is social change, that is, new social transformation models (Forbes Insights and BNP Paribas, 2013). However, experiences in the public and non-profit spheres point to the lack of confidence of Arab diasporas in regional organizations, which could be detrimental to Middle Eastern social start-ups. The Arab social entrepreneurship sphere is nascent, largely unknown, and often disconnected from diasporas. Most organizations or platforms allowing diasporas to be involved in Middle Eastern social entrepreneurship are dedicated either to traditional commercial ventures (as Eureeca, a crowdinvesting platform for SMEs) or to regular non-profits (like Nakhweh, an online platform matching volunteers to non-profits and social initiatives). The combination of social enterprises with either businesses or non-profits is a source of confusion and slows down the emergence of a social enterprise "brand". Recently, few organizations focused on social entrepreneurship started with the aim to embrace Arab diaspora support (such as RISE Egypt in 2013); and some of the existing entities committed to supporting social entrepreneurs in the Middle East are designing strategies to court diasporas (as Ashoka with its Global Diaspora Initiative). Yet there is no proven Arab diaspora engagement model for social entrepreneurship.

**Uniqueness of the Arab context, or the impossibility to replicate diaspora models from other continents in the Middle East**

Successful diaspora engagement models have been celebrated – not least in Israel and India. If their models can serve as inspiration, they cannot be replicated as such in the Arab World.

First, despite a cultural and linguistic identity, each Arab diaspora is fragmented religiously and politically. Individual Arab diasporas are divided along sectarian lines, reproducing national religious divisions. The deep political dissensions that are or were dividing some Middle Eastern countries also affected their diasporas, as in Lebanon. In certain cases (among others, in Syria, Egypt, and Lebanon), diaspora isolation is due to political opposition or even exile. The isolation of diaspora groups is visible online, as shown by the e-Diaspora Atlas of FMSH for Egypt and Lebanon (Severo and Zuolo, 2012; Asal, 2012). This fragmentation is also linked to the absence of governmental coordination. Religious and political divisions within Arab diaspora communities result in a lack of unity and in some cases in counterproductive competition between splinter groups – even in philanthropy – as in the United States (Rignall, 2006).[2] Even though they are strengthened by a pan-Arab sense (see Section " 'Arab diaspora' landscape"), Arab diasporas are not united around a common cause that would transcend their diversity and divisiveness – with the exception of Palestine.

Second, although conflicts and instability in the Middle East are a call for action and instil a sense of urgency, such crises significantly harden diaspora initiatives on the ground (Kleist and Vammen, 2012) and limit the range of involvement options (especially long-term projects), as in Syria, Iraq, and Palestine.

All in all, traditional diaspora engagement models applied elsewhere are unlikely to succeed as such in the Middle East. The Jewish and Armenian diasporas have been cemented by tragedies, have a strong collective memory, share a common religion, and pursue a political agenda – which helps Israeli and Armenian organizations secure diaspora confidence and support. The Israeli government also played a key role in mobilizing the Jewish diaspora. Similarly, peace and stability have been key to involve the Indian diaspora in India's software industry, to promote India as an outsourcing destination. In the early days, innovative models are required to build Arab diaspora trust in Middle Eastern social enterprises.

The following recommendations on Arab diaspora engagement for social entrepreneurship in the Middle East will focus on measures for the next three years, to maximize the relevance of suggestions.

### Promising social enterprise niches for diaspora support

A few sub-sectors (niches) in the social entrepreneurship sphere could be prioritized to initiate diaspora outreach, based on ease to rally Arab diaspora members (rather than on social impact or urgency in the Middle East). The initial focus on social enterprise niches is key to lay the foundation for trust among Arab diasporas. Once the latter have confidence in few social venture niches, engagement mechanisms could be extended to other social areas.

*Socially responsible products and services*

There is a diaspora market for products and services (UNCTAD, 2012) – and thus for socially responsible ones – especially tourism, food and beverage, craft, clothing, and culture (film, music, and books). If social goods and services are more onerous, they would allow diasporas to make an impact in exchange for an actual good or service. Incidentally, international expansion is critical to some social ventures, as the size of most national Middle Eastern markets constrains scaling.

Research outlines the potential of diasporas as buyers. Diasporas are tourists in their countries of origin or ancestry (Newland and Taylor, 2010). In Lebanon, for example, the vitality of the tourism industry owes much to repetitive visits of the Lebanese diaspora, who represents the majority of visitors (Hourani, 2009). Worldwide, diasporas also consume traditional products from their country of origin or ancestry. The diaspora absorb as much as 10 per cent of exports in El Salvador (Newland and Plaza, 2013). In particular, diasporas consume traditional food and beverage products from home (see Table 9.5). Distribution channels for such goods and services exist – offline and to a limited extent online – easing market penetration of social enterprises abroad.

*Social technology ventures*

"Technology for social good" might capitalize on the surge of interest in high technology among Arab diasporas. The latter is evidenced

*Table 9.5*   Arab diasporas as a market for social food ventures

Literature evidenced that food is the "last cultural feature migrant populations [in general] lose, long after the original tongue, the religion, and the way of getting dressed" (Mouawad, 2004, p. 8). Arab diasporas – including second- and third-generation diasporas – are consumers of Middle Eastern food products. In addition, Arab diasporas played a key role in promoting Arab cuisine and launching restaurants and groceries, as the Lebanese diaspora in the United Kingdom (Abdallah and Hannam, 2013). Both factors create demand for imports of traditional Middle Eastern food products from social ventures (like Souk El Tayeb in Lebanon). Arab restaurants and shops have an interest in marketing social food items to build their reputation. In particular, social food ventures could be mentioned on menus, and their products could be made available for sale at restaurants. Distribution channels for food items already exist; and new technologies have facilitated the export of ethnic products to diasporas, as with Lebanese baklavas (Hourani, 2009). In the long run, fool sustainability labels could provide guarantees to diaspora customers by the proliferation of diaspora-led technology initiatives in the Middle East (Abdelkrim, 2013). Some social technology projects already involve diasporas. Thousands of participants worldwide connected to the 2013 MENA+SocialGood Summit, a virtual global conference exploring ways to catalyse technology for social impact in MENA. Founded in 2011, the NYU Abu Dhabi International Hackathon for Social Good in the Arab World – a programming marathon focused on the creation of mobile and web apps for social purposes in the Arab World – attracts each year a number of Arab diaspora participants (as students, mentors, and judges). In fact, the vast majority of the start-ups supported by Arab diaspora organizations are technology ventures (even when these diaspora entities are sector-agnostic). Tech start-ups entail lower risks and offer shorter time to market than other ventures; they also lend themselves well to remote support and transparency, maximizing chances to gain the confidence of Arab diasporas.

*Youth-led and youth-focused social ventures*

Last but not least, social enterprises created by or serving youth could capitalize on the faith of Arab diasporas in young generations and in education. The latter is exemplified, among others, by diaspora scholarship funds and diaspora gifts to leading Middle Eastern universities. AUB and AUC have long had fund-raising antennas in the United States to better tap into their alumni networks abroad. The perceived need for remedies to youth brain drain and youth unemployment in the Arab World exacerbates the relevance of diaspora support to young social entrepreneurs. Emigration of 15- to 24-year-olds from the Arab World doubled from 2.3 to 4.4 million between 1990 and 2013 (ESCWA, 2013). MENA is plagued with the highest youth unemployment rate, namely, 28 per cent in 2012 (ILO, 2013).

Universities are perfect allies to channel diaspora support towards young social entrepreneurs. Academia in and outside the Middle East has demonstrated its credibility among diasporas, for instance, by organizing events and competitions well attended by diaspora members (such as the Wharton MENA Conference and the Harvard Arab Weekend) and by setting up start-up incubators connected to business mentors (e.g. the AUC Venture Lab). Several universities in the region boast large global alumni networks that could be exposed to youth-led and youth-related social ventures through events and electronic newsletters.

Once Arab diasporas have built trust – and engaged – in selected social enterprise niches, mobilization will be easier in the social entrepreneurship sphere as a whole. What kind of involvement can be realistically expected from Arab diasporas?

### Ideal types of engagement between diasporas and social enterprises

Diaspora mobilization objectives need to be in line with diaspora capabilities and aspirations. Involvement strategies should go beyond diaspora wallets to embrace their skill set, network, and country knowledge. Offering the possibility to Arab diasporas to share their intellectual and social capital rather than their wealth would decrease fears of instrumentalization and foster trust.

Social enterprise needs in the region go far beyond financial resources. For one third of MENA entrepreneurs, the first barrier to scaling is generating revenue (Wamda, 2014). Distribution, marketing, advertising, and business development, among others, are key to unlock the growth potential of social start-ups in the Middle East. The following engagement options would help establish mutually beneficial relationships between social ventures and Arab diasporas. The below suggestions are recommended roles for the short run, that is, the coming three years. Models for engagement are depicted in Section "A few models for diaspora engagement" (Table 9.6).

*Ecosystem shapers*

Diasporas boast invaluable skills, experience, connections, and knowledge (of their countries of residence and origin). Those are increasingly leveraged by Arab diaspora organizations to support the development of the entrepreneurship ecosystem in the Middle East.

The LFE model of support to the technology start-up sphere in Lebanon (see Table 9.3) – whereby existing diaspora organizations set up local entities in the Middle East to build the entrepreneurship ecosystem in cooperation with other stakeholders – could serve as inspiration in the social entrepreneurship sphere. Diasporic organizations on the ground would break up the mistrust cycle between diaspora communities and local entities, ensure mutual interest, while limiting large-scale physical return of diaspora members.

*Table 9.6* Recommended involvement of Arab diasporas in social entrepreneurship in the Middle East, in the short term (within three years)

| Recommended role | Details |
|---|---|
| Ecosystem shapers | Active stakeholders in shaping the social entrepreneurship ecosystem |
| Customers | Customers of social products/services (especially sustainable food and beverage, eco-tourism, traditional craft) |
| Brokers | Connecting social ventures to<br>– providers of products/services (regular, discounted, pro-bono)<br>– distribution/sales channels (for international expansion) |
| Advisors | – Punctual mentors/coaches/trainers (with flexibility)<br>– Long-term mentors (young diaspora professionals) |
| Ambassadors | Ambassadors (off and online promotion) |
| Donors | Donors via online crowdfunding platforms (targeting young diaspora members) |

For example, local diaspora entities would be well positioned to improve legal frameworks and infrastructure through discussions with governmental stakeholders, to cooperate with national universities on curricula and training, and to set up social start-up accelerators and impact investment funds with partners in and outside the country.

*Customers*

As mentioned above (see Section "Socially responsible products and services"), some start-ups could market their social products and services abroad to diasporas.

*Brokers*

Arab diasporas could help social entrepreneurs secure regular, discounted, and pro-bono services and products from businesses abroad, especially multinational corporations (e.g. in marketing, advertising, and shipping). Currently, corporate support to Middle Eastern social enterprises is narrow. If any, it tends to come from regional businesses. For example, Timeout Beirut provided complimentary media services to Nabad, the social venture incubator of arcenciel (a major Lebanese social enterprise), and Aramex offered reduced shipping rates to the Awadem Lebanese start-up (an e-commerce platform for socially responsible products from the Arab World). Such offers are driven by corporate social responsibility (CSR) motives. Access to CSR by businesses outside the Middle East is limited for Arab entrepreneurs deprived of personal connections abroad. Arab diasporas could be rallied in finding partners outside MENA. Likewise, Arab diasporas could source distribution and sales (i.e. export) opportunities abroad. Entrepreneurs find it difficult to establish connections to suppliers or distributors by themselves, even though they sometimes do (as RecycloBekia, an Egyptian venture recycling electronic waste in MENA, and whose first customer was a Chinese company). Diasporas would have a high value-added as gate openers and intermediaries. Such help would be punctual and not very time consuming, increasing appeal to diasporas.

*Advisors*

Diasporas are in a position to provide guidance to social entrepreneurs. In the OECD in 2006, 36 per cent of migrants from MENA (and as much of 58 per cent for Egypt) were "highly educated", that is, with tertiary education (OECD, 2012). Figures are usually higher among descendants (i.e. subsequent diaspora generations).

In selected instances (especially among younger diaspora professionals), mentorship can take the form of long-term advisory. This approach is adopted by the Resolution Project, a global non-profit supporting selected students launching social ventures ("Fellows") through remote mentorship by "Guides". Each fellow team is paired for two years with two Guides, who provide coaching for a couple of hours monthly, usually via Skype, calls, and email (Fellow and Guides rarely live in the same country). Resolution support to social entrepreneurs entails not only advisory on social ventures but also personal support, introductions to relevant experts within and outside the organization, and access to training modules, among others. Such long-term mentorship is very valuable to entrepreneurs and rewarding for mentors.

Yet in most cases, diaspora members cannot commit for long periods and are constrained by time. Diasporas need flexible, one-off involvement options, such as punctual mentorship, one-off training sessions or speaking events (in person or through webinars), and high-level remote coaching. Their individual constraints, interests, and experience need to be continuously taken into account. On the website of RISE Egypt, a non-profit diaspora organization dedicated to social entrepreneurship in Egypt, a basic registration form includes ideal involvement options – especially online webinars, one-day training, and long term one-to-one mentorship. Similarly, TechWadi's online form for would-be mentors and coaches (Table 9.4) includes availability in terms of hours per months. Social entrepreneurship organizations gathering diasporic support could even call diaspora members once a year to get an updated view on their professional situation and ability to contribute, making the connection personal, reinforcing trust of diaspora supporters, and maximizing chances of continuing support.

*Ambassadors*

Currently, few Arab business and thought leaders such as Fadi Ghandour (founder and vice-chairman of Aramex) champion local start-ups. This informal ambassador system improves awareness about entrepreneurs and enhances the reputation of new ventures. The ambassador role could be systematized through a system of diaspora champions for Middle Eastern social entrepreneurs. However, attention should shift away from the handful of prominent leaders currently over-solicited to support start-ups in the region. Many Arab diaspora professionals are very successful in their field (e.g. medicine, law, business, government) and are well positioned to promote social ventures, in their circles and globally. A community of diaspora ambassadors for social ventures could be formed following the Endeavor model. In each country where it operates (including Egypt, Jordan, and Lebanon), Endeavor set up a board of directors gathering top national business leaders to support local high-impact SMEs.

*Donors via crowdfunding*

Large-scale diaspora fund-raising and investment in social enterprises should be a long-term objective given the need to generate trust among Arab diasporas. Nevertheless, crowdfunding for social enterprises is likely to attract many young diaspora members (typically under 35). Zoomaal, a crowdfunding platform for innovative Arab projects, sourced about 45 per cent of funding (US$382,500 out of US$850,000) from Arab diaspora donors since its launch in 2013; and the vast majority of contributors are 25–40 years old. The purchasing power of young diaspora audiences is limited. Yet the latter form a vast community that is less risk averse. Young Arab diaspora groups are well positioned to create a buzz and to initiate the online donation movement for social ventures in the Middle East.

In spite of the variety of involvement options in social entrepreneurship, several. approaches are relevant across Arab diaspora initiatives.

### A few models for diaspora engagement

Diaspora projects for social entrepreneurship in the Middle East could be built on several models suggested below.

*Rallying diasporas on their own terms (co-definition, e-contributions, feedback processes)*

Arab diasporas should participate based on mechanisms they subscribe to.

First, initiatives seeking to channel diaspora support towards social entrepreneurship in the Middle East are most likely to succeed if diaspora members are involved in setting up the project, or at least consulted when defining it – instead of being approached to donate time and resources to predefined projects (Kleist and Vammen, 2012). Participation in the design of initiatives (see Section "Ecosystem shapers") would capitalize on diaspora knowledge and experience, and maximizes chances to get diaspora trust and buy-in.

Second, feedback mechanisms should be built into diaspora engagement systems. Motivations to contribute in the social entrepreneurship movement vary. Yet above all, Arab diasporas are eager to see they make a difference. They crave for feedback, as shown in a study conducted among Arab-American philanthropists (Rignall, 2006). Diasporas seek information on the use of funding, skills and time, and they value quantified impact assessments. Transparency is key not only to retain diaspora support, but also to trigger word of mouth and rally other diaspora supporters.

Non-profits and CSR departments of large companies (see Section "Brokers") could help social enterprise in transparency efforts – among others, to define impact metrics to be released online, to represent social impact graphically (e.g. through visualization tools, gamification mechanisms, and movies), and to release financial statements (e.g. through pro-bono audits). The online migration of social ventures could be eased through support of local entities.[3]

Third, electronic involvement options could be leveraged to ease diaspora support. Virtual participation mitigates the cost of contributions, reduces travel requirements, and increases transparency. For some Palestinian diaspora members, e-engagement is the only option, as Israel controls borders. To most Palestinians, virtual channels offer unparalleled convenience: those without an Israeli ID need to land in Jordan and spend another three hours on the road to reach Palestine. Online mechanisms could be leveraged in multiple ways – especially for communication (e.g. via Skype, email) and collaboration (e.g. through websites like Babele, a crowdsourcing platform for turning ideas into social businesses). For example, members of LebNet (a Lebanese–American network of diaspora technology professionals) share knowledge with MENA entrepreneurs via video series on Wamda (an entrepreneurship web portal for MENA) and use Google Hangouts live to access events connecting entrepreneurs with mentors.

Overall, Arab diasporas will be more enticed to join social enterprise initiatives if they agree with the terms of engagement, if projects provide feedback mechanisms and guarantees, and if remote support is possible.

*Dedicated social entrepreneurship platforms*

The social enterprise concept (and its existence in the region) is largely unknown within diasporas and in Middle Eastern countries. Most platforms mix up social ventures with regular non-profits or with traditional commercial start-ups. Social enterprises in the Middle East are unlikely to get diaspora attention on an individual basis. They have an interest in creating a social enterprise brand to educate people on the role and mission of social enterprises and build trust in Middle Eastern social enterprises. Social enterprise standards or labels will take time to implement. In the short term, Internet portals aggregating social ventures in the Middle East would be most helpful. Such websites could focus on a type of support across Arab countries (e.g. socially responsible e-commerce in the Middle East), a social enterprise niche (like technology social ventures in the Arab World), or a country (e.g. Jordanian social entrepreneurship).

Above all, an overarching pan-Arab platform on social entrepreneurship in the Middle East is missing – a "Wamda for social entrepreneurs". Organizations like Consult and Coach for a Cause (C3) support social entrepreneurship but do not play the role of information portal, which limits knowledge about social entrepreneurship in the region. Other websites like BarakaBits cover social entrepreneurship news in MENA (through "good news from the Middle East"), but the topic is one among many subsections and is disconnected from practical support and engagement. A Middle Eastern social enterprise website would capitalize on the pan-Arab sense uniting Arab diasporas. Many successful websites seeking funding and skills for Middle Eastern organizations operate across Arab countries, including Zoomaal (a crowdfunding website for Arab innovative projects) and Nakhweh (a volunteering board for non-profits). A pan-Arab social entrepreneurship platform would create synergies and would address diaspora audiences alongside Middle Eastern stakeholders, limiting the need for special diaspora tools.

If online platforms are necessary to promote Middle Eastern social entrepreneurship among Arab diasporas, early efforts should concentrate on selected diaspora circles.

*Circles of early supporters and communities of allies*

Social ventures in the Middle East are unlikely to rally everyone in the diaspora. Some will be easier to engage than others. The initial focus should be on specific circles (based on criteria such as geography, profession, and age). Once an initial circle of supporters for Middle Eastern social ventures is formed, it will be easier to convince other diaspora members to join the movement through public events showcasing successes and supporters. Social entrepreneurship being an emerging concept, worldwide and in the Middle East, education is needed through individual relationships (on top of online engagement). The founders of RISE Egypt, a diaspora-led non-profit catalysing social entrepreneurship in Egypt, started creating a core community through personal, one-to-one connections, by travelling from city to city (especially in North America and the Gulf).

If diaspora involvement in social entrepreneurship in the Middle East is driven by the will to make an impact, it is also tied to networking and social motives. Organizations catalysing Arab diaspora support for social entrepreneurship could foster connections and bonding between supporters, via discussions, events, and networking opportunities. Communities would instil a sense of belonging to a movement and foster mutual support between members, strengthening the quality and consistency of networks. Communities would also catalyse the energy and ideas of members towards the social entrepreneurship cause.

Communities of supporters could mix diaspora members with nationals living in the Middle East (as RISE Egypt on social entrepreneurship and Bilbaal in Palestine for social initiatives). Such collaborations would foster balanced, equal relationships between diaspora groups and local stakeholders and improve chances of successful collaboration.

In the early days, youth could be instrumental in forming an initial community of diaspora forward-thinkers committed to social entrepreneurship in the Middle East – to promote Arab social ventures and launch diaspora initiatives. Connections between bright, socially minded young diaspora members could be triggered through events (such as the Nexus MENA Youth Summit) or virtual networks that select, connect, and accelerate the development of young leaders (e.g. the Forum of Young Global Leaders at the World Economic Forum).

If the nature of involvement and mobilization mechanisms of Arab diasporas is crucial in the trust-building process, upstream communication is key: access to and interest of diaspora members is conditional upon the chosen communication channels.

### Recommended communication channels for diaspora outreach

Arab diaspora members rarely feel solicited for support and often mistrust organizations in the Middle East. Communication channels are important to ensure broad diaspora outreach, attention, and confidence.

#### Existing diaspora groups and networks

Some diaspora organizations and networks share missions relevant to Arab social ventures – whether they focus on business, specialize in a vertical sector (e.g. health care, technology, finance), are faith-based, or include a philanthropic arm in an organization with networking, religious, or cultural objectives. Their diaspora member database and the personal connections cementing them are precious. Arab social enterprises and organizations supporting the latter (e.g. Nahdet El Mahrousa, the Synergos Arab World Social Innovators programme) have an interest in establishing ties with such diaspora organizations for support. Crowdsourced lists of diaspora organizations could help identify relevant diaspora entities. The KosovoDiaspora.org website prompts its visitors to email them names of diaspora organizations for review, to complement their list. In a more sophisticated manner, the Nakhweh website (dedicated to matching NGOs and social initiatives in the Arab World to volunteers) allows registered members to create organizations' profiles and to suggest modifications (subject to verification). A similar crowdsourcing system could be applied to a database of Arab diaspora entities (instead of NGOs).

In particular, academic diaspora networks could play a significant role in diaspora outreach. Some universities and schools in the Middle East have built strong, global alumni networks. The Lebanese American University (LAU) even built teaching facilities in New York to deepen engagement with diaspora alumni families. Arab universities tend to be trusted both by diasporas and local communities owing to their educational mission. They are usually considered as unbiased and are more likely to be immune from political and religious affiliations. Support to social entrepreneurship would contribute to building the image of Middle Eastern universities. The latter could convene social enterprise competitions or host social entrepreneurs as speakers during alumni reunion events (this is common practice with non-profit and business leaders). Universities in the region could also share information with alumni on Arab student social entrepreneurs via their newsletters. As for universities in Europe, America, and other continents, they could host Arab social ventures competitions and Arab social entrepreneurship conferences, through their Arab departments and student societies (following the model of the Arab Startup Day at the Harvard Arab Weekend).

*Social media and video*

If diaspora organizations are established and secure communication channels, social networks (Facebook, Twitter, YouTube, LinkedIn, and others) are promising awareness raising platforms for Arab social entrepreneurship globally. So far, Arab diaspora engagement initiatives are overwhelmingly focused on North America despite the existence of Arab diaspora communities on all continents.

Social media is at the reach of any social enterprise in the Middle East. A study among 17 Lebanese social entrepreneurs showed that over four in five social enterprises "market their organization through social media" (Feghali et al., 2012, p. 5). Donner Sang Compter, a Lebanese blood donation non-profit, successfully built its brand thanks to Facebook, Twitter, and YouTube pages.

Yet emerging social start-ups have limited time to promote their activities on social networks. To them, the power of social media lies in pages aggregating the stories of Arab social ventures, to keep audiences engaged and create awareness around a social enterprise movement (rather than around individual social ventures). For example, in each Arab country, a Facebook page could be set up to tell stories of its social entrepreneurs in pictures (with captions), the way it is done on the "Humans of New York" Facebook page (through stories of New Yorkers).

Lastly, video would be an ideal tool not only for raising diaspora awareness about social ventures and marketing them (thanks to video pitches and documentaries) but also for showcasing social enterprises that benefited from diaspora support (to encourage other diaspora members to follow suit). The high YouTube penetration in the Arab World is promising for social video: "more than two hours of [Youtube] video are uploaded every minute" and the region ranks second for video views worldwide (Salem et al., 2013, p. 28). Videos on Arab social ventures could be shared not only in the form of reality television shows (as "El Mashrou3", a reality TV show about young business and social entrepreneurs in Egypt) and popular Arab shows (such as Ahmad Al Shugairi's Ramadan Khawater show), but also through social media campaigns (like #MyArabWorld, a campaign highlighting stories of Arab youth transforming society) and on websites (leveraging the crowdsourced model of BarakaBits).

*Physical places*

If social networks and videos offer convenient outreach possibilities, awareness raising and communication campaigns could meet Arab diasporas where they are physically. Diaspora members naturally transit through places where they could be exposed to social ventures in the Middle East. These locations include embassies and

*Table 9.7*   "Invest on board" by Turkish airlines: promoting Turkish start-ups in planes

In late 2013, Turkish Airlines, in partnership with Etohum (a Turkish start-up accelerator programme) launched a campaign promoting Turkish entrepreneurs. The latter pitch their start-ups in short videos accessible during flights, in business and economy classes. Videos are renewed every month. Such a promotion system could be replicated for social start-ups with Middle Eastern airline carriers, on routes popular among Arab diasporas, at periods of return (e.g. summer, Christmas). Videos could include crowdfunding options and links to social media

*Sources:* Turkish Airlines, http://investonboard.com/#apply, Dalakian (2013).

consulates (on site and online), airports and airplanes – especially in airport lounges and in-flight (see Table 9.7), foreign branches of Middle Eastern banks, and above all Arab restaurants and groceries abroad – where diasporas gather and network on a regular basis (see Table 9.5). Promotion of social enterprises would be a brand-building tool for these organizations.

All in all, involvement options, engagement models, and communication channels are of high importance for Arab diasporas to gain confidence in social ventures in the Middle East. Chosen frameworks should be guided by national diaspora specificities.

## A call for research on Arab diasporas

There is no universal (or Arab) diaspora engagement strategy, hence the need for quantitative and qualitative data on each diaspora. Governments in the region are overwhelmed by other priorities. Research on Arab diasporas could be conducted by universities in countries of origin (as done at the Lebanese Emigration Research Centre or LERC at NDU in Lebanon) and by universities in host countries (such research could be coordinated via academic departments such as the Centre for Palestine Studies at Columbia University in the United States). Research results could be released to the public. Data collection could include both quantitative and qualitative inputs, about demography, groups, aspirations, behaviours, and engagement. For example, the LERC collects newsletters and magazines published abroad by diaspora organizations, creates short profiles of prominent diaspora members, and started building a Lebanese diaspora database.

The LERC even partnered with Relief International to identify potential diaspora members who could be interested in specific investment opportunities (based on their interests and home villages). Academic diaspora research could be carried out with the financial support of diaspora alumni (via donations) and data inputs from governments and international organizations. The World Congress for Middle East Studies (WOCMES), a discussion forum gathering researchers, professors, students, and professionals (started in 2002), could be the opportunity to launch research collaboration on Arab diasporas across universities. Online networks of academic researchers dedicated to Arab diasporas could be set up by national diaspora groups, as RISE Egypt is doing (through a global, virtual think tank arm dedicated to social entrepreneurship in Egypt).

New ways to collect data on diasporas could be explored, by leveraging technology. Initiatives include online surveys (such as the World Bank's i-MENA survey launched in 2014 and targeting high-killed Lebanese diaspora returnees), social network analysis on diaspora dynamics, and collaborative online research tools (fed by diaspora inputs). One interesting initiative was launched by the FMSH, namely, the e-Diasporas Atlas, which maps connections between diaspora websites.

### Responsibilities and cooperation

In the early days, diaspora engagement could be initiated by diaspora organizations and by local social entrepreneurship stakeholders (such as social venture incubators and impact seed funds). Both types of entities are responsible for reaching out to each other to jointly launch initiatives for Arab social entrepreneurship. That is how, for example, the LIFE Lebanese diaspora network organized discussions with stakeholders in Lebanon before co-launching LFE to boost the technology entrepreneurship ecosystem in the country. Conversely, Ahmed El Alfi of Sawari Ventures in Egypt recently prompted ABANA, a pan-Arab diaspora network of financial professionals based mainly in the United States and Canada, to create its forthcoming online mentorship programme.

Universities could also trigger discussions between Arab diaspora members (including groups) and local social entrepreneurship actors, by convening discussions and events.

As seen earlier, partnerships of diaspora networks with businesses, public entities, academia, and international organizations are key in diaspora engagement. Such collaborations not only improve the relevance and impact of diaspora initiatives, but also strengthen diaspora organizations themselves.

## Conclusion

There is potential for Middle Eastern social enterprises to get support from diasporas. Yet the need for research on each Arab diaspora is urgent to ensure successful engagement in each country. Building diaspora trust around a social enterprise brand in the Middle East should be a priority. Overall, the fragmentation and mistrust of Arab diasporas require innovative engagement models in the early days. Arab diasporas – especially existing diaspora networks – should be involved or at least consulted in the design of social entrepreneurship initiatives, to ensure ownership and confidence in the latter. Most importantly, diaspora engagement models for social ventures in the Middle East should go beyond financial contributions, not only to create trust, but also to meet the needs of social entrepreneurs in the region. Arab diasporas could be targeted as shapers of the social entrepreneurship ecosystem, customers of social products and services, brokers (through connections with suppliers and sales channels abroad), mentors (with flexible involvement options), and ambassadors. Arab diasporas deeply long to make an impact, hence the importance of feedback processes. Transparency mechanisms are fundamental to gain the trust of Arab diasporas and to keep them engaged. Engagement should be incremental and initially focus on few social enterprise niches and restricted circles of diaspora supporters, to allow for optimizations, maximize chances of success, and create trust through personal relationships. The sense of belonging to a pan-Arab community among diaspora members should be an invitation to build pan-Arab platforms and mechanisms for support. Arab diaspora mobilization in social entrepreneurship should be taken as an opportunity to test new communication tools, levering new channels, especially social video and physical places (such as aircrafts and restaurants). Initiatives should strive to create communities of Arab social entrepreneurship supporters, encompassing both local individuals and diaspora members (especially among youth). Diaspora engagement endeavours should involve trustworthy allies, especially universities in and outside the Middle East (for research, communication, and incubation of youth-led social ventures). Ultimately, the best way to encourage Arab diaspora to support social enterprises in the region is to create and showcase a handful of success stories of social enterprises that succeeded with diaspora help.

## Acknowledgements

To Lebanon. And to Kim Issa and her family.

## Notes

1. Palestine is sometimes referred to as "the Silicon Valley of NGOs".
2. Pan-Arab groups might run lower risks of internal political and religious quarrels thanks to membership diversification. Similarly, secular and a-political organizations tend to insulate diaspora organizations from internal conflicts.
3. Eureeca (a global investment crowdfunding platform for SMEs) specifically set up mechanisms in the Middle East to assist entrepreneurs individually in preparing business material to be submitted online.

## Bibliography

Abdallah, A. and Hannam, K. (2013). "Hospitality and the Lebanese Diaspora: A Critical Perspective", *E-Review in Tourism Research (eRTR)*, 10(5/6), 19–37.

Abdelkrim, S. (12 December 2013). "Three Ways the Arab Tech Diaspora can Stimulate Regional Development", *Wamda*.

Agunias, R. H. (2 November 2009). "Committed to the Diaspora: More Developing Countries Setting Up Diaspora Institutions", *Migration Policy Institute, MPI*.

Agunias, D. R. and Newland, K. (2012). *Developing a Road Map for Engaging Diasporas in Development: A Handbook for Policymakers and Practitioners in Home and Host Countries*. Geneva: International Organization for Migration – IOM and Migration Policy Institute – MPI.

Alquhali, M. (2013). "Expatriates and Development in the Republic of Yemen. A Work Paper Presented at the International Dialogue on Migration", Ministry of Expatriates Affairs.

Ancien, D., Boyle, M. and Kitchin, R. (26–28 January 2009). *Exploring Diaspora Strategies: An International Comparison*. Workshop Report, NUI Maynooth.

ANIMA Investment Network (2014). *Innovation and Entrepreneurs Newsletter*, available at http://www.animaweb.org/uploads/Innovation& Entrepreneurs_jan-2014_EN.pdf, January.

Aridi, A. (14 July 2014). "World Bank Wants to Help Lebanese and Tunisian Diasporas Give Back", *Wamda*.

Asal, H. (2012). *Community Sector Dynamics and the Lebanese Diaspora: Internal Fragmentation and Transnationalism on the Web*. Paris: Fondation Maison des Sciences de l'Homme, Programme de Recherche TIC-Migrations, Projet e-Diasporas Atlas.

Ashoka (2013). "Global Diaspora Initiative", available at https://www.ashoka.org/diaspora.

Asi, M. and Beaulieu, D. (2013). "Arab households in the United States: 2006–2010", *U.S. Census Bureau American Community Survey Briefs*, ACSBR/10–20.

Aspen Institute (2013). *Partners for a New Beginning, Status Report*. Washington, DC: Author.

Balderston, K. (18 November 2011). "Unleashing the Power of Diaspora Entrepreneurs", *International Diaspora Engagement Alliance – IdEA*.

Batrouney, T. (28–29 June 2001). *Australian-Lebanese: Return Visits and Issues of Identity*. Paper Presented at the Conference on the Lebanese Diaspora, Beirut.

Bejjani, G. (2012). *Proposal for Launching the High Tech Industry in Lebanon*. Lebanese International Finance Executives – LIFE.

Beyond Reform and Development – BRD/I Group (2012). *Social Enterprise Momentum*, available at http://www.scribd.com/doc/101725917/BRD-The-Social-Entrepreneurship-Momentum.

Brand, L. A. (2007). "State, Citizenship, and Diaspora: The Cases of Jordan and Lebanon". Working Paper No. 146. San Diego, CA: University of California, Center for Comparative Immigration Studies, CCIS.

Buckner, E., Beges, S. and Khatib, L. (2012). *Social Entrepreneurship: Why Is It Important Post Arab Spring? Online Survey Report*. Stanford, CA: Stanford University, Center on Democracy, Development, and the Rule of Law – CDDRL, Program on Arab Reform and Democracy.

Byblos Bank – Economic Research and Analysis Department (1 May 2011). "The Global Crisis and Expatriates' Remittances to Lebanon: Trends and Elements of Resilience", *Focus*.

Byblos Bank – Economic Research and Analysis Department (5 October 2013). *Lebanon This Week*, 325, 2.

Calvert Foundation (2013). *Calvert Foundation Developing Impact Investing Initiative for Diaspora Communities*, available at http://www.calvertfoundation.org/press/releases/416-diaspora-initiative-kellogg-grant, 15 July.

Cohen, R. (2008). *Global Diasporas – An Introduction*. New York: Routledge.

Dalakian, G. (15 October 2012). "Kiva, Silatech Launch Microsite for Micro Lending in the Arab World", *Wamda*.

Dalakian, G. (12 November 2013). "In-Flight Investing: Turkish Airlines Lets Startups Pitch to Passengers", *Wamda*.

Debass, T. and Ardovino, M. (2009). *Diaspora Direct Investment (DDI): The Untapped Resource for Development*. Washington, DC: United States Agency for International Development – USAID.

Dialogue on Mediterranean Transit Migration – MTM, Interactive Map on Migration – i-Map (2013). *Migrant Entrepreneurship, Migration and*

*Development*. Background paper prepared for the MTM i-Map expert meeting, 12–13 June, Marseille.

Doherty Johnson, P. (2007). *Diaspora Philanthropy: Influences, Initiatives, and Issues*. Boston, MA: Harvard University: The Philanthropic Initiative – TPI and Cambridge, MA: The Global Equity Initiative.

*The Economist* (19 November 2011). *The Magic of Diasporas*.

Economic and Social Commission for Western Asia – ESCWA (2013). *Social Development Bulletin on Migration and Youth*, 10.

Eldin, A. S., Zidi, A., Khallaf, M., Farouki, N. T., and El Taraboulsi, S. (2013). *Giving in Transition and Transition in Giving – Philanthropy in Tunisia, Egypt and Libya 2011–2013*. Cairo: American University of Cairo – AUC, John D. Gerhart Center for Philanthropy and Civic Engagement.

El Gamal, M. (n.d.). *How to Unlock Arab Philanthropy*, available at http://voices. mckinseyonsociety.com/mahmoud-el-gamal-arab-philanthropy/. McKinsey on Society, Voices.

European Bank for Reconstruction and Development – EBRD and World Economic Forum – WEF (2013). The *Arab World Competitiveness Report*. Geneva: World Economic Forum – WEF.

Feghali, T., Abuatieh, E., and Dandan, J. (2012). *Social Entrepreneurship in Lebanon: Context and Considerations*. Beirut: American University of Beirut – AUB, Darwazah Center for Innovation Management and Entrepreneurship.

Fondation Maison des Sciences de l'Homme, ICT Migrations program. *e-Diasporas Atlas*, available at http://www.e-diasporas.fr/.

Forbes Insights and BNP Paribas (2013). *BNP Paribas Individual Philanthropy Index: Measuring Commitment in Europe, Asia, Middle East*. New York, NY: Forbes.

French Ministry of Foreign Affairs (2012). *Harnessing the Skills of Migrants and Diasporas to Foster Development: Policy Options*. Paris: Directorate General of Global Affairs, Development and Partnerships of the French Ministry of Foreign Affairs.

Hilal, J. (2007). *Relations Between Palestinian Diaspora (al-shatat), Palestinian Communities in the West Bank, and Gaza Strip*. Paper prepared for the Migration and Refugee Movements in the Middle East and North Africa, 23–25 October. Cairo: American University of Cairo – AUC, The Forced Migration and Refugee Studies Program.

Humanitarian Policy Group – HPG and Overseas Development Institute – ODI (2012). *Syria Crisis: The Humanitarian Response*. London: Author.

Hourani, G. (2007). *Lebanese Diaspora and Homeland Relations. Migration and Refugee Movements in the Middle East and North Africa*. Paper prepared for the Migration and Refugee Movements in the Middle East and North Africa, 23–25 October. Cairo: The American University of Cairo – AUC, The Forced Migration and Refugee Studies Program.

Hourani, G. (2009). "Diaspora and E-Commerce: The Globalization of Lebanese Baklava", *Palma Journal*, 11(1), 105–137.

Institut De Recherche Pour Le Développement – IRD. *Programme d'Aide à la Création d'Entreprises Innovantes en Méditerranée – PACEIM*, available at http://paceim.ird.fr/.

International Labor Organization – ILO (2013). *Global Employment Trends for Youth 2013: A Generation at Risk*. Geneva: Author.

International Labor Organization – ILO (2014). *Where Is Unemployment the Highest?*, available at http://www.ilo.org/global/about-the-ilo/multimedia/maps-and-charts/WCMS_233936/lang–en/index.htm.

International Labor Organization – ILO. *The TOKTEN (Transfer of Knowledge Through Expatriate Nationals) Programme*, available at http://www.ilo.org/dyn/migpractice/migmain.showPractice?p_lang=en&p_practice_id=26.

Investment Development Authority of Lebanon – IDAL (2013). *Invest in Lebanon*. Document presented at the Euromed Migration III, 24–25 September. Slovenia.

Ionescu, D. (2006). "Engaging Diasporas as Development Partners for Home and Destination Countries: Challenges for Policymakers", *IOM Migration Series*, 26.

Johnson, B. and Sedaca, S. (2004). *Diasporas, Emigres, and Development – Economic Linkages and Programmatic Responses*. A special study of the U.S. Agency for International Development (USAID) Trade Enhancement for the Services Sector (TESS).

Khater, A. (2001). *Inventing Home: Emigration, Gender, and the Middle Class in Lebanon, 1870–1920*. Berkeley and LA, CA: University of California Press.

Kitchin, R. and Boyle, M. (2011). *Diaspora Strategies in Transition States: Prospects and Opportunities for Armenia*. Maynooth: NIRSA, National University of Ireland.

Kiva (2013). *Kiva Arab Youth: Progress in Promoting Financial Services for Youth in the MENA Region*. Document presented at the CGAP Silatech Workshop on Youth Financial Inclusion, March, Rabat.

Kleist, N. and Vammen, I. (2012). *Diaspora Groups and Development in Fragile States – Lessons Learnt*. Copenhagen: Danish Institute for International Studies – DIIS.

KosovoDiaspora.org – KD, available at http://kosovodiaspora.org/about/.

Kumar, R. Social Enterprise (n.d.). *Social Enterprises: It Takes a Network*, available at http://voices.mckinseyonsociety.com/social-enterprise-it-takes-a-network/. McKinsey on Society, Voices.

Kuznetsov, Y. (2013). *How Can Talent Abroad Induce Development at Home? Towards a Pragmatic Diaspora Agenda*. Washington, DC: Migration Policy Institute, MPI.

Labaki, B. (2006). *The Role of Transnational Communities in Fostering Development in Countries of Origin: The Case of Lebanon*. Paper Prepared for the United Nations Expert Group Meeting on International Migration and Development in the Arab Region, Beirut, 15–17 May.

Lamloumi, J. (2013). *Entrepreneurship Education in the Arab States: A Joint Project Between UNESCO and StratREAL Foundation, UK – Final Evaluation Report*. Bonn: United Nations Educational, Scientific and Cultural Organization – UNESCO.

Marinova, N. (2010). "Transnational Homeland Involvement of the US-Based Lebanese Diaspora". Working Paper No. 15, Global Migration and

Transnational Politics. George Mason University, Center for Global Studies, Fairfax, VA.

Mayard, A. (2014). "PACEIM Offers French-Style Incubation to North African and Lebanese Entrepreneurs", *Wamda*, 3 February.

McCormick, B. and Wahba, J. (2001). "Overseas Work Experience, Savings and Entrepreneurship amongst Return Migrants to LDCs", *Scottish Journal of Political Economy*, 48(2), 164–178.

Moammed bin Rachid Al Maktoum Foundation – MBRF and United Nations Development Programme Regional Bureau for Arab States – UNDP/RBAS (2009). *Arab Knowledge Report 2009*. Dubai: Al Ghurair Printing & Publishing House L.L.C.

Mouawad, H. (2004). *Modernity and Tradition of Lebanese Food Consumption Between Standardization and Particularisms*. Paper prepared for the 11th conference of the Economic Research Forum, ERF, Beirut.

Mourtada, R. and Salem, F. (2012). *Social Media, Employment and Entrepreneurship: New Frontiers for the Economic Empowerment of Arab Youth?* Dubai: Dubai School of Government – DSG, Governance and Innovation Program.

Mowafi, M. and Farag, N. (2013). *Leveraging the Capacity of the Egyptian Diaspora to Promote Social Entrepreneurship and Innovation in Egypt.* available at http://conf.aucegypt.edu/ConfAdmin/ybakr_images/Nadine%20Farag%20-%20Egyptian%20Diaspora%20Paper.pdf.

Newland, K. and Tanaka, H. (2010). Mobilizing Diaspora Entrepreneurship for Development. In K. Newland (ed.), *Diasporas: New Partners in Global Development Policy* (pp. 25–59). Washington, DC: Migration Policy Institute – MPI.

Newland, K. and Taylor, C. (2010). Heritage Tourism and Nostalgia Trade: A Diaspora Niche in the Development Landscape. In K. Newland (ed.), *Diasporas: New Partners in Global Development Policy* (pp. 94–125). Washington, DC: Migration Policy Institute – MPI.

Newland, K., Terrazas, A. and Munster, R. (2010). *Diaspora Philanthropy: Private Giving and Public Policy*. Washington, DC: Migration Policy Institute, MPI.

Newland, K. and Plaza, S. (2013). *What We Know about Diasporas and Economic Development*. Washington, DC: Migration Policy Institute, MPI.

Organisation for Economic Co-operation and Development – OECD (2010). *Entrepreneurship and Migrants*, Report by the OECD Working Party on SMEs and Entrepreneurship, Paris.

Organisation for Economic Co-operation and Development – OECD (2012). *Connecting with Emigrants: A Global Profile of Diasporas*. Paris: Author.

Orozco, M. (2008). *Tasting Identity: Trends in Migrant Demand for Home Country Goods – Summary*, available at http://www.thedialogue.org/PublicationFiles/DNA%20Paper%20Series%20-%20Tasting%20Identity_11-18-08-Summary_FINAL.pdf.

Özden, C. (2006). *Brain Drain in Middle East & North Africa – The Patterns under the Surface*. Paper Prepared for the United Nations Expert Group Meeting on International Migration and Development in the Arab Region, Beirut, 15–17 May.

O'Hannelly, P. (23 January 2013). "Harvesting the Iraqi Diaspora", *Iraqi Business News*.

Palestinian Central Bureau of Statistics – PCBS (2014). *Press Release on the Results of the Labour Force Survey, October–December 2013*, available at http://www.pcbs.gov.ps/site/512/default.aspx?tabID=512&lang=en&ItemID=1022&mid=3171&wversion=Staging.

Palestinian Information Technology Association of Companies – PITA (2013). *ICT Exporting and Connecting Diaspora*, available at http://www.slideshare.net/EngLinaShamia/ict-exporting-via-connecting-diaspora.

Ratha, D. and Mohapatra, S. (2011). "Preliminary Estimates of Diaspora Savings. World Bank Migration and Remittances Unit", *Migration and Development Brief*, 14.

Ratha, D., Mohapatra, S. and Silwal, A. (2011). *Migration and Remittances Factbook*. Washington, DC: World Bank, Migration and Remittances Unit.

Riddle, L. (2008). "Diasporas: Exploring Their Development Potential", *ESR Review*, 10, 28–35.

Rignall, K. (2006). *Insights on Arab-American Giving: A Report from the Collaborative of Arab-American Philanthropy*. A project of the National Network for Arab-American Communities and Arab Community Center for Economic and Social Services.

Saddi, J. and Soueid, R. (2011). *Accelerating Entrepreneurship in the Arab World*. A World Economic Forum Report in Collaboration with Booz & Company. Geneva: World Economic Forum, WEF.

Salem, F., Mourtada, R. and Alshaer, S. (5 June 2013). "Transforming Education in the Arab World: Breaking Barriers in the Age of Social Learning", *Arab Social Media Report, Dubai School of Government – DSG*.

Schneider, N. (n.d.). *Returning Experts Programme – Centrum für Internationale Migration und Entwicklung – Centre for International Migration and Development*.

Schroeder, C. M. (2013). *Startup Rising: The Entrepreneurial Revolution Remaking the Middle East*. New York: Palgrave Macmillan.

Schwab Foundation for Social Entrepreneurship. Available at http://www.schwabfound.org/.

Severo, M. and Zuolo, E. (2012). *Egyptian e-diaspora: Migrant Websites without a Network?* Paris: Fondation Maison des Sciences de l'Homme, Programme de Recherche TIC-Migrations, Projet e-Diasporas Atlas.

Sirkeci, I., Cohen, J. and Ratha, D. (2012). *Migration and Remittances during the Global Financial Crisis and Beyond*. Washington, DC: World Bank.

Smart, A. and Hsu J.-Y. (2004). "The Chinese Diaspora, Foreign Investment and Economic Development in China", *The Review of International Affairs*, 3(4), 544–566.

Storey, D., Fanelli, A. and Méndez, J. G. (2012). *New Entrepreneurs and High Growth Enterprises in the Middle East and North Africa*. Paris: Organization of European Cooperation and Development, OECD and International Development Center, IDC.

Syrian American Medical Society (20 March 2013). *NGO Coordination Meeting for Humanitarian Relief to Syria*. Syrian American Medical Society.

Tabar, P. (2009). "Immigration and Human Development: Evidence from Lebanon", *Human Development Research Paper* – HDRP, 35.

Tabar, P. (2011). *Lebanon: A Country of Emigration and Immigration*, available at http://www.aucegypt.edu/gapp/cmrs/reports/documents/tabar080711.pdf.

Terrazas, A. (2010). *Connected Through Service: Diaspora Volunteers and Global Development*. Washington, DC: Migration Policy Institute.

Terrazas, A. (2010). *Diaspora Investment in Developing and Emerging Markets: Patterns and Prospects*. Washington, DC: Migration Policy Institute.

United Nations Development Programme – UNDP – Capacity Development Group (2007). "Case Evidence on Brain Gain", *Capacity Development Action Briefs*, 1.

United Nations Office for the Coordination of Humanitarian Affairs – OCHA (2014). *Humanitarian Bulletin – Syrian Republic*, March, 45.

United Nations Statistics Division. *UN Data*, available at http://data.un.org/.

United Nations Volunteers (2008). *TOKTEN*, available at http://www.unv.org/fileadmin/docdb/pdf/2008/TOKTEN_factsheet_01.12.2008.pdf.

United States Agency for International Development – USAID and Western Union. *African Diaspora Marketplace*, available at http://www.diasporamarketplace.org/about-african-diaspora-marketplace.

Wamda Research Lab (2014). *Enhancing Access, Assessing the Funding Landscape for MENA's Startups*. Beirut: Author.

World Bank – Office of the Chief Economist (2014). "Growth Slowdown Heightens the Need for Reform", *MENA Quarterly Economic Brief*, January 2014, 2.

World Bank. *World Bank Open Data*, available at http://data.worldbank.org/.

Wyne, J. (2014). *The Next Step: Breaking the Barriers to Scale for MENA Entrepreneurs*. Beirut: Wamda Research Lab.

Zohry, A. and Debnath, P. (2010). *A Study on the Dynamics of the Egyptian Diaspora: Strengthening Development Linkages*. Cairo: International Organization for Migration.

# Index

Lightning Source UK Ltd.
Milton Keynes UK
UKOW06n2200030815

256321UK00003B/14/P